Contents

Foreword	v
Introduction	vii

7-ON

Clark in Sarajevo Catherine Zimdahl	1
Tsunami Ned Manning	69
The Sweetest Thing Verity Laughton	135
Third Person Noëlle Janaczewska	191
Perfect Stranger Hilary Bell	237
Porn.Cake Vanessa Bates	285
The Daphne Massacre Donna Abela	337
About the Authors	*395*

Foreword

Dorothy Hewett once argued that Australians were afraid of the imagination, and suspicious of eloquence. This is certainly challenged by the group of playwrights that form 7-ON, who dare to play with both imagination and language.

These are seven distinct voices—all different from each other, each striking when considered alongside more mainstream playwriting voices we tend to encounter in this country. These seven highly experienced playwrights are intimately familiar with the languages of theatre; each commands their language with native skill. Some of the plays are written in verse—rhymed, half-rhymed, or dependent on rhythm. Their varied rhythmic and structural dialogue offers a great gift to actors.

I would argue that all good texts have something in them that resists being understood. The secret of good playwriting is that the characters feel intimate, yet enigmatic enough to draw us in. The audience yearns to see more revealed, to join the characters on their journeys. Good playwriting leaves us looking in, wondering how we got here, even after we think the playwright has let us in. That is true of all the plays in *7-ON A Collection*. They all keep us curious, different though they are in story, form, structure and language.

I was intrigued that in a collection written by seven playwrights, each play leaves us on an ambiguous note at their end. There are no answers, only infinite directions in which to go. We sense that something is still hidden in the text, not quite fully exposed. We're more than satisfied, yet we want more. And on we read, savouring the work of this group of playwrights who will continue on, long past these twenty years they have shared.

Thank you, 7-ON.

Dr May-Brit Akerholt

Introduction

7-ON was born in the upstairs room of a Paddington pub in 2005. We emerged organically, serendipitously, from a group of Sydney playwrights who had been meeting casually over a few months. As often happens with informal arrangements, participant numbers were dwindling. We were the last ones standing, and we wanted to do more than talk about theatre—we wanted to see our work produced and in front of audiences. That's how you truly develop as a playwright.

We began with an aim to support each other's individual careers, but also were curious to explore what collaborating with each other could produce, and to see where else our collective might lead.

Our first venture as 7-ON was *The Seven Needs,* which was part of the Griffin Theatre Company's 2007 season. We divided up psychologist Abraham Maslow's hierarchy of needs and each wrote a ten to fifteen-minute piece. Those scripts were published in the anthology *Short Circuit* (Currency Press, 2009).

In 2007, we also established our blog at sevenon.blogspot.com. It served as a platform for updates on individual and collective activities. Although we ceased posting in 2024, it remains online as a record of our many and varied undertakings.

With a grant from the Australia Council (now Creative Australia), we tackled an adaptation of Nietzsche's *Thus Spake Zarathustra*, staged at the University of Wollongong in 2008. We developed the immersive *Long Shadows* during a Sydney Theatre Company workshop in 2009. That same year, we received commissions from ABC Radio National for their series *Old Texts Revisited*; two of those scripts received AWGIE Awards. Other key 7-ON projects include *Platonic* (Hothouse Theatre development, 2013) and *We Are The Ghosts Of The Future*, an immersive performance experience (The Rocks Discovery Museum, 2015).

As you'll see from the seven plays in this collection, we're seven minds that don't think alike—something we have always viewed as a strength. We're writers with very different sensibilities, interests and voices. But we speak as one voice when it comes to our belief in the transformative power of our art form and its place in Australian culture.

In an arts ecosystem of intense competition, the members of 7-ON champion each other's work. We offer advice and encouragement to each other and, sometimes, words of caution. If a concern with social justice unites us as a group, so too does generosity. 7-ON is one for all and all for one, but never one-size-fits-all.

From intimate dramas that interrogate personal identities to broader narratives exploring societal shifts, 7-ON's repertoire showcases versatility and a commitment to bold and adventurous storytelling.

Our individual works have graced stages across Australia and internationally. Between us we have garnered more than fifty awards. Over the years, each of us has extended their creative practice—into audio scripts, screenplays, poetry, novels, nonfiction books, children's literature and the visual arts.

We like to think that 7-ON has made— and continues to make— significant contributions to Australian theatre, not only through our individual award-winning works but also through our collective advocacy for playwrights and playwriting, sustainability for the arts, for diversity and gender equity.

As well as the aforementioned *Short Circuit*, we have published two anthologies of short plays: *No Nudity, Weapons or Naked Flames* (Federation Press, 2012), a book of monologues designed for educators, students and theatre practitioners, and *Sharp Darts: Chamber Plays by 7-ON* (Currency Press, 2021).

After three collections of short scripts, we wanted more. A question we often asked ourselves was: if you had the opportunity to publish a full-length play, which one would you choose? The seven plays in *7-ON A Collection* are those individual choices.

In 2025, 7-ON reached a landmark: we are twenty years old. This collection is our birthday gift to ourselves and—we hope—to the writing and theatre community. It is a celebration of collaboration, resilience, friendship and longevity.

7-ON. Keeping on.

7-ON Playwrights
Donna Abela, Vanessa Bates, Hilary Bell, Noëlle Janaczewska,
Verity Laughton, Ned Manning and Catherine Zimdahl

CLARK IN SARAJEVO
Catherine Zimdahl

Clark In Sarajevo was commissioned by the Melbourne Theatre Company and first produced by Griffin Theatre Company at the Stables Theatre, on the lands of the Gadigal peoples of the Eora Nation, Sydney, on 17 April 1998, with the following cast and creatives:

CLARK CANT	Jamie Jackson
LALA / JASMIN / DELORES / VILLAGER / CHORUS	Jeanette Cronin
BORIS / SNIPER / OLD MAN / PRISONER / VILLAGER / WOMAN IN QUEUE / SAFET / JESUS / DOG / PEACEKEEPER / CHORUS	Justin Smith
ANDJA / FATA / PUPPY / SENELA / ELISABETH / VILLAGER / MOTHER OF DYING SOLDIER / CHORUS	Paula Arundel
HENRI / AHMET / CHORUS / COMMANDER / VILLAGER / CHUCKIE / WOMAN IN QUEUE / UN OFFICIAL / FATHER OF DYING SOLDIER / DOCTOR	Michael Beckley
HARIS / MARK / MILITIA COMMANDER / CANADIAN PEACEKEEPER / DYING SOLDIER / DOG / CHORUS / DEAD SOLDIER	Benjamin Winspear

Director, Ros Horin
Dramaturgs, Peter Matheson, Ruth Little
Designers, Karin Thorn, Nicola McIntosh
Composer, Sarah de Jong
Lighting, Mark Trubridge

CHARACTERS

CLARK	VILLAGER 1
LALA	VILLAGER 2
ANDJA	VILLAGER 3
HARIS	WIFE
CITIZENS	MILITIA COMMANDER
SNIPER	CHUCKIE
CANADIAN PEACEKEEPER	DELORES
HENRI	OLD WOMAN
PUPPY	YOUNG WOMAN
FATA	UN OFFICIAL
BORIS	DYING SOLDIER
OLD MAN	DYING SOLDIER'S FAMILY
SENELA	SAFET
ELIZABETH	JESUS
MARK	DOCTOR
JASMIN	DOGS
PRISONER	PEACEKEEPERS
COMMANDER	DEAD SOLDIER/VILLAGER
VILLAGERS	

NOTE ON CASTING

This play can be performed with a minimum of six actors, four male, two female.

ACT ONE

SCENE 1: PROLOGUE

The sound of the ocean.

Out of the darkness CLARK *is slowly revealed. He is in glasses and trench coat.*

He gazes out at the audience, the CHORUS *behind him.*

CHORUS: Clark Cant scratches his tummy and looks out at the sea, wondering—

    CLARK *scratches his tummy.*

CLARK: Why do I have to be me?
    I eat, drink, walk, talk
    I ache, sigh, moan, yawn
    I think, think, thought, thought.
CHORUS: Clark Cant slumps at fate
    Something is drowning he looks he waves.

    CLARK *waves.*

CLARK: I know who I am and what I believe.
    I know where my place is in the map of history.
CHORUS: Clark Cant reports

    He takes out his notebook and pen.

CLARK: The calm seas of democracy
    The waves of monotony
    oceans and oceans of everyday misery
CHORUS: Clark Cant looks out at the sea
    The sea of circling sharks.
    He wants to be new.
CLARK: Leave this stupid job, do something for myself.
CHORUS: Clark Cant looks but he can't see
    the gravity
    the call to catastrophe
    he just feels kind of

CLARK: Hungry.

> CLARK *stands.*

I need something more, the taste of a war.

> *He sticks out his thumb follows his direction in a figure eight— the* CHORUS *follows him.*

CHORUS: He hitches a ride to the Balkans.
CLARK: I'll find one good reason to have been born.
CHORUS: He checks in to the Holiday Inn.
CLARK: That's Cant with a C. No, no apostrophe.

> *He is shown his room.*

CHORUS: He wants to see Sarajevo under siege.
He wants to write it all down.

> *He opens his notebook.*

His senses are heightened,
He looks at his hand—
CLARK: What a piece of work is man!
CHORUS: A bomb explodes through the window of the hotel.
The guy from the *New York Times* screams.
CORRESPONDENT: Get down you idiot, do you have any idea what is going on over by the fence?
CHORUS: He peeks out the window, braving the sniper fire.

> *He scribbles it down.*

CLARK: A woman shot her handbag flung up stuck in mid-air stays—
CHORUS: Clark Cant thinks the strangest thing—
CLARK: This is the safest place to be.
CHORUS: He sleeps.

> CLARK *tilts his head to one side and starts snoring.*

He cries out in his sleep.
CLARK: I am here so therefore I am not.
CHORUS: And over breakfast he is asked
CORRESPONDENTS: What? What? What are you not?

> *Long pause.* CLARK *is uncomfortable. Looks at his watch.*

CLARK: Well I better get a move on. You see, I missed

Saigon, I somehow overlooked Lebanon and I really don't know, uh-uh, where I was when the Gulf War was on.

CHORUS: Clark Cant rises up. He is offered a helmet and a bullet-proof vest. He shakes his head.

He takes out his pen.

CLARK: With my pen, my weapon, my wand
I am protected from all that is wrong.

He clicks it down.

SCENE 2: THE CITY

CHORUS: Clark Cant steps out into sniper alley. One hundred and fifty metres from the front line.
He sees a sign.

He gets out a phrasebook to read the sign.

CLARK: 'Beware sniper.'

Gunshots like thunderclaps.

CHORUS: But Clark Cant walks on.
He follows the river.
He sees cathedrals, a synagogue, a mosque.
He walks down Marshal Tito Street.
He walks on and on and on
until he turns, circles, wonders

The CHORUS scatters back away from him.

CLARK: Am I lost?

He looks around.

It appears to be a kind of marketplace.
And yet it's so strangely empty of anything that anyone could possibly want.
I am vaguely troubled by the thought—if there is nothing, then What can be sold? What can be bought?

LALA notices CLARK, comes forward, catches his eye, smiles.

LALA: Hey are you from the West?
CLARK: Yes. How did you guess?

LALA: I don't know just popped into my head.
We must have been meant to meet.
CLARK: Yes.
LALA: My name is Lala.

> *She puts out her hand to shake.*

CLARK: My name is Clark C—

> *He puts out his hand to shake.*

LALA: Can you get me out of here? Just me, my mother, my kid—

> *But before their hands meet* CLARK *pulls his hand back.*

CLARK: I can't. I can't because I have greater responsibilities.
LALA: Are you with the UN? Can you get me a job?

> ANDJA *notices* CLARK. *Comes forward to him.*

ANDJA: Are you lost? Do you need assistance … ?

> LALA *starts talking to* ANDJA *in Serbo-Croatian but it is mouthed and can't be heard. It is obvious what is being said—'Back off, I saw him first.' While this is happening* CLARK *ponders—*

CLARK: Am I lost?
ANDJA: I would love to show you my city and our ways of survival—
LALA: I could show you things you've never seen.
ANDJA: My husband, is a soldier, he has so many stories to tell.

> CLARK *takes out his notebook and pen.*

CLARK: Oh. A soldier.

> *He turns to go with* ANDJA.

LALA: But Clark we were meant to meet.

SCENE 3: ANDJA AND HARIS' APARTMENT

CLARK *stands facing* HARIS *and* ANDJA. ANDJA *is in her late twenties and* HARIS *in his mid-thirties.* HARIS *is a soldier.*

ANDJA: I found him at the markets.

> *Pause.*

He's a reporter.

CLARK *puts his hand out to shake—he speaks but we can't hear what he is saying.* ANDJA *translates.*

He says he's pleased to meet you.

HARIS *shakes his hand.*

Please smile.

HARIS: Tell him to take his shoes off.

ANDJA *speaks to* CLARK. *Again, we can't hear what she is saying.*

CLARK *nods takes his shoes off.*

ANDJA: [*nodding and strained smiling at* CLARK] Make friends with him, just try—

I'm gone tomorrow—

HARIS: And you bring a stranger home?

ANDJA: I need to know you'll have a chance, a connection, whatever— I don't know … you don't know maybe visas, wherever—

HARIS: What are you trying to do? Turn me into a beggar?

CLARK *brings a bottle of whiskey and a packet of Marlboros out from his trench coat and gives them as a gift.* HARIS *takes them.*

Have you told him what I used to do before all of this? Did you tell him?

HARIS *opens the cigarettes.*

I am an architect. Tell him.

ANDJA: I told him. He said there would be a lot of work for you after the war.

HARIS *shakes his head. Points a cigarette at him.*

HARIS: I bet he hasn't even had an education. I—

CLARK *starts talking, again we can't hear what he says.* HARIS *stares at him.*

What's he want?

ANDJA: [*smiling and nodding at* CLARK] He wants to ask a question.

ANDJA *smiles and gestures for* CLARK *to sit. Gives him a glass. Opens the whiskey, pours the drinks.*

CLARK *opens his notebook and asks the question. Again his lips move but we can't hear what he says.* HARIS *and* ANDJA *look at him*—ANDJA *translates.*

ANDJA: He says 'Islam. Islam.

Pause—translates.

Can this really be a holy war?

Pause—translates.

Is it really a race war? Because

Pause—translates.

from what I read in the guide book

Pause—translates.

you seem to speak fairly much the same language

Pause—translates.

and to be honest from what I can see you all seem so, so ... European.

Pause—translates.

White. White, even.'
He's only staying for tonight—

CLARK *starts talking again.* ANDJA *continues to translate as he speaks.*

He says—

Pause.

'I'm sorry if that came out a bit rude.

Pause—translates.

Since the thaw of the Cold War it's hard to know which side to be on.

Pause—translates.

Who's the enemy, who are the allies, who are the ones worth dying for.

Pause—translates.

It's maybe just me I'm having this mid-life thing, I don't want any confusion, just ... just ... just ...

*Pause—*CLARK *searches for the word.*

clarity.'

HARIS: He's come here to tell us his problems?

> ANDJA *gets the giggles.* HARIS *starts to laugh too. They keep on laughing more than is warranted, hysterical.*
>
> CLARK *tries to join in but doesn't understand the joke.*
>
> *They laugh until they are worn out. Then they both gaze into space.* HARIS *absently takes her hand. Long pause.* CLARK *raises his glass.*

CLARK: Here I am a stranger from the West—

> HARIS *looks up at him,* ANDJA *keeps looking down but translates silently for* HARIS.

I was lost at the market and you, my good friends, my friends that I will have forever, you in all your suffering opened your doors to me. If I could be so bold, it leads me to believe that suffering is, in its own way, truly ennobling.

> *He lifts his glass.*
>
> *They both stare at him.*
>
> *Later. Both really drunk. It's the early hours.* CLARK *is asleep, snoring lightly.*

HARIS: No more spirits?

ANDJA: All gone. We should sleep.

HARIS: I miss you, I miss you, I miss you already.

> ANDJA *nods.*

ANDJA: If we sleep we'll miss our lives.

> *Pause.* HARIS *gets up suddenly, paces, possessed with sorrow.*
>
> *Looks at* CLARK.

HARIS: How can he sleep so sweetly? As if he has no substance. Thin as air I could put my hand right through him.

ANDJA: Haris.

HARIS: Oh god my my nerves so frayed my fingers are falling out of their skin.

> I could kill someone or something.

Pause.

Him.

CLARK *wakes, looks around half-asleep.*

CLARK: What?

Then he falls back to slumber.

HARIS: I could get a grenade and I could pull the pin. Thud. Kill me this stupid fucking misery. There is nothing to—I could I could I could I could take my gun blast the air between his ears away what's to stop me what? The police? The warlords? The UN? Snap. There is nothing to stop—

ANDJA: I know who you are.

Pause.

I feel sick.

Pause. He stares at her. Softens.

HARIS: Where?

She shakes her head.

In your head? Honey you'll be safe soon.

ANDJA *moves away from him.*

Andja? Come on. Really?
Don't, don't be afraid—oh for god's sake—

ANDJA: That smell of gun, all over you.

HARIS: Don't look at me that way—

ANDJA: Sometimes when you come home—

HARIS: Like you can't wait to get away.

ANDJA: I think, I think what the hell is that smell that stink, god, the stench of death

HARIS: No.

ANDJA: On your breath.

HARIS: I'm hungry. It's hunger.

ANDJA: I want to know. Where did you go? Where have you been?

HARIS: What?

ANDJA: You hurt me when you love me.
You go too deep, too fast, too hard.

HARIS: I just, I just want to
ANDJA: I don't know, like you want to
HARIS: forget myself
ANDJA: break my heart.

> *Later* HARIS *is asleep.* ANDJA *is awake. She looks down at her watch, grabs her bag and goes. The mortars start.*
>
> HARIS *wakes. Looks around for* ANDJA.

HARIS: Andja. Andja.

> *He shoves* CLARK *awake.*

[*To* CLARK] Did you see her? Did you?

> CLARK *grabs his phrasebook.*

CLARK: [*hesitantly*] I-do-not-understand.
HARIS: What did she say? What?
CLARK: [*looking in phrasebook*] Thank-you-for-your-kind-hospitality—

> HARIS *pulls his boots on. Grabs his gun, runs out the door, pounding down the stairs.* CLARK *picks up his shoes and follows him.*
>
> *They go in a rectangle shape as if they are going down stairs.*
>
> HARIS *pauses on the stairs to turn to* CLARK *for his opinion.* CLARK *just nods.*

HARIS: The road. It'd have to be closed. Don't you think?
All these mortars flying about. Too dangerous. Don't you think? The UN wouldn't risk a convoy being blown to bits. Would they? Would they?

> CLARK *just nods.*

SCENE 4: ON THE STREET

They join a crowd of people running. They're standing in one spot, then they move in the stylised shapes of running. They carry things— shopping bags, water containers, babies, wood ... with each shot, they dodge, twist, turn. It becomes a dance.

A shot rings out.

CITIZEN 1: Every day I run this way. The same way to work. It's funny. Before the war I despised work. I use to sit on the tram and think—'When when when is my life going to begin?'

A shot.

CITIZEN 2: I just think to myself I think I am brighter than this. Good with numbers. There must be a math to solve it. An equation to tell me whether the bullet is in front or behind me. It's just a puzzle—a puzzle—if a sniper shoots a bullet from a distance of fifty metres with a velocity of blackness and the speed of darkness how many people can he possibly kill?

Shot. Shot. Shot.

HARIS: I feel the glaze of the sniper's eye upon my cheek, thigh, back, chest. But I try not to think. Run, run as fast as I can. No two days the same, a different route.

Shot.

CITIZEN 3: I carry my talisman—some American dollars, my mother's wedding ring.

Shot. Shot. Shot.

CITIZEN 2: I carry an autographed photo of Tito.
CITIZEN 1: I carry the Quran.

Shot

CITIZEN 3: I don't stop for anyone, that's what they want, you go to help them and the sniper picks you off. So I don't stop, if they fall serves them right, they must have done something bad in a previous life.

Shot. Shot. Shot.

CITIZEN 2: I go exactly the same way every day, I don't deviate, my brother my neighbour my mother went the wrong way and now they're not here, I won't make the same mistake.

Shot.

HARIS: I make myself believe that my heart floods my body and fills me to the brim with love, love that I've turned into light. I'm as invisible as air.

Shot. The bullet spirals around the crowd, everyone ducks in turn except CITIZEN 1.

CITIZEN 1: No-one can run faster than a speeding bullet. You can't beat fate. Everyone hates a realist but if that bullet has your name on it—there is nothing you can—

> CITIZEN 1 *gets shot, falls backwards and is caught by the others. They bring* CITIZEN 1 *to the ground. A couple get shot in doing this. Those that run off get shot.* HARIS *tries to drag one of the injured to safety and gets shot. Eventually everyone is shot dead except* CLARK.
>
> *He stands in the middle of the carnage. He tries to control himself so he doesn't look down.*
>
> *He pulls out a white hanky, waves it, crosses the front line.*

SCENE 5: THE SNIPER

CLARK *consults his phrasebook.*

CLARK: I would like very much to speak with a sniper who is fluent in English.

> CLARK *turns and faces the sniper.*

My name is Clark.

> *He is a young man, thin and moving in slow motion.*

SNIPER: We've met. I had you in my sights. It was day or night. Infrared sights. I can see you in the light or the dark. Yes I was going to kill you but I was called away.

CLARK: Thanks.

> CLARK *clicks down his pen and looks down at his notebook for his questions.*

So you, you kill civilians right?

SNIPER: You could be army, you're of age. I don't kill civilians, killing civilians is a war crime. If I need target practice I shoot dogs and cats. That's it.

CLARK: Uh-huh. Um, yeah, um, I've just come from there and I've seen civilians get killed.

SNIPER: They kill their own people, that's what they do, to make us look like monsters. That's what they do. Do I have two heads? This is a war and people die in wars. This is a holy war. Write it down.

CLARK *writes it down.* SNIPER *turns and takes position with his gun.*

CLARK: Are you from … ?
SNIPER: I grew up here. Yes.
CLARK: You've met Muslims before?
SNIPER: Yes. But they are just pretending to be Muslims really. They were forcibly converted in the Ottoman Empire.

    CLARK *writes it down.*

CLARK: In what year was this?
SNIPER: In the fourteenth century. They really are Serbs really.
CLARK: Did you have many friends down there? Muslims?
SNIPER: Yes. But I didn't know then what they were planning—an Islamic State.
CLARK: Do you hate your friends now?
SNIPER: No. Sometimes if the phones are working, I'll call them to say hello.
CLARK: I beg your pardon?
SNIPER: Just for a chat.
CLARK: What do they say?

    Friends as a CHORUS *face front.*

FRIENDS: I can't believe you call us as if nothing has happened.
SNIPER: Let's not talk about the war.
FRIENDS: Your cousin told us where you are.
SNIPER: I was thinking—do you remember when we were little and—?
FRIENDS: Why?
SNIPER: I was just thinking about it. When we played Cowboys and Indians down the river and you'd say 'we are liberating Yugoslavia from our little sisters!'
FRIEND 1: How is your sister?
SNIPER: She's good I think good.
FRIEND 2: Where are you going to go after this?
SNIPER: I'll stay here.
FRIEND 3: You won't be able to stay here.
SNIPER: They say that there is work in South Africa.
FRIEND 1: Sometimes I am going down the street and I think are you staring at me? Are you? You and your evil eye.

SNIPER: I hang up. I don't have to listen to that. I'm a soldier.
CLARK: When did you sign up?
SNIPER: 1992. I never thought much about these things—nations and states.

Then one day my sister was taken and hurt.

My parents could not stop crying. They remember all that happened before.

How I could sit back and watch them finish us off?

I always had a very good eye. I was a good shot. I signed up.

Here I am. I feel nothing. I visit my sister. I know she doesn't want me around. I don't know why but I can't look her in the eye.
CLARK: Is it hard to kill?
SNIPER: What do you think?
CLARK: I beg your pardon?
SNIPER: [*slowly*] Do you think it would be hard to kill?

CLARK *writes his own answer down.*

CLARK: Yes. I-am-incapable-of-such-a-thing.
SNIPER: I would love to be you.
CLARK: I—I—

He quickly looks over his questions.

Is it hard to kill?
SNIPER: At first I dreamt ... No. Not now, no, at first ... but now I never ever let their eyes find me.

CLARK *looks up from his notes, looks him in the eye. Their eyes lock.*

The stare seems to propel him backwards down the stairs and out into the street.

SCENE 6: THE FOOD LINE

He walks on the spot. He looks out up high in the distance.

CLARK: There, there is the sky. A break in the clouds. The creamy blue sky in all the grey. Eyes of a dove.

The sound of a truck slowly comes into earshot. His eyes strain to see as the sound of the truck gets closer. His eyes follow the truck as it circles around.

CLARK *turns and there is a* CANADIAN PEACEKEEPER *standing on the back of a truck piled with food parcels.*

CLARK *turns and moves toward the* CANADIAN PEACEKEEPER. *As he does so, in the opposite direction a crowd of people form a queue before the truck. It is important that* CLARK *does not come from the hungry queue to the truck but rather from the perspective of the* CANADIAN PEACEKEEPER.

CANADIAN PEACEKEEPER: Hiya. How are you doing?

CLARK: I saw your blue helmet I thought it was the …
   I'm a reporter.

CANADIAN PEACEKEEPER: We're not at liberty to talk to the press.

CLARK: Yes, of course, of course. Would you be so kind as to allow me to watch over your shoulder?

The CANADIAN PEACEKEEPER *looks around to see that none of his superiors are about. He puts a hand out to* CLARK *pulls him up on the truck.*

CANADIAN PEACEKEEPER: No questions.

CLARK: As you wish.

CLARK *puts away his notebook and pen.*

The CANADIAN PEACEKEEPER *goes to give a parcel but turns back to* CLARK.

CANADIAN PEACEKEEPER: When people get hungry they get weird you know. But this is still my favourite thing to do. Body retrieval that's the worst. There was this dead boy and he was trapped in ice. We had to use ice picks to chip him out. How about that? Me and my friend it made us sick. But this is my favourite. People are hungry and you give them what they want. And that's a good thing. You look right into their eyes and you think these people are so miserable and I look them right in the eye and I say—

He hands out a food parcel.

'God bless, God bless' and I want them to know that I know and I nod like this.

He nods.

These guys they think I'm way too green but it's so terrible what's happened here.

He hands out a food parcel.

God bless. You just want to do your best.

He hands out a food parcel.

God bless. Some of them are vets from the Gulf and they are like fuck you know 'we're feeding the fucking Arabs'.

He hands out a food parcel.

God bless. I try and say that's not the case.

He hands out a food parcel.

God bless. But when people get hungry they get weird and they start doing stuff and it makes me not want to give a shit about anyone.

He hands out a food parcel.

God bless. They start up you 'cause they think you're from the West that you got everything.

He hands out a food parcel.

God bless. But they don't know your circumstances.

He goes to hand out a parcel when LALA *carrying a bunch of flowers steps up to retrieve it.*

God bless.

LALA: God bless?

CANADIAN PEACEKEEPER: God bless.

LALA: Is there a god?

CANADIAN PEACEKEEPER: I—I—

LALA: Because when I eat the food from these food parcels it makes me believe that there is no god. I don't mean to be ungrateful but it's more than a bit bland. I mean the biscuits the biscuits are killing me. Honey listen it wouldn't look good for the UN if we all died of food poisoning.

CANADIAN PEACEKEEPER: [*nodding*] God bless.

> CLARK *looks at her. She goes.* CLARK *gets down from the truck. Waves goodbye to the* CANADIAN PEACEKEEPER *and follows* LALA.

SCENE 7: LALA AND HENRI

LALA *stops, waiting for* HENRI. CLARK *goes up to her.*

CLARK: Hello.

> *She doesn't acknowledge him.*

Hello.

It's me. Remember? We were meant to meet. We met at the marketplace.

LALA: Of course I've met you, I've met so many of you. How can I re—

> HENRI *the peacekeeper enters with a* PUPPY *trailing him.*

HENRI: Ah Lala ma cherie!

LALA: Hey where have you been? I've been waiting for hours. Three hours. I got the flowers.

HENRI: Lala. This is a wonder. How can I thank you? I cannot find the words to express my grat—

LALA: Say it with deutschemark Henri.

> *He smells them.*

HENRI: Beautiful.

> *Takes out some money from his wallet—looks at* CLARK.

So you have a bodyguard now?

CLARK: Oh no I'm a—

> *He looks down and sees the* PUPPY.

Oh a puppy.

> CLARK *bends down to pat the* PUPPY.

HENRI: I found him in a burning house. I fed him and now what do you know? He loves me.

> CLARK *gets down on the ground to play with the* PUPPY.
>
> HENRI *gives some cash to* LALA.

LALA: It's not enough.

> HENRI *shrugs.*

You asked for flowers and I get you flowers and these are the only fresh flowers in the whole of Bosnia.

HENRI: You're exaggerating.

LALA: Henri, there is a war on. It's winter, nothing is growing. It's—

HENRI: Have any idea how much we get paid?

LALA: Like I fucking care?

HENRI: Fucking nothing with a few crumbs for danger money. But those bastards those UN officials—now those bastards—you never see them—have you ever seen them—

LALA: Look I'll take my business somewhere else.

Cursing under her breath, she turns to go.

HENRI: Hey!

He puts out his hand with another bill in it.

You're taking me for a ride.

She smiles, takes the money, gives HENRI *the flowers. She then gestures to the flowers.*

LALA: Someone I know huh?

HENRI: It's a secret.

LALA: But I've run my feet off for you. I bloody have. It's Nermina isn't it? Well her husband isn't going to be too impressed.

HENRI *shows no reaction.*

Come on Henri. All the things I do for you. Really I mean it, that's it, no more errands for you, nothing. I don't need much but I do need just a bit of gossip—and I love love, tell me a love story in the middle of a—

Bam bam bam.

Who is she?

HENRI: He.

LALA: Ho ho ho.

HENRI: [*insulted*] Hey!

He leans forward whispers in her ear.

LALA: [*whisper to a roar*] Francois? Francois? Francois MITTERAND!

HENRI: Shh!

LALA: [*whispering*] He's coming here?

HENRI: Yes it's a great day.

We've been out all morning, there is so much to be done, we had to find a bed we couldn't let the president sleep in a cot. And good linen and we put some curtains up, made the room fit, well, almost fit for a president. Now flowers. We're all just sweating that the electricity will be burning, the water will be running, the toilets will be flushing and—

LALA: [*breathless*] He's coming to help us? Lift the embargo, send in NATO. It's going to be over.

HENRI: He truly is a great and a powerful leader on the world stage.

LALA: Is it going to be over? What do you think?

HENRI: If you ask me Henri …

LALA: Tell me.

HENRI: I can't speak for my president but if you ask me Henri …

LALA: I'm asking.

HENRI: I would say …

Long pause.

… give up, surrender, your chances of winning are …

He shakes his head.

LALA: [*to* CLARK] Hey you, you whatsyourname what do you think?

The PUPPY *is licking* CLARK'*s face.*

CLARK: Huh?

HENRI: A real soldier does not come back from the front and put his regular clothes on.

LALA: [*to* CLARK] Do you think it's all over for us?

CLARK: Oh.

HENRI: A real soldier does not have his mother make him a cut lunch to eat in the trenches.

LALA: What do you think?

CLARK: Ah, well I would say. Hmm.

HENRI: A real soldier knows how to march and how to hold a gun—

LALA: We don't have any guns! [*To* CLARK] Tell me.

CLARK stands up.

CLARK: You know what goes up must come down and um everything is up in the air but eventually it has to come back to the ground.

LALA: [*pointing to* CLARK] See? See? It's going to be fine. Listen to him.

    CLARK *smiles.*

HENRI: You see Lala this, what you call, pluralism idea, this interbreeding—black, white, red ... I Henri think—give it up, it is not worth the bloodshed.

LALA: Give me back my flowers.

HENRI: I paid good money.

LALA: I want my flowers back.

HENRI: You asked my opinion.

LALA: Yeah well call me a fool for asking. I mean Henri you don't even know what the word means. Your culture is so pure, so sophisticated, so clean—

He kisses her on both cheeks.

HENRI: My president is coming.

    HENRI *goes. Clicks his fingers at the* PUPPY. *He follows* HENRI *off.*

CLARK: Those flowers, those flowers made me think that it's important to just grab those moments of, of, of, um, beauty don't you think, in, in, in a time of hate and—

LALA: Are you with the UN? Can you get me a job? One with perks. A career path. No black market. I can't do black market it's getting too scary. Yes? No? What about just airlifting me the hell out of here?

CLARK: I'm a reporter.

LALA: You need an interpreter?

    You have to have an interpreter I speak Spanish, English—my English is pretty damn opulent wouldn't you agree?

    You gotta armoured car? Huh? No. Oh. Such is life. My name is Lala and I am very—

CLARK: Lala?

He takes out his notebook.

Is this a Muslim or Serb or Croatian name?

Pen poised for the answer.

LALA: It's such a boring question.
CLARK: Oh.
LALA: But even still I'm very pleased to meet you.
CLARK: Clark.
LALA: So it's a deal.
CLARK: Er …
LALA: Clark we were meant to meet.

SCENE 8: THE HOLIDAY INN

CHORUS: Clark Cant catches his breath as he steps into his room at the top of the Holiday Inn.
CLARK: I really wish they would get that elevator fixed.
CHORUS: Clark Cant looks out the window upon the blazing night of the siege of Sarajevo.
    He has an epiphany.
CLARK: Sarajevo at siege … it's all a mystery to me.
CHORUS: Clark Cant pulls up a chair and reads a book on Balkan history.

He takes out a book from his trench coat.

CLARK: Just to get a handle on things.
CHORUS: Clark Cant reads and reads and reads …
CLARK: I get fragments, some concepts, a few personalities, the Sultans, the Ottoman Empire, the Caliph, the Turk, the Habsburgs, the king, the archduke, the president. I get bits and pieces … I understand intellectually the murders, the screams … if you think too deeply you could have bad dreams.

SCENE 9: LALA'S APARTMENT

CLARK *stands at the door.*

LALA: Hey Clark!
CLARK: I couldn't sleep.
LALA: Take your shoes off and come in.

    CLARK *takes his shoes off.*

CLARK: I have so many questions, that perhaps you can answer—the how, the who, the what, the when, the where, the why?

LALA: Clark maybe you should meet my mother.

> LALA's *mum* FATA *and* LALA's *child* BORIS *appear and welcome* CLARK.
>
> *There are distant sounds of mortars shuddering the city in the background.*
>
> FATA *clasps his hand in hers.*

FATA: Thank you, thank you for taking my girl under your wing.

> CLARK *nods, unsure.*

CLARK: This is a very charming apartment. The rugs are very nice.

> *They are hung up on the wall. He touches one tracing a pattern.*

LALA: And this is my boy Boris.

> *She kisses him.*

My darling one, my darling please don't grow up to be a killer. Please don't.

> BORIS *lifts his hands up and roars like a monster.* LALA *meows.*
>
> BORIS *roars.* LALA *meows.* BORIS *meows.*

FATA: She is very artistic.

> LALA *pulls canned foods and extra things out of her coat.*

Before the war she was useless, but now she is remarkable. My mother told me and I remember it that during WWII, that it is quite common, that some useless people come to the fore during a war. It is a very strange phenomena. I'm very proud, very proud. Still she killed her father.

LALA: I did no such thing.

FATA: With all her drugs and music and running around.

LALA: My father died of laughter.

CLARK: Laughter?

LALA: You know, it was the last of the great state ceremonies. They rolled on Tito, because they had to, because he's almost completely dead and his lackeys are propping him up and my father is whispering to me 'Look at their faces look at them, look how frightened they are, look how frantic they are to keep him alive, look at them thinking how can we keep him alive what do we do if he dies how will we hold onto our power?'

> Then my father got the giggles, and he was trying not to giggle because it was dangerous but he couldn't help it, and the more he tried not to laugh the more he laughed, for the life of him he couldn't stop, tears rolling down his cheeks, howling his head off. He just couldn't stop.
>
> *Pause.*

Until he stopped.

CLARK: I'm sorry.

LALA: Ah Clark you had to be there.

> *Pause*—BORIS *is grabbing at* LALA*'s bosoms.*

Boris I'm sorry darling but you're too old to be breast fed. The milk is gone.

> BORIS *starts crying.*

Oh baby, baby. You can't cry, not today—it's your birthday.

> BORIS *claps.*

CLARK: It's the little fella's birthday. And how old are you?

LALA: At this moment time is irrelevant.

> LALA *takes out a lighter and flicks it alight.* BORIS *blows it out. She lights it again.* BORIS *blows it out. She lights it again.* BORIS *blows it out.* BORIS *claps again.*

Blow it out.

> BORIS *blows it out. She lights the lighter again.* BORIS *blows it out again. She lights it once again.* BORIS *blows it out.*
>
> CLARK *takes out his notebook.*

CLARK: If you don't mind me asking—how do you bear the cold?

LALA: We bicker, bickering keeps us warm.

FATA: Don't listen to her she talks a lot of babble. We get along very well.

CLARK: Seriously that's what everyone wants to know. How do you bear it?

LALA: We bear it.

CLARK: The cold, the dark, the hunger, the fear. You just bear it. How?

LALA: We just bear it.

> CLARK *writes it down.*

CLARK: They-just-bear-it.
LALA: But what I can't bear—
FATA: Our guest—
LALA: is that the knowledge—
FATA: is hungry—
LALA: of what is happening here is known and yet—
FATA: Our guest—
LALA: nothing can be done? How can it be? Why is it that when you come from the West you only want to know about how many coats I have to wear to keep from frostbite or how do I choose what to burn to stay warm?
FATA: Darling.
LALA: I don't understand.

> CLARK *looks at them both.*

The wolf is in the house our heads are in his mouth and you really want to know where I dump my shit after I shat it?

> BORIS *starts to grr grr.*

> FATA *opens up a cloth.*

FATA: Bread.

> *Pause.*

CLARK: Hmm. You know things are happening.
LALA: Are they?
CLARK: You just don't know it because you're here but I've been there. There's a momentum.
LALA: Really?
CLARK: Believe me.
LALA: Then when?
CLARK: Soon. Didn't we move heaven and earth to liberate Kuwait? We kicked ass. Huh?
FATA: Listen to him.
LALA: You said yourself what goes up must come down why not now?
CLARK: You have to have more faith.
LALA: Are they waiting for the slaughterers to be exhausted with slaughtering?

BORIS *stops growling and starts meowing.* LALA *suddenly notices him. She pats his face.*

CLARK: There are a lot of things that you and I can't possibly understand. But believe me—all this will pass.

LALA: Yes. It will. Soon.

SCENE 10: IN THE BASEMENT

Fierce shelling.

CLARK *and* LALA *sit in a dark basement. It is crowded.*

A thin man, AHMET, *comes in, nods to the others and takes a seat.*

LALA: Clark have you got a cigarette?

CLARK: How long will we be down here?

> *He gives her a cigarette.*

LALA: When the shelling gets going like this it could be all night.

> CLARK *takes out his book on Balkan history and reads.*
>
> *A slightly disoriented young girl,* SENELA, *enters and takes a seat. She sits very still, staring.*
>
> *An* OLD MAN *looks at her.*

OLD MAN: You can't sit there. [*To the others*] She can't sit there. That's Andja's seat.

LALA: Andja's gone.

OLD MAN: Andja sits there. [*To* SENELA] Get out of Andja's seat.

> SENELA *doesn't move.*
>
> LALA *gets up from her seat.*

LALA: Andja can sit in my seat. I don't want to sit down anyway. It's boring.

OLD MAN: She doesn't sit there. She sits there.

LALA: She's gone on a convoy. She got out.

OLD MAN: [*pointing at* ANDJA] She sits there. And she talks to me. She's not a peasant. Lovely, sophisticated girl. Her husband is a architect. Now he is a soldier and he defends the city.

The others look at LALA—*all know* HARIS *has been killed. Except for* CLARK *who doesn't understand the language and continues reading.*

It's the peasants that have ruined my city. My beautiful city. My gateway to the West. I stand at the well and [*to* SENELA] the peasants push in the line. An old man out of the way. Thirsty. Spit in the street. Backward. Blackmarket thugs. No respect. Get out, get out of my sight!

    SENELA *starts screaming.*

Screaming. See. No manners. Shut up!

    She continues screaming.

LALA: Hey kid come and sit over here.
OLD MAN: Who are these strangers? [*At* SENELA] These strangers in my nation?
LALA: Come on kiddo. I've got cigarettes.

    LALA *goes over to* SENELA.

[*To the* OLD MAN] Okay you back off.
[*To* SENELA] See that guy, see him—

    SENELA *stops screaming.*

He's a reporter. He takes messages.

    SENELA *looks at* CLARK *and smiles.* CLARK *smiles back not understanding what is going on.*

    LALA *manages to coax* SENELA *away from her seat.*

Clark? Clark?! Please!
CLARK: What?
LALA: I told her you'd take a message out for her.

    SENELA *smiles at him half-crying and frightened.*

CLARK: Well you shouldn't have done that Lala, make promises.
    If I start taking messages out I start getting involved I stop being objective, if I stop being objective I stop performing my duties as a—
LALA: Look Clark this shelling is going to go all night. Do you really want to sit in a basement all night with everyone screaming? Because if she keeps going we are all going to start screaming—

CLARK: I don't want the responsibility of—
LALA: I'll get it on a convoy. Just pretend.

> CLARK *turns to a clean page of his notebook out. Clicks down his pen.*
>
> LALA *nods to* SENELA. SENELA *wipes away the tears.* LALA *translates—it is a silent translation.*

SENELA: To Hollywood USA. Dear Mr Mel Gibson—

> CLARK *snickers.* LALA *says something to him to shut him up.*

I'm fourteen years old. I think you are very handsome and I know you are married but I would like to meet you anyway.

My phone number in Sarajevo when the phones are working is two-seven-eight-six-three-one-nine.

If the phones are not working you could come straight over to my apartment it is Ivana Place seven-forty-five. If no-one is there I will go to my best friend's place her name is Mira and she lives at Tiber Avenue twelve-one hundred. She has a lovely cat named Sara. If you call and no-one is there she may have gone to Austria with her family. I hope she doesn't because I'll miss her. If she has gone perhaps I will stay with my aunty and uncle their address is …

> *She can't remember.*

… I will write you again with their address just in case.

All my love, Senela.

> LALA *takes the notebook and pen out of* CLARK*'s hands and gets* SENELA *to sign it and give it a big lipstick kiss.* SENELA *goes back and sits down,* LALA *stays talking to her, we can't hear what she is saying.* AHMET *the gaunt man comes over to* CLARK.

AHMET: Please could you take a message out for me too?
I can't write in English.

> CLARK *looks at* LALA. *Like 'Look what you've started'. She ignores him.*

Please, please if there is a chance that you can reach her. My cousin.
CLARK: Okay. This is it. No more.
AHMET: Nerida Brown,

Three-six-one-one West Eleventh Street. Zip code seven-seven-four-five-one, Ohio State, USA.

Dear Nerida ...

There is a long pause as AHMET *is stuck for words.* CLARK *is impatient. The pause becomes agonising.*

I have arrived home safely after four months in a concentration camp. Warm regards, Ahmet.

SCENE 11: RED CROSS LANDCRUISER

MARK, *the Red Cross Field Officer hands* CLARK *a helmet and a vest.* ELIZABETH *and* CLARK *are sitting next to each other in the landcruiser.*

MARK: Helmets. Vests.

He reluctantly takes it. She hands him a card.

ELIZABETH: And your Field Delegate card, just so you know who you are. Keep it on you at all times. Just follow us and do what we say. For god's sake don't take notes.

MARK *and* JASMIN *get into the landcruiser.*

CLARK *and* ELIZABETH *sit facing the audience and the others face the other way.*

MARK *turns to them.*

Clark this is Mark. He's our driver, fellow doctor and singing instructor.

MARK: Really, someone has to do it. Hi Clark.

CLARK: Hello.

He starts up the engine.

ELIZABETH: And this is Jasmin our interpreter. Clark.

Clark is a journalist.

JASMIN: Good.

She turns and takes his hand.

I'm glad you're coming to see it.

CLARK *smiles.*

They start driving. It's very fast.

MARK: Seatbelts kids.

ELIZABETH: You know the prettiest sight on a war-torn Sarajevan night? It's when the electricity comes on for that brief time and the traffic lights flicker and of course no-one pays the slightest bit of attention you can't—but just a bit of colour. Look, look there Clark over there is the bridge where Archduke Franz Ferdinand the Second was assassinated. That's the spot they say the First World War began.

> CLARK *bends to look but it whizzes past.*

CLARK: I should have brought my camera.

> *Later. Still on the road.*

CLARK: Jasmin, excuse me—is this a Serb, Muslim or Croat name?

JASMIN: I really don't feel—

MARK: Jasmin you don't have to answer—

JASMIN: I can answer the man. The answer is I don't feel like anything—

ELIZABETH: We are all neutral—

JASMIN: I feel it's just life that matters ... that's what I want to believe ... but maybe not. I try and hold on to this—but perhaps it doesn't matter, perhaps it just doesn't—

MARK: Oh I think it's time for a song.

> JASMIN *laughs.*

ELIZABETH: Clark when you work for the Red Cross you become neutral.

This is precisely why we can do our work. When we wear the emblem it's like an invisible shield that allows us to attend to the victims of war regardless of who they are and where they are from.

MARK: [*sings*] That's the theory anyway.

> JASMIN *laughs a bitter laugh.*

> *Later. Still on the road.* MARK *teaches* JASMIN *a song. It's starting to get dark.*

ELIZABETH: ... Basically our job is to try to instil some basic code of conduct—to get the warring parties to hold to the Geneva Convention. That is to not kill prisoners of war, to torture, to murder civilians. We are doing our best. But when you are dealing with irregulars, who are drugged, who are sometimes just children who have no comprehension that whatever they do now they will have to live with for the rest of their lives ... you sometimes just feel so ... so ...

CLARK: Useless?

ELIZABETH: [*sharply*] I wouldn't do this if I thought it was useless.

MARK: Hey you kids, you settle down in the back there otherwise I'm just going to turn the car around and we're going to go home.

ELIZABETH: I'm sorry Clark. It's just hard. It's a paradox. It's hard to hold a paradox in your head without going mad.

Pause.

We've been out here and we've had people pleading 'get us on a bus get us out.' They've heard what's happened in the other villages. They believe the militia are coming. So we've put them on a bus, got them out, sometimes. The question is have we saved lives or have we assisted in the process of ethnic cleansing? Or done both?

ELIZABETH *looks at* CLARK. *He doesn't appear to be listening.*

Clark?

CLARK: It's a lot to take in. Great slabs of information. How much further?

It becomes night.

They stop and unload a couple of backpacks. They take out torches and walk.

SCENE 12: THE DETENTION CENTRE

They face toward the audience. CLARK *looks around the camp.*

CLARK: Oh ... oh ... oh.

ELIZABETH: Mark, Clark, can you get started? Jasmin let's get the paperwork done.

They go off.

CLARK: This is a ... er ... um ... it's a bit of a mess. It's a bit of a mess.

MARK *unloads medical scales.*

CLARK: So they all get to go home?

MARK: Today is a detainee exchange.
CLARK: Good.
MARK: We have to choose the fifty weakest.

> CLARK *nods. Looks around like 'But there are hundreds'.*
>
> MARK *gestures to a very gaunt* PRISONER *to be weighed. The* PRISONER *holds out his detainee card.* MARK *takes it and starts writing down details.*
>
> *The* PRISONER *is too feeble to take off his shoes and be weighed.*

Can you give him a hand Clark?

> CLARK *looks at the* PRISONER. *He nods. But doesn't move.*
>
> JASMIN *and* ELIZABETH *re-enter.*

ELIZABETH: [*to* MARK] No-one seems to be able to tell us where the commander is.
MARK: [*to* CLARK] Help him take his shoes off.

> MARK *goes over to* ELIZABETH *and* JASMIN.

If the negotiations have broken down already we would have been told.

> *They confer silently.*
>
> CLARK *gingerly kneels down to help the* PRISONER *take his shoes off. The* PRISONER *puts his hand on* CLARK*'s forehead to balance.*

CLARK: You'll get to go home soon. Back to your wife and kids. Everything is going to be right as rain, there is no need to panic. You'll look back on this horrible time and you know what you're going to do? You're gonna laugh.

> *The* PRISONER *steps up on the scale.* MARK *turns back to the* PRISONER *and checks his weight. Writes it down.*

Righto. Not long now. You just, you just keep the faith. That's the ticket. We're gonna get you out of here.

> MARK *gives the* PRISONER *back his card. The* PRISONER *goes.*

You got him on the list. He should be on the list there. The list to go.

> *Silence.*

What are we saying here? The man can't even take off his own shoes.

Pause.

He touched my forehead.

MARK: Just cool it.

CLARK: I told him he was gonna go home. I don't get it. How do you make these decisions? On what grounds?

ELIZABETH: Remember where you are Clark.

CLARK: You're just a bunch of amateurs. That's what you are.

ELIZABETH: Please Clark be calm.

CLARK: What if we … ?

He gestures to the PRISONER *and himself.*

And I … ?

He gestures to himself and the PRISONER.

And he … ?

Gestures to himself.

CLARK *reels back at the thought.*

Oh for crying out loud.

MARK: This is not the time.

ELIZABETH: Clark?

CLARK: Who is in command?

MARK: It doesn't—

The COMMANDER *comes on.* MARK *steps in front of* CLARK.

ELIZABETH: Ah! There you are.

She smiles and shakes his hands as JASMIN *silently translates.*

As you can see we have the paperwork.

MARK: [*to* CLARK] Clark could you come here for a moment. I need some help here, I really need your help. Please.

He leads CLARK *over to the backpack.*

ELIZABETH: [*to the* COMMANDER] The paperwork is all in order.

The COMMANDER *looks over the papers.*

MARK: Look at me Clark. We need an inventory of our medical supplies.

Can you just count them up. It's important. Here's a clipboard and a pen.

> CLARK *starts searching through the backpack, pulling out bandages.*

> ELIZABETH *is offering the* COMMANDER *a pen to sign the documentation for the exchange. He takes it but keeps staring at* JASMIN.

ELIZABETH: If you could just sign and date.

CLARK: One ... two ... three ... four ... five ... six ...

> *The* COMMANDER *starts talking to* JASMIN. *It still can't be heard but it is threatening, accusing her.* JASMIN *is shaking her head.*

ELIZABETH: What's happening? Jasmin? What's he saying?

> MARK *stands up.*

MARK: What's going on?

> JASMIN *is shivering. Petrified, can't speak.*

> CLARK *looks up at the terrified* JASMIN. JASMIN *looks at him for a fleeting moment. He looks back at the inventory.*

CLARK: Ten, nine, eight, seven, six, five, four, three, two, one.

> *The* COMMANDER *throws the clipboard at* JASMIN.

You're good people, you know, doing this, coming out here like this, doing what you do.

MARK: Thanks Clark.

> MARK *goes over to them.*

It's okay Jasmin. We'll sort it out.

ELIZABETH: Our interpreter is neither a traitor or a spy do you understand? Jasmin please translate this. Can someone translate this please? If you threaten our people we will withdraw our humanitarian aid. Do you understand? Can someone please translate this for me?

CLARK: I mean it, you're good, through and through. Well I best be off. It's very hot. I think I'll just get some air. Good.

SCENE 13: CLARK IN THE COUNTRYSIDE

CLARK *walks and walks, through the countryside. he breathes deep, looks up at the trees, the dappled light on his face.*

CLARK: The sunlight through leaves like stained glass windows.

>CLARK *takes off his shoes.*
>
>*The sound of a stream.*
>
>*He wanders over to it.*
>
>*He has a drink.*

It tastes of the sweetest reverie.

>*He wades into the stream and follows it up and off.*

SCENE 14: THE VILLAGE

In a village, a group of people gripping onto each other.

VILLAGERS: Do you hear it? The tanks. Have you heard what they've done? Feel the ground. The ground is shaking. Sh-sh-sh-sh-sh-ak-ak-ak-ak-kkkkkk-king-king-king. Oh my god, they're coming, they're coming. This is somewhere else, this not here, this is Africa, Asia, Central America, this is another hemisphere, this is another Europe, another century, another decade, this is not—Oh my god—they're here—

>CLARK *enters.*

CLARK: Hello. My name is Clark and I appear to have lost my bearings.
   I followed a river that became a stream that became a trickle until it became …
   I'm trying to get back to Sarajevo. It's getting a bit late and—

>*There is a thump thump thump thump, rumbling of tanks getting louder and louder.*

VILLAGERS: Who is he? He must be the UN.
CLARK: I was wondering if I could stay the night.
VILLAGERS: He has to be the UN.

CLARK: I'm a bit worried about bears.
VILLAGER 1: He is the UN.

> *They run toward him.*

VILLAGERS: Please. They're coming. They're coming for us. Over the bridge. They're coming. They're coming. They're here. Help us.
VILLAGER 2: He's not the UN. Look at him.
VILLAGERS: Where are the Blue Helmets? They're on the way.
VILLAGER 2: He's not the UN. Look at him.
VILLAGERS: Who is he?
VILLAGER 2: He's a lily-white liberal who doesn't believe in evil.
CLARK: Hey I understood that and—
VILLAGERS: They're coming. They're coming. They're in the square.
VILLAGER 1: Make it a safe haven.
CLARK: A safe heaven?
VILLAGERS: Haven.
CLARK: Me?
VILLAGERS: You.
CLARK: [*rising to the occasion*] Alright.

> *Pause. Dramatic flourish.*

This is a safe haven. A haven of safety. A civil society free from tyr—

> *With* CLARK's *arms outstretched, they stand behind him. The* COMMANDER *comes on, heavily armed. Stands still. Those behind* CLARK *scatter.* CLARK *puts his arms down, shrinks back. Silence.*

> *The* COMMANDER *takes out a revolver and casually walks around the* VILLAGERS—*they cower as he looks at each of them.*

> VILLAGER 3 *runs with his* WIFE *to the* COMMANDER.

VILLAGER 3: Here here are my papers, you see. See we are the same. And my wife. There.

> *The* COMMANDER *looks at them, nods, like 'It's okay'.*

I've grown up here and this place is alright. You get your odd bad apple, but people are reasonable. There is no need—

> *The* COMMANDER *stares at him.*

> VILLAGER 3's WIFE *is trying to pull him back.*

WIFE: Shh.
VILLAGER 3: If anyone has even given me a hard time there always been someone else that—good people.
WIFE: Shut up.
VILLAGER 3: There is a balance.

You're obviously very hardworking people and you are just doing your job—

Finally he settles on one, a man who falls to his knees begging for mercy. The COMMANDER *moves forward to execute him.*

VILLAGER 3 *points to the cowering villager.*

And really trust me, you shouldn't waste your precious energy on these people. He's nothing. Don't waste your—
WIFE: [*trying to drag him away*] Shhh. He doesn't mean it. No he's lost his mind. He's mad. Don't listen.
VILLAGER 3: I beg of you he's just like me and I'm like you—
WIFE: He's not himself.

The COMMANDER *puts a pistol in* VILLAGER 3*'s hand.*

COMMANDER: Kill him.
VILLAGER 3: He came to our party when our first baby was born. He lent me his tractor when mine broke down. He took my mother to the doctor and—

COMMANDER *puts a gun to* VILLAGER 3*'s head.*

The cowering villager is whimpering.

He's my friend and I tell him jokes I make him laugh.

Do you like jokes? I can tell you a joke I can make you laugh.

Have you heard the one about the three guys? There was this Englishman, a Frenchman and an American and they were going to … I … I … can't remember … think, think, oh yeah anyway the American says or the German guy says 'but there isn't enough choice!' No it's the other way round, that's the punch—
COMMANDER: Kill him.

CLARK *moves forward takes out his notebook and pen.*

CLARK: I'm a reporter.
VILLAGER 3: I'm a simple man.

CLARK: This is my pen.
VILLAGER 3: I beg of you he's my friend.

    CLARK *taps his pen on the notebook.*

CLARK: I'm reporting this. I'm reporting this in real-time.
COMMANDER: I can't stand cowards.
WIFE: Just do it. Kill him.

    She walks away.

VILLAGER 3: Forgive me. Forgive me.

    He shoots him.

CLARK: I saw that.
VILLAGER 3: [*weeping*] What have you made me do?

    He starts at the COMMANDER *who pistol whips him back to the ground.*

CLARK: I'm making a citizens' arrest. You're under arrest. What's your name Sonny Jim?
COMMANDER: 'What's your name Sonny Jim?'

    COMMANDER *laughs.*

CLARK: My name is Clark Cant that's with a C and no apostrophe.
COMMANDER: Do you think we can live together?
CLARK: Not if you're going treat each other like that!

    COMMANDER *gives* CLARK *a knife.*

CLARK: What's this?
COMMANDER: Help us carve it up.

    With one hand, the COMMANDER *pulls* VILLAGER 3 *up by the hair.*

CLARK: Look I'm—

    COMMANDER *puts a gun to* CLARK*'s eye.*

I—I …

    Blackout.

END OF ACT ONE

ACT TWO

SCENE 1: A FIELD

It is night. Fog. Green night-vision.

CHORUS: Clark Cant stands in no-man's land.
CLARK: Where is everyone?
CHORUS: Whisper.
 There is no-one here. No-one to remember this.
 No-one is here. Nothing happened.
CHORUS 1: Something something something something.
CLARK: What?
CHORUS 1: I said something something something something.
 The rest of the CHORUS *'Shh! Shh!' at* CHORUS 1.
CLARK: I don't know I—
 Confused, panicked, he starts running.
 I've got to find a road.
CHORUS: He stumbles onto the Highway of Brotherhood and Unity.
CLARK: Where does it go?
 Headlights upon him. He stands waving his arms flagging down a convoy.
 Please please I want to go back to Sarajevo!

SCENE 2: THE CONVOY TRUCK

CHUCKIE *is driving.* CLARK *sits in between* DELORES *and* CHUCKIE. CLARK *is shivering in shock. It's still night.*

CHUCKIE: I'm having a heck of a time. I just signed up for another six months 'tour o' duty'. Back home I'd be another asshole hauling my ass from one side of the country and back gone all mean with meaninglessness—
 Gun shots.

Jesus wept!

[*To* CLARK] Yeah I saw the ad in the paper I saw a little bittie bit on CNN that they needed drivers for humanitarian purposes I thought to myself—Yo! Ten-four ten-four I think we got ourselves a convoy.

He laughs.

I'm having a heck of a time. Are you having a heck of a time Delores?

DELORES: A hell of a time. What about you Clark are you having a hell of a time?

CLARK *shivers.* CHUCKIE *looks at him.*

CHUCKIE: Let's just bump up the heat here you're looking all frostbit.

CLARK: Cold very cold.

DELORES *writes in a notebook.*

DELORES: I'm writing my thesis.

CLARK *nods.*

For my degree.

CLARK: F-F-F-Freezing.

DELORES: In creative writing.

CHUCKIE: Man! She's a poet!

DELORES: It's going to be a book of poetry. Yeah. I was just at this refugee camp and every night the women they sing and dance and clap.

She claps.

That's where I got this scarf for one deutschemark from a little old lady who had no teeth. I put it on my head like this when I need to write a poem.

CHUCKIE: Man! She's a poet!

DELORES: I'm pretty fucking inspired at the moment, yeah.

CHUCKIE: You see Clark it was in this damn fool country ... Can you call it a country? I mean what is it? What is it Delores?

Pause as DELORES *waits for inspiration.*

DELORES: It's a state of mind.

CHUCKIE *looks impressed.*

CHUCKIE: Well that's where we met. Uh-huh. Let's see it was oh twenty-two—
DELORES: No as I recall it was twenty-four hours ago.
CHUCKIE: Well she's my closest bestest buddy.
DELORES: Because the things we've seen … it's as if we're soul mates, I mean it's not sexual really—
CHUCKIE: It's spiritual.
DELORES: It's spiritual, yeah …
CHUCKIE: I know we're gonna be friends for forever and ever.
DELORES: I'm closer to Chuckie than anyone I've ever known.
CHUCKIE: That's what's so wild and thorny about a place like this moments are like days and days are like months and months are like years and years what the hey—let's just call them light years. So's before you know it you're as old as them sages walking on clouds.

DELORES *puts her hand on* CLARK*'s shoulder.*

DELORES: Clark I had no idea I came here to learn how to live.
CHUCKIE: Man I am sure-as-heck convinced only good can come from all of this.

CLARK *shivers.*

The convoy continues on, through the night. They get to Sarajevo. They drop him off …

SCENE 3: THE NIGHT

He walks on, stumbling through the flashes of mortars … .

CHORUS: Clark Cant walks through the night
through the heaviest bombardment
of the siege of Sarajevo
CLARK: It doesn't look right to my naked eye
before it looked
like the Fourth of July
CHORUS: Clark Cant is breathless

The mortars intensify. It is blinding.

CLARK: Am I dead?
Am I alive?
To blackness.

SCENE 4: THE QUEUE

Morning. LALA *is standing in the food line.*

LALA: See that building over there that ugly grey apartment tower
YOUNG WOMAN: Which one? They're all grey.
LALA: The greyer one—I threw myself off it I did.
OLD WOMAN: Rubbish.
LALA: I did years ago. Didn't want to live. And you know what happened?
YOUNG WOMAN: No.

>LALA *re-enacts it.*

LALA: A great big gust of wind came up from under and blew me back up onto the ledge. Cuts and bruises. Cuts and bruises.
OLD WOMAN: No!
LALA: Swear to God. And you know what?
YOUNG WOMAN: What?
LALA: I'm so glad I lived. You know why?
OLD WOMAN: Why?
LALA: [*expansive*] Because life is really ... something!

> *They crack up laughing.* CLARK *enters backwards. He sees* LALA. *Stumbles to her.*

CLARK: Lala! Lala. Hello. It's me, it's Clark. It's me. I'm back.
LALA: So did you raise the dead? Warm and fed. Bring them home?

> *Pause.*

CLARK: My heart went out ... it ... it ... it went out ... my heart went out ... Where?

> *He looks at* LALA. *Like he will fall to bits. She tries to distract him.*

LALA: Hey hey Clark hey hey don't go away, you know what?
CLARK: What?

LALA: See that building over there, the grey one, I threw myself off it I did because I didn't want to live and you know what happened?
CLARK: Yes.

She stops and looks at him.

You fell off the building and you crashed down to the ground and you died.

LALA *is shocked into an unusual silence.*

LALA: [*quietly*] You've got to lighten up.

LALA *suddenly becomes agitated, can't stand still at all.*

Can you do me a favour?
CLARK: I'd do anything for you, for anyone, that's just the way I am.
LALA: Just wait here.
CLARK: I'll come with you.

He takes out his notebook, finds a page.

LALA: Clark I have to see a peacekeeper about a blowjob.

CLARK *looks shocked.*

There are nicer girls than me getting down on their knees.

LALA *goes.* CLARK *smiles to the others, awkward. They nod. Keep on talking to one another.*

The queue moves forward. CLARK *receives the food parcel. His head bowed. He doesn't want to be seen.*

SCENE 5: LALA'S APARTMENT

CLARK *delivers the food parcel.*

FATA: Please Clark come in.

FATA *gestures for him to come in and sit down. He doesn't want to. She insists. He takes off his shoes.*

CLARK: Lala asked me to …

He gives her the parcel.

She's on her way.
I didn't recognise your apartment.

He looks around.

All the windows have gone.

FATA: Yes yes a big fire. We got it out.

She takes the food parcel from him.

Thank you. Come, come sit.

She puts the food parcel on the table.

Opens it up. CLARK *looks into it.*

CLARK: There isn't much.

FATA: There's flour, oil, some dried beans, powdered milk, oh there's no sugar—and these—

She holds up a package.

These are biscuits from the Vietnam War—

She looks closely at it.

1967. We've been afraid to eat them.

CLARK: I'll eat one.

She gives him one. He opens it and eats it.

A little bitter. I think it's okay.

LALA *enters talking.*

LALA: You think you know someone but you don't—

CLARK: I beg your pardon?

LALA: No-one can ever know anyone. I've been trapped—

FATA: The viper?

LALA *nods.*

LALA: [*to* CLARK] For three weeks this sniper has had his nest down at the end of the road. This guy this guy has a trademark, he wounds but doesn't kill, he wounds so you just slowly … so you just slowly …

CLARK: Die?

LALA: I guess that's one way of putting it. Anyway so there I am—

FATA: We don't care. If you get killed you can complain.

LALA: What about if I get wounded?

FATA: You can whinge.

LALA: I found out who he is—it's—

FATA: I heard.
LALA: He was the sweetest guy.

She empties her coat on to the table. Matches. Cigarettes. Sugar.

FATA: [*seeing the sugar*] Ah! Sugar. Sugar. Isn't she remarkable? Isn't she?

LALA *looks at him.*

CLARK: [*quietly*] Yes.

FATA: Everyday she goes to the well. Everyday. She's a good kid, a good kid, I can't do much with my hip. She's a good kid. A rotten mother but a good kid.

LALA: Where's Boris? Where's my baby?

FATA: Shh! Sleeping.

LALA: [*sing-song*] Boris! Oh Boris.

She goes over to the corner.

There you are! Yes yes yes! Wake up! Come and play!

FATA: Shh!

BORIS *wakes up irritable and confused. He wants to go outside. He tries to get to the door. He starts crying. He is more insistent. They try to lead him away.*

He hasn't been outside for a month. Only to the basement. He is tired of the darkness

BORIS *becomes more difficult. He wants to go outside. He bangs his head on the floor.*

With BORIS's *tantrum* CLARK *becomes more uncomfortable and agitated. His stunned presence changes.*

LALA: Come on my darling. You'll get to go out soon. Do you know why? Remember the planes? NATO is coming for us. Yes they are.

BORIS *is inconsolable.*

Aren't they Clark?

CLARK: I don't know—

BORIS *stops crying and stares at* CLARK.

LALA: You don't know what?

CLARK: I don't know—

Pause.

LALA: [*to* FATA] He knows something. [*To* CLARK] Something is happening isn't it? They're sending in NATO aren't they? The siege the siege is going to be over isn't it?
CLARK: I think …
LALA: What do you think?
CLARK: They're afraid.
LALA: Of what?
CLARK: The ghosts.

They stare at him. He fumbles in his coat for a book, finds it.

I read a book. The history. It makes perfect sense to me—the ages old rivalries, ancient tribal, centuries and centuries of killing each other like animals. It's written in blood. You see? Even the president of the United States no matter how powerful he can't do battle with the ghosts of history, can he? Can he do battle with the ghosts of history?
LALA: He can if he doesn't believe.

BORIS *starts screaming.*

CLARK: Crying child. It gets inside.
LALA: Stay here.
CLARK: Outside. Outside. Outside. Outside.
FATA: Sugar and water he's in shock.

Bombardment begins. CLARK *is trying to get out.*

Bombs pound the apartment. LALA *and* FATA *try to stop* CLARK *from going.*

But he goes.

SCENE 6: IN THE STREET

CLARK *stretches his arms out. Looks up to the audience.*

CLARK: I know you're there. I know you can see me in the dark.
    Here take me take me here is my heart
    eyes of infrared
    there's the devil not me

come on wing me
write me a history that will
forgive and forget me
kill me.

Nothing happens.

CLARK *moves to another position.*

Kill me.

Nothing happens. He moves to another position.

[*Softer*] Kill me.

He waits but once again nothing happens. MARK *and* ELIZABETH *the Red Cross delegates rush past* CLARK, *carrying armfuls of paper.* CLARK *sees them ...*

SCENE 7: RED CROSS ON THE STREET

He reaches out to touch them. To know they are real.

They are rushing so much, dropping papers. ELIZABETH *is trying to pick up* MARK's *and* MARK *is trying to pick up* ELIZABETH's.

CLARK: Elizabeth. Mark.
ELIZABETH: We thought we lost you.
MARK: You look possessed.
CLARK: You're here.
MARK: Geneva has ordered us out.
ELIZABETH: We're pulling out of Bosnia.
CLARK: God no—

ELIZABETH *reaches to touch* CLARK, *to balance herself.*

ELIZABETH: They took Jasmin.

MARK *grabs a hold of* CLARK *too.*

MARK: She was taken.
CLARK: Where? Where did they take her?

They don't answer.

I'll be your interpreter. Teach me a song.

They start to go. Stumbling dropping papers. Picking them up.

But your emblem, your emblem, your invisible shield of neutrality.
MARK: The snipers use it to adjust their infrared sights—
ELIZABETH: All we do bringing food, medicine … all a weapon of war. Can you imagine it? Can you imagine it? Two hours flying time from Geneva—
MARK: Come with us Clark. There is nothing you can do.

He shakes his head.

CLARK: But what will happen? What will happen?

They go, a trail of papers left on the ground.

SCENE 7: CLARK AND THE MANDATES

CLARK *at the UN office. He has his shoes in hand.*

CLARK *is on the floor with a whole batch of papers.* CLARK *searches for the right paper. Finds it.* UN OFFICIAL *sits at his desk.*

CLARK: [*feverish, whispering*] Resolution seven-sixty (1992): 'The Council, acting under Chapter VII of the Charter of the United Nations, decides that certain prohibitions contained in resolution seven-five-seven shall not apply.'

CLARK looks for resolution 757 in the mountain of papers, finds it, reads it. Nods.

Yes, yes, yes. See. Listen to this—

CLARK goes back to resolution 760.

'With the approval of the Committee established by resolution seven-two-four.' Okay, resolution seven-two-four—

Again he looks under the mountains of papers, finds it, laughs, reads it.

Uh-huh, uh-huh, uh-huh—

Looks back at resolution 760 and reads again.

Under the simplified and accelerated 'no objection' procedure, to commodities and products for essential humanitarian need.' You get it? You see? They're meant to be read against one another, the mandates, they're—

UN OFFICIAL: The mandates Clark, are as inscrutable as the Quran.
CLARK: Is that so?

> CLARK *writes down everything the* UN OFFICIAL *is saying.*

UN OFFICIAL: Are you really going to allow yourself to become a weapon of war? Call yourself a journalist you're meant to be as impartial as us. But are you? They want to shame us. They want NATO intervention. So Clark are you too, going native on us?
CLARK: I have every right as a citizen of the—
UN OFFICIAL: Then put your damn shoes on man. Next you'll be lining up for rations.
CLARK: There are rumours of mass graves.

> *Pause.*

UN OFFICIAL: Do any of your people care to cast a glance on our successful peacekeeping operations?
CLARK: What exactly are you doing?
UN OFFICIAL: I would have thought you'd know, now that you and your CNN cronies have got yourself a permanent seat on the Security Council. Do you have any idea how impossible it is for us to do our work? By demonising the Serbs it's almost impossible to get them to negotiate, they too, of course, have a case to be heard—
CLARK: I've seen Sarajevo under siege, I've seen the concentration camps, I've seen the villages—
UN OFFICIAL: The Croats have committed war crimes as well and the Bosnian Muslims well it's just a matter of time before their crimes are uncovered. You see, Clark everyone is equal and we're impartial.

> *A strange bomb-falling sound.*

TURN AWAY FROM THE WINDOW!

> *Bomff!! Wind blast. Crash. Dust. Pitch black.*

[*Coughing*] Clark?

> *Pause.*

Clark? Are you all right?

> CLARK *moans.*

Clark?

CLARK: I'm pinned under something—
UN OFFICIAL: Keep talking and I'll find you—
CLARK: Ah, er ... Is, er, is, is Sarajevo really a safe haven?

The phone rings, it's muffled under something.

UN OFFICIAL: Have you heard the one about the five Bangladeshi peacekeepers who between them had one gun?
CLARK: N-no.

UN OFFICIAL *lights a match.*

UN OFFICIAL: They had one gun.

Pause.

Do you know how many UN soldiers we asked for to create these safe havens?
CLARK: Uh-uh.
UN OFFICIAL: One hundred thousand although we said we could possibly get by with seventy-five thousand. Boutros Boutros-Ghali asked the Security Council for thirty-four thousand. Do you know how many were authorised?

The UN OFFICIAL *seems to be looking in the wrong direction.*

CLARK: I'm ...
UN OFFICIAL: Seven thousand, six hundred were authorised. How many have been deployed? Well I'll tell you, fewer than five thousand UN soldiers have been deployed. As an organisation we are bankrupt. Do you know why?
CLARK: Still here. I'm ...
UN OFFICIAL: Because the United States and Russia have not paid their debt!

The UN OFFICIAL *finds the phone. Picks it up.*

Yes yes been hit bad. Yes.

Pause.

And find out whose mortar that was. Who the hell fired on us? Find out!

He slams down the phone.

CLARK: [*fading*] Did you fire on your own people to gain sympathy to your cause?
UN OFFICIAL: Oh very funny.

SCENE 8: CLARK IN HOSPITAL

It is chaos. There is no sound. Shadows behind sheet partitions. CLARK *is in a hospital bed staring up at the ceiling.*

CLARK: That poor man. That man. I wonder what will happen to him. Lying on the bed like that with the earth calling him. What will become of you mister? Are you a reporter? That's a notebook there. There's no need to cry. A tear drips slowly down from your eye. You'll be alright whoeveryouare. Whatshisname. A memory of something someone said of what? Of what? Crushing misery into strength.

> *A* DYING SOLDIER *lies there. Around him is his family. His mother is trying to feed him with soup but he's not conscious. His father and sister are trying to stop her, trying to convince her it's no good, he's almost gone. Father is kissing him on the forehead. Sister is gripping his hand. It's very quiet.* CLARK *watches them.*

And that poor man too. He'll be alright. You'll be right soldier. Just a scratch.

> SAFET *enters.*
>
> SAFET *speaks to* CLARK *but it can't be heard. He carries over his arm, some white sheets.*

Who is he talking to?
SAFET: I am talking to you. In English. I'll make an effort just for you.
CLARK: Me? Me? ME!

> CLARK *realises his situation. Checks himself. A bandage around his head.*

Oh boy. Oh boy. Oh boy.
SAFET: Fifty DM. Burial cloth.
CLARK: Ahhh. Oh god no I'm not Muslim.
SAFET: Well you want it anyway?
CLARK: No! I'm not going to die!

CLARK *makes himself stand up.*

SEE? I'M FINE!!

SAFET: You never know. You need penicillin?

CLARK: Get away from me you sick filthy war profiteer!

SAFET: I don't sell weapons of war. Fuck you.

> SAFET *goes over to the family and the* DYING SOLDIER. *He offers his condolences. The father buys the sheet.*
>
> CLARK *drags himself off over to the soldier's father.*

CLARK: You creepy bastard you get away from him.

> *Takes the money off* SAFET *and gives it back to the father, grabs the sheet from him but as he does the sheet flies back into his face and over him.* CLARK *panics trying to get the burial sheet off himself.*
>
> *Finally he casts it off. Pushes his way through the family and over to the* DYING SOLDIER.

[*With authority*] He is going to be alright.

> *The family look hopeful.* CLARK *takes command. He goes over to the fading soldier and puts his hand on his forehead.*

Get up. I SAID GET UP. GET UP.

> SAFET *tries to pull* CLARK *away. But members of the family push* SAFET *away. Hopeful for a miracle.*

GET UP! GET UP! GET UP AND WALK!

> *The* DYING SOLDIER *makes one last lunge for life. He thrusts himself up. The family gasp with joy. But then the* DYING SOLDIER *plunges back down dead.*

[*Smiling*] He's sleeping.

> *The family grief tableau.*
>
> LALA *enters.*

LALA: Clark. Clark.

> CLARK *tries to write but he can't, becoming more horrified.*
>
> CLARK *seems like something has hit him.*

CLARK: Strange sensations.

> *He tries to continue to write. His head flies to the side.*

A rifle butt to the head.

> *He is flung forward.*

A knife in my back.

> *He looks down.*

I'm on fire!

LALA: I heard you'd been in the wars. Are you alright?

CLARK: Shh. Shh. Shutup.

> *Tries to write, stops.*

I can't spell!

> *Writes.*

It's the pen, it's …

> *He drops the notebook and pen.*

How the hell can I tell the … uh-oh.

> *He spins around.*

I've grown horns and a tail. Am I flesh or fowl?

LALA: Florid as a flower, you fucking idiot.

Come on come on let's get out of here—

> *He takes* LALA*'s hand.*

CLARK: Yes. Let's go, it's time, it's time to evolve.

> *He begins to walk in a spiral taking* LALA *with him.*

LALA: Oh Clark. Lets not hang about.

CLARK: Upwards to a kinder, gentler place.

LALA: This place just gets me down.

CLARK: We're stepping up the spiral staircase—the DNA to find the gene responsible for this misery.

LALA: Honey listen you need a holiday.

CLARK: And when we find it do you know what we're going to do?

We're going to rip it out and kill it and after we murder it we're going to preemptive-genocide it and after we do that we'll slaughter it, and after we slaughter it, we have to preemptive-genocide it and after we murder it, we have to kill it and after we rip—

And then then we'll be free and then we'll mutate a few genes and then we'll grow some wings. I behold a map of the human genome. A gene for everything and everything will be known before we are born, before we are formed, a foetus, a zygote, a twinkle in someone's eye—

CLARK *is now in the centre of the spiral. He is spinning like a whirling dervish.*

LALA: You look like someone I've met before.

He stops and stares at her.

CLARK: Huh?

LALA: I cracked up once—it's no big deal.

CLARK *nods solemnly. He opens an imaginary notebook and writes it down with an imaginary pen.*

CLARK: Uh-huh.

LALA: Same place different time.

The hospital was filled with everyone who thought they were …

JESUS *comes to him.* CLARK *puts his hand out to shake. But* JESUS *bows to him.*

JESUS: I am Jesus.

CLARK *writes it down.*

Christ. Son of—

CLARK: Yeah yeah yeah. In the beginning was the Word and the Word was good—

JESUS: No the Word was God. But God is good so it doesn't matter.

CLARK *looks down at his palm, checking the two words.*

CLARK: Actually I beg to differ because there is only one zero in God and there are two zeroes in good. So there. And therefore. And furthermore and so on IF you don't know how many zeroes there are then then how can you possibly be God?

CLARK *gestures to his imaginary friend.*

JESUS: My good friend Mohammed will address your doubt—

CLARK: Go ahead. Move me.

> CLARK *does a handshake into the air. Then waves his hand around feeling for him.*

I don't get the image thing, Mohammed. You want to sell something you have to be seen. Big deal, big deal you're invisible. I can fly. See? I am flying. I've got ideas. Big ideas. Bigger than—

> *Stops, looks down.*

What are you doing?

JESUS: I am washing your feet.

> CLARK *looks horrified.*

CLARK: La La La La La La La!
    I don't feel very well.

LALA: Well there was this doctor …

CLARK: [*panicking*] I can't hear what you're saying.

LALA: This doctor I saw
    I would look him in the eye
    I would never have thought—

> *The* DOCTOR *enters.*

> *The* DOCTOR *sits down.* LALA *sits down facing him.*

CLARK: Who is that man?

DOCTOR: What is the mood today?
    What is the feeling of the people?

CLARK: What he's saying?

DOCTOR: A cure is a curious thing.
    To make the soul sing.

CLARK: What is this place?
    What are you doing here?

LALA: I had too many opinions, too many jokes.

> LALA *lights a cigarette.*

CLARK: I can't hear you.

DOCTOR: What is the mood today?
    What is the feeling of the people?

LALA: Have another cigarette watch the smoke.

DOCTOR: To make the soul sing.
   A cure is a curious thing.
CLARK: [*to* LALA] Your lips are moving but nothing is getting through
LALA: When you're young and stupid, you're young and stupid
DOCTOR: a hand on the pulse, look inside me
LALA: i was hanging about, buzzing around
DOCTOR: let me hypnotise
LALA: everything so ordinary I'd scream to myself.

> CLARK *starts to get hypnotised, drawn closer and closer to the* DOCTOR *but fighting it.*

DOCTOR: you're getting dreamy
LALA: sitting in the cafes, in the clubs
DOCTOR: dreamy
LALA: 'ah it can't happen here'
DOCTOR: dreamy
LALA: spinning out
DOCTOR: i'm getting taller
LALA: because this is it?
DOCTOR: i'm getting warmer
LALA: because this is all?
CLARK: who is that man?
LALA: wound up here, I'd look at him
   laugh my head off
   who could believe in you?
DOCTOR: i'll save you from yourself
CLARK: what is he saying?
   sounds so soothing
DOCTOR: blow the breath into me
LALA: couldn't have done much
DOCTOR: let the furies out
LALA: but I could have done more
CLARK: he makes me feel like a baby
LALA: blew it i was just so bored
   i never thought … we didn't think
DOCTOR: fi fie
LALA: he would become

DOCTOR: foe fum
LALA: what he became
DOCTOR: feelings
LALA: they gave him an army
DOCTOR: look out my eyes
LALA: aimed the guns to the city
CLARK: what is this craving?
DOCTOR: i'll bring you home
    deaf blind and dumb
    is it love?
    it's near enough
LALA: oh god
DOCTOR: to kill is to cure
CLARK: i can't understand a word!
DOCTOR: the hurts inside
LALA: how i squandered the word hate
CLARK: please, tell me, Lala I beg of you
    who is this man where does he come from?
LALA: it takes my breath away
  i never thought today would be today

>LALA *stands.*

dogs running down the street with human hands in their mouths!!!

>*She spits into the* DOCTOR*'s face.*

CLARK: spell it out

>LALA *starts to hit the* DOCTOR, *bash him and kick him off the chair like a rag doll.*

LALA: We can't live together??? We did live together!

>*He slumps to the ground. Still.*

CLARK: I think he's dead.
LALA: Oh yeah give him a folk song and he'll rise up again.

>LALA *walks off.*
>
>*He is left alone.*

CLARK: everyone just wants a song to sing to themselves so they don't feel so alone

The CHORUS *surround him and lead him gently out of the spiral.*

CHORUS: a verse a chorus a verse a chorus a bridge a verse a chorus a chorus—

CLARK: So alone.

CHORUS: not alone, anything you've ever thought someone's thought it all before, all the feelings you've ever felt, they have all been felt before, everything you've touched everywhere you've walked it's all been done before, a verse, a chorus, a verse, a chorus a bridge

CLARK: the weight the gravity

CHORUS: it's not much further now—

CLARK: of who I think i am

CHORUS: can't you see the ground?

> CLARK *looks down. Shakes his head.*

CLARK: i appear to have lost my shoes

CHORUS: yes.

CLARK: I don't know what to do.

CHORUS: walk this way, around this corner, step back, a mortar, down, a bullet—

CLARK: but what do I do?

CHORUS: just do what anyone would do

> *The* CHORUS *back away from him.*
>
> CLARK *stands for a moment as the swirling noise of war erupts around him. He then smiles.*

SCENE 9: HENRI THE PEACEKEEPER AND THE DOGS

In the background CLARK *goes to each member of the* CHORUS *asking for something. They direct him on to another.*

In the foreground HENRI *the peacekeeper enters carrying a food parcel.*

After CLARK *approaches each member of the* CHORUS *they become* DOGS *and run to* HENRI.

HENRI *stands amongst them.*

They swirl around him. They are licking him and playing.

HENRI: I'm not the enemy. Am I? No. Not me.

They lick his face. He pats them.

My friends, my friends, my four-legged, three-legged—

He starts feeding them.

I'm not the enemy, oh no. How can I be a peacekeeper if there isn't a peace to keep? Answer me that? What? The cats have got your tongues? When we came through the villages the peasants came out with plum brandy, they just wanted to touch us. That's true. They wept 'thank you thank you. God bless. God bless'. They called us heroes. You are a hero they said. That's what they said my friends.

HENRI *shoves one of the* DOGS *away.*

Macaroni get out of it! Now they yell at us in the streets—yes 'if the UN was around in WWII we would all be speaking German now!' I've done my best.

The last CHORUS *member points* CLARK *in the direction of* HENRI.

CLARK: Are you Henri?

The DOGS *turn on* CLARK, *growling protecting their master.*

HENRI: What is it to you?

CLARK: They said to go see Henri. They said he'll find you anything you need.

Are you Henri?

HENRI *clicks his fingers. The* DOGS *stop growling. He begins to feed them from the food parcel.*

One of the DOGS *attacks another.* HENRI *whacks him away. The* DOG *goes for him.* HENRI *slaps him.*

HENRI: Do not bite the hand that feeds you.

DOG *cowers.*

Beg.

SCENE 10: LALA

LALA *enters, stands, waits.* CLARK *comes up behind her.*

CLARK: Lala!

> *She startles.*

LALA: Don't ever come up behind anyone alright?

> *She quickly stuffs some money into her jacket.*

You could get your head blown off alright?

CLARK: Alright.

LALA: Okay.

> *She notices his bare feet.*

Hey say Clark you need some shoes? You could do with some shoes. I can get you some shoes. What about a suit? You could do with a suit. I can get you a suit, a fine Italian suit from Milan. Huh'? We may be war-torn but it's important to keep up appearances.

CLARK: You look tired.

LALA: Yeah well you look like a lunatic.

> *Pause.*

What? What? What do you want?

CLARK: Nothing.

LALA: Oh yeah.

CLARK: I found a way out. Please.

LALA: Good for you Clark. Have a nice life.

> *Pause.*

CLARK: Bring just one bag each. You and your mother and Boris, you're going to go away from this. I found a peacekeeper. There's a convoy tomorrow morning.

> LALA *says nothing. Strange exhaustion.*

I've arranged it. You don't have to worry.

> LALA *still says nothing.*

There isn't much time to say goodbye to people but—

LALA: If we leave we'll lose our apartment.
CLARK: It's so ruined. The apartments above and below you. Bombed. The people in the basement
LALA: They're mad
CLARK: Call Boris a mongrel.
LALA: He's an angel! He's beautiful!
CLARK: I know.
LALA: I don't think there is an outside world.
CLARK: Lala this is it. It's time to go.
LALA: There's a ceasefire every five minutes.
CLARK: They only last moments.
LALA: I don't know how to catch a tram, even walk down a street.
CLARK: Let me give this to you.
LALA: I want the past, I want my friends, I want my friends alive—

> *Pause.*

If we all leave what will be left?
CLARK: I don't know.

> LALA *looks at her watch.*

LALA: I have to get to the marketplace.
CLARK: There's your mother and Boris, you have to consid—
LALA: Don't do this to me. I'm concentrating. I can cope. I have to concentrate. Time has stopped still—

> *They stop and stare at each other.*

CLARK: I promise you it's freely given. It's a good thing. It's good.
LALA: With all the bullshit things I've had to do. I've got to concentrate. All the miserable things you know. Who knows. God.
CLARK: Please.

> *He starts emptying his pockets.*

Whiskey, cigarettes, vitamins, antibiotics, a satellite phone, running water ... no no running water ... no electricity ... sorry ...

> LALA *looks at* CLARK.

LALA: Yes it's good. You're good okay.

> CLARK *starts laughing like he's going to die. She goes.*

SCENE 11: THE DEAD SOLDIER

The bombardment gets louder and louder. Two PEACEKEEPERS *are frantically loading bodies onto a truck. They lift up a woman and place her on the truck. Her handbag is on the ground.* CLARK *lifts it up and gives it to them.*

CLARK: Do you need a hand with him?

> CLARK *points to a* DEAD SOLDIER *on the ground.*

PEACEKEEPER: He's going to have to find his own way to the morgue. Can't touch him. Orders from on high. To remove a dead enlisted man would be an act of partiality. Could destroy the peace process.

> *The* PEACEKEEPERS *go off.*

CLARK: Good taxpayers' money.

> *The truck with all the bodies piled high moves slowly off. The* PEACEKEEPER *jumps onto it and waves goodbye.*

PEACEKEEPER: [*bitterly*] How I long for the glory days of classical peacekeeping when we watched borders and ballots …

> CLARK *puts his hankerchief gingerly over his face and lifts the* DEAD SOLDIER *over his shoulder. He gets too heavy and* CLARK *starts to drag him, until finally* CLARK *is exhausted.*

CLARK: The thing is … I, um … is it's not you it's me I need an armoured car. I called my editor I said to him get me an armoured car. But he just ummed and ahhed. A lot of the reporters here you see, their papers ship them in an armoured car. I'm not complaining there are worse off then me, yourself included but lately I've become afraid of the dark. I just want an armoured car, the helmet and bullet-proof vest, I feel every bit of me that's exposed … so anyway I best go … I gotta get going … I have to go and touch someone or kiss someone or just fuck someone, I don't care who, oh no I do I do, I just have this urge to reproduce.

> CLARK *starts to walk off.*

DEAD SOLDIER: Don't go.

CLARK *stops turns back. The* DEAD SOLDIER *is still just lying there.* CLARK *turns to go.*

I want to tell you Something.

CLARK *slowly turns around.*

Closer.

CLARK *goes over to him.*

CLARK: Yes?

DEAD SOLDIER: Do you remember how my hand quivered?

CLARK *goes to run but the* DEAD SOLDIER *grabs his ankle.*

CLARK *falls.*

How my spirit banged about inside of me. Let me out. Let me in. Shed the skin. Death can't kill me I think I said.
   I fought I fought
   the blade the blood.

CLARK *is trying to crawl away.*

You killed me, you killed me, you killed me
   You're dead.
   It will be born into another form.
   Who will you sacrifice?
   Cast it out into your wife your kid?
   Will you remember what you did?

CHORUS *rise up behind them. Pull the* DEAD SOLDIER*'s head back by the hair. Put a knife in* CLARK*'s hand.*

How you thought it's me or him?
   This is what you did.

CLARK: I DIDN'T I DIDN'T I DIDN'T I DIDN'T—

CLARK *plunges the knife into him.*

SCENE 16: AT LALA'S APARTMENT/EPILOGUE

FATA *ushers* CLARK *in.*

FATA: Clark come in. Lala she won't be long. Come have supper. Are you hungry?

He shakes his head.

Sit. Sit.

    CLARK *waits with* FATA *and* BORIS.

    FATA *is lighting the lighter.* BORIS *blows it out again and again.*

CLARK: Is it always the little fella's birthday?
BORIS: Yes!
FATA: Yes.

    It is later. BORIS *starts crying.*

CLARK: Please don't.
BORIS: Mama, mama …
CLARK: Please don't. You see if you start crying for your mother. We'll all start crying for our mothers. And then where we would be?

    FATA *is shaking, she gets* BORIS *some paper and crayons.*

FATA: Boris here. Draw anything, anything you want.

    BORIS *starts drawing.*

He likes it best when the electricity comes on. I let him switch the lights on and off.

    Pause.

The lady doctor told me that the children who survive the best are the ones that have diaries, but because Boris is so young I give him crayon and paper.

    They wait and wait and wait. FATA *quietly wipes tears away from her face.* BORIS's *picture starts to come to life. The apartments. People and soldiers and kids. Bombs. Explosions. Ambulances. Blue helmets. Fire. A cartoon* CLARK *emerges—notebook in hand.*

    BORIS *starts to grow up before our eyes. Picture still.*

BORIS: My name is Boris and I was a child in the Siege of Sarajevo.
    I have two memories. Drawing this picture and stranger who said—
CLARK: I want hindsight.
BORIS: I was told when I went to Italy that I wouldn't go outside.
    I watched the satellite cartoon channel for ten days and nights.

I am looking for Lala Senad.
She lived in an apartment on this street.
I am her son and even if she is dead, I just want to tell her I'm alive.

CHORUS *gather around* CLARK. *They speak quietly to him, overlapping one another. This becomes a whisper, until it is so faint, it can barely be heard.*

CHORUS: Clark Cant scratches his head and looks down at his feet—
CLARK: I want to go, I want to go home.

He gets up. Rips off his glasses, rips his tie loose.

CHORUS: You can't go home.
CLARK: I want to forget
CHORUS: with all of your senses
CLARK: all that I've tasted, touched, smelt, seen, heard
CHORUS: surrender
with every last ounce of your strength
CLARK: I can't—
CHORUS: surrender
CLARK: I can't
I can't
I can't

Pause.

it's in my breath, it's in my skin, it bangs at my heart, it says, it's here, it's here
CHORUS: it's here
CLARK: surrender
CHORUS: surrender
CLARK: i thought i was ... i know I'm not ... what? what?
CHORUS: imagination ran away nowhere to run
surrender
hands up high. reach for the stars
surrender

CLARK *points to his body.*

CLARK: it's my head, my body

Points to head.
it's neither here
Points out.
nor there
Points to himself.
it's not quite black
Points up.
or white
Gestures down.
i'm neither either or
i'm i'm …
Looks at his hands.
my god …
i'm bloody

                              THE END

TSUNAMI
Ned Manning

CHARACTERS

HARRY WALSH. Eighty-five-year-old ex-journalist.

TOM WALSH. His forty-five-year-old son. A politician.

MEI LING YOUNG. A twenty-five-year-old Chinese-Australian woman. An activist.

GERALDINE (GERRY) ROBERTS. A forty-three-year-old Chief-of-Staff.

NOTE

— Indicates the line is cut off by the next speaker.

… Indicates an unfinished thought.

PROLOGUE

MEI LING, *Chinese-Australian woman in her twenties.*

MEI: An old man called Yugong lived in a house that faced two great big mountains called Taihang and Wangwu. The two mountains troubled him because the mountains blocked his people's path to the Han River. One was beautiful but its beauty was dangerous because of what was hidden beneath it. The other was rugged and foreboding and openly defiant.

The river was pristine and offered unlimited resources to the people.

He gathered his family around him and suggested they flatten the mountains.

Everyone, except his wife, thought this was a wonderful idea.

'No wonder your name means *foolish old man*', she told him.

'You can't even shovel the snow off the path. How do you expect to move a mountain?'

Yugong smiled. He told her he had spent a lifetime moving mountains.

'Don't give me that silly smile. Where are you going to dump the soil and the rocks?'

Everyone answered at once.

'We will dump them into the Bohai Sea.'

'And what will happen to the land around the Bohai Sea?' she asked.

But no-one heard her. They rushed off and smashed the rocks and dug up the soil. They carted the rubble in wicker baskets to the edge of the sea and tossed it in the Bohai Sea. Basketload after basketload. Even the little boy who lived next door to Yugong joined in.

All year round, in summer and in winter, the workers toiled away trying to move the mountain.

When Zhisou, whose name meant 'wise old man' told him he would never complete the task before he died, Yugong laughed at him.

'Don't you realise that I have a son and he will have a son and he will have a son?'

Zhisou despaired. Moving mountains was not that simple.

It took more than time.

ACT ONE

SCENE ONE

Some time in the near future.

An Institution for Old People. One of the few in the country.

An old man is wrestling with a paragraph. He is writing with a fountain pen in an exercise book.

His world is like a diorama of the writer's garret. Notes are scattered over the floor.

HARRY: 'Ferret. Ferret. Ferret?'

> *A knock at the door.*
>
> MEI LING, *a Chinese-Australian woman in her twenties enters. She is dressed in the uniform of a carer and carries cleaning gear.*
>
> *He carries on without paying her any attention.*

Did I tell you I had a ferret when I was a kid? Well, I didn't actually have one. But I knew someone who did. Or knew someone who knew someone who did. Great for sniffing out …

> *He sees* MEI LING *and freaks out, standing and knocking his chair over in the process.*

Who … who are you?

MEI: Hi.

HARRY: Hi?

MEI: Hello.

HARRY: What … what do you want?

> *She indicates cleaning gear.*

You're not Polly.

MEI: No. I—

HARRY: Where's Polly?

> MEI *starts cleaning.* HARRY *panics.*

HARRY: Hey ... hey!!
MEI: Yes, sir?

He spells it out.

HARRY: *Where is Polly?*
MEI: I ... I don't know.
HARRY: You don't know?
MEI: No, sir.
HARRY: She ... she's my carer ... my ... I'm used to her.
MEI: I'm sorry—
HARRY: She understands me. Knows me.
MEI: I won't get in your way, sir.

She cleans.

HARRY: I don't know you.

She cleans.

I'm working. I've got work to do. I can't have ... anyone ...

She cleans.

Don't ignore me!
MEI: I'm not ignoring you, sir—
HARRY: Sir?
MEI: Mr—
HARRY: No-one's called me sir—
MEI: Sorry Mr—
HARRY: Walsh.
MEI: I know.
HARRY: This is very ... unsettling ...

MEI *moves a few things around to clean.* HARRY *is confused.*

What are you doing?
MEI: Getting the job done.
HARRY: No-one told me.

She cleans.

You think they'd tell me.
MEI: Sorry.
HARRY: They don't tell me anything.
MEI: They don't tell anyone anything.

He eyes her suspiciously.

HARRY: I don't like … change.

She comforts him.

MEI: It's okay, Mr Walsh. I'm not going to do anything to upset you. I'm just here to look after you.

She picks up the notes scattered on the floor.

HARRY: Don't touch those!

She freezes.

No-one told you to touch those!
MEI: Sorry … I'm ju— What do you want me—
HARRY: Leave them.
MEI: Where?
HARRY: Where they were.
MEI: On the floor?
HARRY: That's where they were, isn't it?
MEI: Yes … but …

A stand-off. Eventually she drops the notes.

Better?
HARRY: I … I don't …

MEI *picks up the chair. He resists.*

MEI: Here. Why don't you sit—
HARRY: I don't want to sit!

She releases him and backs away.

MEI: Okay, okay. I don't want to cause any trouble. I don't want to upset you. I'll just finish this and leave you in peace.

She steps over the notes and continues cleaning.

Beat.

HARRY: Polly never touches my personal papers.
MEI: Okay.
HARRY: I'm used to Polly.

She cleans, walking on eggshells. He watches her.

Where did you come from?

MEI *points outside.*

Out there?

She nods.

How is it?

She shrugs. He watches her as she cleans around him. He isn't making it easy for her.

What do you want?
MEI: To get this done. Excuse me …

He totters out of the way.

You all right?
HARRY: I'm … I don't know anymore.
MEI: I won't be long.

He waves his hands dismissively before making his way to sit. He exhales.

Beat.

HARRY: Where did you say you were from?
MEI: I didn't.
HARRY: Well?
MEI: None of your business.

He enjoys her response.

HARRY: Oh!
MEI: Sorry. I'm under a bit of pressure. I'm just following orders.
HARRY: Like everyone.
MEI: That's right. Like everyone.

He springs up and offers his hand.

HARRY: I'm Harry.

She is surprised by this sudden change of tack. He pushes his hand towards her. She has no alternative but to shake his hand.

MEI: Good to meet you.
HARRY: You going to …

He indicates that she introduce herself. She plays along.

MEI: Mei.

HARRY: What's the Mei …
MEI: Ling Young.
HARRY: Young. What's the Mei Ling Young story?
MEI: I dunno. Not much. Why do you wanna know?
HARRY: In me blood … sorry … in *my* blood.
MEI: Busybody?
HARRY: Something like that.
MEI: I dunno, I'm just a—
HARRY: Yes?
MEI: Nothin'. Just a temp.
HARRY: Just a temp?
MEI: Uh-huh.
HARRY: Who knows you're here?

She freezes momentarily.

Mmm?
MEI: What sort of a question is that?
HARRY: One that's touched a nerve.

She moves.

MEI: Like I said, I'm like everyone else.
HARRY: Is that right?
MEI: Uh-huh.
HARRY: You're not, you know.
MEI: You can think what you like.
HARRY: I think you're hiding something.
MEI: Mr Walsh—
HARRY: Harry.
MEI: Harry …
HARRY: That's better.
MEI: Can you just let me get this over and done with?
HARRY: Old habits.

She cleans. He deliberately gets in her way.

Always sniffing.
MEI: Excuse me.

He moves so she can clean.

HARRY: Always searching … looking for the …

MEI: Mr ... Harry ... I've got nothing to tell you and nothing I want to tell you.
HARRY: Pity.
MEI: Didn't you say you had work to do?
HARRY: No.
MEI: Weren't you ...

She indicates typing. He looks at her quizzically.

Don't let me ... interrupt.

He watches, trying to work her out. She ignores him and cleans. Eventually he returns to his work. He writes, searching for the right phrase, crossing words out, writing new ones.

She sneaks the odd glance at him.

HARRY: 'I have spent a lifetime trying to *ferret* out the truth. I have assiduously avoided rubbing shoulders with the politicians that I have written about ... '

He re-reads this last sentence.

'I have assiduously ... '

He looks at her, seeking her approval. She shrugs.

Pretentious?
MEI: Bit.

He crosses it out and writes. Reads.

HARRY: 'I have done this without fear or favour and this book is a record of the events I have witnessed and the people I have written about.'

He looks.

Better?

She nods. He re-reads. Likes it. Loves it.

Done! Finished. Finished!

He raises his arms in triumph.

You are witnessing a moment in history.

She stares.

An Olympic moment.

He looks to the Gods.

NOW …

With a great flourish, he closes the exercise book and tries to tie some string around it. His hands are shaking and he is finding it hard to do it.

MEI: Want me to help?
HARRY: Would you?
MEI: Sure.

She ties it up neatly.

Where will I put it?
HARRY: Leave it there. My son will send someone to take it to the typist. A courier person.
MEI: Ohhh …
HARRY: Yes. I like to write longhand …

He mimes cursive writing.

When I was younger … working … I obviously typed but now I get someone to do it for me.
MEI: Okay …
HARRY: There lies a lifetime's work.

She looks around the room.

MEI: Nearly done.

He pours himself a drink as she gets back to work.

He toasts.

HARRY: Cheers. Feels good. Bloody good.

She works. He wants to engage.

It's a book.

She works. He strikes a pose.

My *magnum opus*!
MEI: Yeah?

She keeps working, almost grudgingly humouring him while she works.

What's in it?

HARRY: Words.
MEI: Really?
HARRY: Musings. Reflections.
MEI: About?
HARRY: The state of play.
MEI: Who's gonna read it?
HARRY: Everyone. I hope.
MEI: Cool.
HARRY: You've got to keep 'plugging away'.
MEI: Is that right?
HARRY: 'Rolling the rock up the hill'.
MEI: Must be a good feeling.
HARRY: It's life, isn't it?
MEI: Writing … finishing a book.
HARRY: Writing keeps me sane.
MEI: Keeps you *what*?
HARRY: You know … it's all relative.

> *They share a laugh. He makes a decision and then gets down on his hands and knees and takes a shoe box of old clippings out from a hiding place.*

HARRY: I've been a writer ever since I can remember. When I was a kid, I used to write poems.
MEI: I don't have time to read your poems.
HARRY: Oh. That's a pity. I thought …

> *He laughs.*

Don't worry, I wouldn't inflict them on anyone.

> *She smiles, humouring him.*

We had quite a bit of influence, 'back in the day', as you say.
MEI: We?
HARRY: I was a journo. Wrote for the papers. I was the senior correspondent for a paper in the National Capital and a member of the Press Gallery. I reported on everything from governments being sacked to apartheid in South Africa to wars in Asia. Tried to report what was really going on.
MEI: Really?

HARRY: Back then, we … it was different.
MEI: Oh?
HARRY: I called it the way I saw it. The way it was. The facts.
MEI: The facts.
HARRY: Yes.
MEI: What are the facts?
HARRY: The truth.
MEI: Oh. The truth.
HARRY: I was a 'truth seeker'.
MEI: Didn't editors tell you what to—

He laughs.

HARRY: Tell us what to write? No way. Wouldn't have been game. My job was to try and shine a light on what was outside the frame.
MEI: My job is to clean your room.

HARRY takes a faded clipping out.

HARRY: Stuff like this.

He shows it to her. She rubs it in her fingers.

MEI: Feels …
HARRY: Yes?
MEI: Fragile.
HARRY: It is.

She reads.

MEI: 'The Napalm Girl and Me' by Harry Walsh.
You wrote this?
HARRY: Yep.
MEI: 'She was about the same age as my little sister. She was running down the road and the agony was etched on her face. Behind her was a curtain of smoke and flames and utter devastation. The fact that she was naked made it more poignant. As though humanity was stripped bare.'
Wow.
HARRY: The photo of that girl became one of the iconic images of the twentieth century. I was standing next to the guy who shot it. He was taking photos and I was … I don't know what I was doing. I was covering the war.

MEI: The Antarctic War?
HARRY: An old war.

> MEI *hands it back to him.*

I won a big international prize for that.

She looks at him blankly. He laughs.

It was published in the *Washington Post*. In America. It's a big paper ... prestigious ... big circulation ...

She gets back to work.

Not impressed?

She shrugs. He folds up the paper and puts it away.

MEI: How did you get stories out? You know ... stories the ... 'authorities' ... didn't want to get out?
HARRY: The landscape was different back then.
MEI: You were big?
HARRY: I had my fifteen minutes. Enjoyed them too. Too much. The prize became the story. The story got lost in ... my indulgence. I came home and ...

> *Indicates writing.*

Got back to what I was good at. Telling stories. 'Ferreting'.
MEI: Ferreting.

> *Mimes scribbling.*

HARRY: Scribbling. Listening. Watching. Observing. Questioning.
MEI: Cool.
HARRY: This ... 'tome' ... has been a labour of love. Something to get up in the morning for. That's why I'm celebrating. It's going to ruffle a few feathers.

> *A ringtone.* HARRY *looks at his mobile.*

MEI: Are you going to ...

> *He stares at it.*

You want me ...

> *He prevents her seeing who is calling.*

I was only trying to help ...

The ringtone continues. MEI *does some final checks and picks up her stuff. The ringtone stops.* HARRY *stares at the device the call emanated from.*

HARRY: Not today. No-one is going to rain on my parade.
MEI: Sorry?
HARRY: Not even His Master's Voice.
MEI: I'm done. Can I get you anything?
HARRY: Expects me to drop everything.
MEI: You can buzz—
HARRY: As though I haven't got anything better …
MEI: If you need anything. See ya!
HARRY: Hold on!

He pulls another story out of the shoe box.

This one might interest you.
MEI: Oh?
HARRY: Have a gander and let me know what you think.
MEI: I might not be back … Polly …
HARRY: You'll be back.

She exits.

He pours himself another drink and toasts.

To 'The Ferret'!

SCENE TWO

TOM *is backstage with* GERRY.
She is making some final alterations to a document.
He is checking to see if HARRY *has arrived.*

GERRY: I think you have to acknowledge him. This other stuff's good.

She reads.

'Raised on the knee of … '? Bit clichéd, don't you think? It would be like saying, 'it has been my bread and butter' …
TOM: Where the fuck is he? I sent a car—
GERRY: He's respected …
TOM: Was.

GERRY: What about, 'I have been raised to cut through … '
TOM: It's going to look bad if he isn't there. People will ask questions.
GERRY: Don't worry about it. Everyone knows he's got dementia.
TOM: Even so—
GERRY: They won't be surprised if he isn't there. You need to acknowledge him though.
TOM: Bitter old bastard.

She writes.

GERRY: 'I have been raised to cut through to the core of a problem. To be able to decipher the obfuscation of others. For that and for the standards he has set for himself and, by extension, for all of us, I am eternally grateful to my father, Mr Harry Walsh.'

Applause.

TOM: He's such a prick.
GERRY: No. We won't say that.
TOM: He missed my sixteenth birthday because he had to cover some bloody speech.
GERRY: Get over it!
TOM: Now he's going to …
GERRY: You're nervous.
TOM: I am.
GERRY: You can do great things.
TOM: Can I?
GERRY: You can.
TOM: With you in my corner.
GERRY: 'Eyes on the ball'.
TOM: Do we want this?
GERRY: We do. And so do they. Just remember this. You are the guy everyone wants to fall in love with.
TOM: Everyone except my father.

GERRY checks the time.

GERRY: Let's go.

She gives him the document.

We've got mountains to move.

A red light flashes.

They both look up. He straightens himself up.

Go get 'em.

She hands him a baseball cap with 'Australia Rules' emblazoned on it.

He puts on the cap, adjusts his tie as the lighting changes and the scene is transformed.

We hear the strains of something appropriately uplifting as TOM *walks onto a stage, waving at his adoring fans who respond with a deafening roar.*

The scene has the feel of an American Presidential Convention.

He speaks with a confidence that belies the earlier personal exchanges. He is a charismatic public speaker.

TOM: Fellow citizens of this fine country, I am humbled to stand before you as your Prime Minister. I am excited by the challenges, motivated by the possibilities, driven by the responsibility, moved by the honour.

We stand on the cusp of greatness. We must seize the opportunities that come our way. We cannot let the politics of envy stand in the way of progress.

We have choices to make. Hard choices. Tough choices. There will be some pain, but it will be worth it in the long run. There will be decisions made that will not please everyone. I cannot resile from the hard calls I will have to make. I accept the mantle of accountability. I am accountable to you all.

With that in mind, I pledge that I will ensure that this great country continues to grow and that no-one will stand in the way of our achieving our goals.

Cheers.

We hear a lot of noise from those who regard achievement as something to be ashamed of. I am not ashamed. I am proud. The more we achieve as a nation, the more wealth we create, the better for all. When business thrives, the rest of us thrive. I will lead a government that makes it possible for business to go about its business without the constraints of a union movement that stands in the way of progress. There is nothing wrong with a fair day's pay for a fair day's work. As long as the fair day's work is done, not spent complaining. On my watch, the union movement will no longer stand in the way of progress. Nor will those who bespoil our wonderful natural environment with 'swindle sticks' that do nothing but kill enterprise and divert our attention from the real challenge. And that is lowering costs.

Applause.

Like everyone, I support the movement to green energy, but it won't come at the cost of keeping the lights on. That is why my government will continue to develop nuclear energy despite the naysayers. The 'experts' whose 'reports' are untried and untested.

We will be a government that gets out of people's lives and lets them get on with living. We will encourage people to work hard and enjoy the rewards of that work.

Making a profit isn't a crime. Our future depends on it. We will continue to cut taxes for those corporations whose investment in this country's resources will ensure a better future for everyone.

Applause.

On a deeply personal note, I wish to acknowledge the debt I owe to my family. In particular, my father. I am the son of a great journalist. I have been raised to cut through to the core of a problem. To be able to see past the obfuscation of others. For that and for the standards he has set for himself and, by extension, for all of us, I am eternally grateful to my father, Mr Harry Walsh.

Applause.

Therefore, my friends:

Let us unite with purpose. Let us move forward with certainty. Let us walk as one.

Anthemic music and tumultuous applause as TOM *acknowledges the crowd.*

He raises his arms like a prizefighter who has knocked out an opponent.

SCENE THREE

HARRY *is pretending to be occupied.* GERRY *has bought him some electrical IT equipment straight from a computer specialist. She is unwrapping it.*

GERRY: He asked me to drop this in.
HARRY: Too busy?

She looks at him before returning to unwrapping.

GERRY: So …
HARRY: What?
GERRY: You know …
HARRY: Oh, that.
GERRY: Yes Harry, that.
HARRY: You really want to know?
GERRY: We're pretty busy …

Beat.

HARRY: Not only was it dishonest. It was meaningless. An empty vessel … full of sound and fury, signifying nothing.
　　What was worse, it was badly written. It's bad enough that he appropriates my good name, you'd think he could have at least strung a few decent phrases together.
GERRY: He didn't write it.
HARRY: Can't even write his own acceptance speech!
GERRY: I did.
HARRY: Oh. You …
GERRY: Not all of it.
HARRY: Well …
GERRY: The good bits.
HARRY: You should have asked me.
GERRY: Sure, Harry. We gave up asking you years ago.
HARRY: Yes, well … I have a reputation to uphold.
GERRY: I thought you weren't going to watch it?
HARRY: I wasn't. It was like a flood. You couldn't avoid the bloody thing.

Beat.

GERRY: We've looked at your book.
HARRY: Who gave you—
GERRY: Checking for typos.
HARRY: Oh, yeah …
GERRY: You can't publish that.
HARRY: Who says?
GERRY: Not in its present form.
HARRY: Since when—
GERRY: You need to edit it.
HARRY: Do I just?
GERRY: You know you do.
HARRY: The thought police …
GERRY: I'm sorry.
HARRY: Do you have any idea—
GERRY: I do.
HARRY: You want me to—
GERRY: Just the chapters that—
HARRY: Matter?
GERRY: The ones that might—
HARRY: Cause embarrassment?
GERRY: You are his father.
HARRY: You're telling me?
GERRY: The father of the Prime Minister.
HARRY: Yes.
GERRY: That carries certain—
HARRY: Responsibilities?
GERRY: It's an honour.
HARRY: Depends.
GERRY: Father to the nation.
HARRY: Come off it!
GERRY: Where did he get his—
HARRY: Ambition?
GERRY: Passion. Drive. Commitment.
HARRY: He wanted to prove he could go one better—
GERRY: Bullshit, Harry! He wanted to live up to the impossibly high standards you set him and the only way he could do that was by—
HARRY: Standing for everything I've fought against?

GERRY: That's unfair.
HARRY: It's the truth.
GERRY: Don't let your own failures cloud your judgement.

Beat.

He needs you.
HARRY: Sure.
GERRY: He does.
HARRY: Who are you kidding?
GERRY: We all need you. The nation needs you. We need you now more than ever.
HARRY: Me?
GERRY: You have been there, Harry. We need you to show us the way. To be our moral compass.
HARRY: A washed-up, has-been—
GERRY: Better than a 'never-was'!
HARRY: S'pose.
GERRY: Come on. Do you want to comment on the news or make it?
HARRY: What does that mean?
GERRY: You know exactly what it means.

Beat.

HARRY: Why did he have to … you know … the day I sent my book off!
GERRY: Put it this way, I don't think he planned it. He didn't know George was going to be caught fucking the work-experience girl on his desk and would have to resign.
HARRY: Timing is everything.
GERRY: Sure is.
HARRY: That book means everything to me.
GERRY: I know it does.
HARRY: I can't change—
GERRY: Harry.
HARRY: It's my … you know … you only get one chance to set the record straight.
GERRY: As you say, 'timing is everything'.

Beat.

Think of yourself as a young man. Dreaming of a better future. That's your son. That's what he's inherited. He's you, writing all those stories, exposing the truth, trying to make the world a better place.

HARRY: Fat lot of good it did!

GERRY: Imagine what it would be like if you hadn't? That's what motivates him. Sure, he wants to prove himself to you. What son doesn't?

HARRY: Huh!

GERRY: You've fought your fight. Smell the roses, Harry. Not everyone gets to enjoy this—

She waves her arm, indicating the room.

HARRY: You want me to compromise—

GERRY: We all have to compromise Harry.

She notices the notes on the floor. She picks them up and puts them in the bin.

We're offering you a lifeline, Harry. Your choice. He's a good man. And a good son.

Beat.

HARRY: Are you having it off with him?

GERRY: I beg your pardon?

HARRY: You're like his—

GERRY: What?

HARRY: You do all his dirty work for him.

GERRY: I'm going to ignore that remark, Harry. I have a job to do and I'm going to do it. I tell you what, though. I'm not putting up with your shit.

She goes to leave.

HARRY: Wait.

GERRY: Yes?

HARRY: What's …

He points at the package.

GERRY: He does care about you.

HARRY: What is it?

GERRY: You don't know how lucky you are.

She returns to the package and unwraps the latest in computer technology.

This will make your life a bit easier. Speak into this and it'll write it for you.

HARRY: A dictaphone?

GERRY: Sort of. Makes editing a piece of cake.

HARRY: Editing?

GERRY: Yes Harry, editing.

HARRY: How am I …

GERRY: I've downloaded your book on to it. All you have to do is speak into this microphone—

HARRY: Doesn't look like a microphone—

GERRY: And it'll cut it for you.

He peers at the device.

HARRY: Or what?

GERRY: You'll work it out.

HARRY: Is that a threat?

GERRY: Please, Harry. Be reasonable. I've got to go. Cheer up. No more …

She mimes cursive writing.

Welcome aboard. It's a new dawn, Harry.

She leaves.

HARRY *takes the notes out of the bin and carefully re-arranges them.*

SCENE FOUR

MEI *is cleaning* HARRY*'s room. She makes sure the coast is clear and takes photos of his notes. She hears a noise and hurriedly returns to cleaning.*

HARRY *enters wearing a towel. He's been in the shower.*

HARRY: Oh. Sorry. I didn't realise …

She tidies, carefully stepping over notes.

What was your name again?

She pretends not to hear him.

That's right. Mei.

She keeps working. He dresses.

I've got a head for names.

He sees the notes are out of place. He picks them up. She freezes.

These were—
MEI: I didn't look at them. I was just tidying—
HARRY: No. No. It's all right. Did you read—
MEI: Listen, Mr Walsh …
HARRY: Harry.
MEI: Harry. Whatever. I nearly lost this job because of you.
HARRY: Did you read that story I gave you?
MEI: You trying to get me in trouble?
HARRY: I thought you might …
MEI: I just followed instructions.
HARRY: What are you going on about?
MEI: Your daughter reported me. Told them I left the place in a mess. Told them I wasn't as good as … whoever.
HARRY: I haven't got a daughter.
MEI: I'm on notice.

She cleans feverishly.

I'm lucky they didn't kick me out.
HARRY: What?
MEI: I can't lose this gig.
HARRY: Really?
MEI: I need the money.
HARRY: Surely there are better things to do than wipe the arses of the living dead.
MEI: You think that's funny?
HARRY: I think a girl like you is wasting her time looking after people like me.
MEI: You've got no idea, have you?
HARRY: Tell me.
MEI: Just let me do my work.

HARRY: Please. Tell me. I want to know.
MEI: It's okay. Just …
HARRY: I can't help you if I don't know.

> *She pauses.*

I can help you. Tell me.

> *She cleans.*

MEI: I need this job. I have to pay the rent or I'll be out with them.
HARRY: Sorry. I've been … locked in here … I've lost … am losing … touch.
MEI: Don't make jokes about shit you know nothing about.
HARRY: I tried—
MEI: —What?
HARRY: To get out. To see.
MEI: Yeah?
HARRY: I tied some sheets together and tried to … Douglas-Bader-style … the sheets tore and I broke my leg. Not very … edifying.
MEI: They don't let you out?
HARRY: Oh, they let me out, but they don't let me see what I want to see.
MEI: What do you want to see?
HARRY: What's really happening.
MEI: It might—
HARRY: Yes?

> *Beat.*

MEI: It's pretty crap.
HARRY: You've got me interested.

> *She indicates the room.*

MEI: This is … not many … you're lucky.
HARRY: I know I'm one of the privileged—
MEI: You better believe it!

> *Beat.*

HARRY: I am interested. To know. I mean, shouldn't a young woman like you be going to university?

MEI: I was. I had to defer like a lot of my friends. It was a choice of being homeless and finishing my degree or postponing it and getting some work till I save enough to live on.

HARRY nods.

HARRY: What were you studying?
MEI: International Studies.
HARRY: Your English is very good.
MEI: It should be. I was born here.
HARRY: Oh …
MEI: I'm Australian, Harry. Third generation. My father came out after Tiananmen Square—
HARRY: Hawkie?
MEI: I need to save enough to go overseas and finish my PhD.
HARRY: Don't they support you?
MEI: The uni? You're kidding, aren't you? The days of supporting young people to study died when you guys fucked it for us.

He nods.

So if you don't mind, I'll get on with this.
HARRY: I wrote a piece about what the end of free tertiary education meant—
MEI: People like you write shit. We live it.

Beat.

HARRY: I'll make sure you don't lose your job.
MEI: You got that much influence?
HARRY: I have now.

MEI looks at him.

Don't you know?
MEI: What?
HARRY: You don't, do you?
MEI: I don't know shit. Why don't you just shut up and let me get this work done.

He watches her. She works quickly and efficiently.

HARRY: I'm the Prime Minister's father.

No response.

Didn't you hear?

Beat.

Mei?

MEI: I heard.

HARRY: It's true.

MEI: Yeah and I'm He Xiangning.

HARRY: Who?

MEI: You don't know everything, do you?

Beat.

She was a Chinese feminist and artist.

She works as he finishes getting dressed.

HARRY: I'm sorry. I really am sorry. My son's Chief-of-Staff. She's a bit of a control freak.

Beat.

She works. He watches her.

I'm on your side.

She stops.

MEI: I know.

He picks up the notes.

HARRY: I try and … piece together what I can.

He hands them to her.

Here. I like the feel. You know … the feel of …

He looks at his notes. She works.

We could …

MEI: Yes?

HARRY: Be a team.

She stops. He picks up the device GERRY *left.*

If you can help me get this to my publishers, I'll be … Avenues will open. Avenues that have been closed down for years. You could be my eyes and ears. I can't get out and about. Not by myself. Not anymore. Once my book hits the streets, I'll be …

MEI: You'll become relevant again?

He laughs.

HARRY: There's always a market for the truth. Even in this day and age.

Beat.

What do you reckon?

She looks around the room and collects her cleaning gear.

MEI: I'll think about it.

She exits.

HARRY *looks at the device, pushes it to one side and start 'scribbling'.*

SCENE FIVE

TOM *and* GERRY *are watching an address* TOM *has made to the National Press Club.*

TOM: 'Now we have migration down to manageable numbers, we can focus on giving Australian jobs to Australians. Reducing permanent migration was part of that. So, too, was restricting the number of international students coming here to study. We owe it to Australians to put them first.

We have a message for those people who have been lucky enough to come to this country. Don't bring your troubles with you. If you want to be accepted into the great country, become an Australian. A true Australian.

From today, we are banning the wearing of national or religious symbols in our schools. You are free to practise your religion but you are not free to force it on the rest of us.

The last few decades have seen a huge amount of waste. Bleeding hearts trying to assuage their 'guilt' with handouts. Those days are well and truly over. We are proud of our history. Proud of the great Australians who built this country from the ground up. I'm happy to say that those years of hand-wringing about our perceived ills are well behind us.

Let us move forward together. United.'

GERRY *switches off the recording.*

GERRY: That should play well in the regions.
TOM: And the 'burbs.
GERRY: Indeed. Well done.

GERRY applauds.

TOM: What are you applauding me for? It's your baby.
GERRY: But you delivered.

She reveals a bottle of French champagne on ice and two flutes.

TOM: Oh!

GERRY kisses him.

GERRY: And on time!

She opens the champagne and pours two glasses.

TOM: Well … you—
GERRY: We.
TOM: I can already feel the knives in my back.
GERRY: They'll love it. 'Aussie jobs for Aussies'.
TOM: Oi! Oi! Oi!

They toast each other.

No, we've got to seal this deal with the Chinese.
GERRY: We will.
TOM: No distractions.
GERRY: No distractions.
TOM: Might even get a nod of acknowledgement from the old bastard.
GERRY: I wouldn't hold your breath.
TOM: Cheers.
GERRY: Cheers! I'm very proud of you.
TOM: Yeah …
GERRY: 'No guts, no glory'?
TOM: You're amazing.

He kisses her.

GERRY: It's important.
TOM: Sure.
GERRY: It is.
TOM: We do what we can.
GERRY: We do.

He entwines his arm around hers and they sip champagne. He lowers her glass and kisses her. She is not sure how to respond. She goes to speak but he puts his finger to her lips and then kisses her again. She pulls away.

TOM: What?

She straightens herself up.

GERRY: Cheers.
TOM: No-one can …
GERRY: There are precedents.
TOM: Come on …
GERRY: These things have a way of coming back to bite you.
TOM: Ten minutes?
GERRY: Especially when they are rushed.

She kisses him.

'Eyes on the ball.'

TOM *groans.*

Save it for later.

He laughs. They kiss.

TOM: After we win the Chinese over?
GERRY: Then we'll have something to really celebrate.

He laughs.

TOM: There are some benefits to this job.
GERRY: There are lots of benefits to this job!

SCENE SIX

HARRY *is lying on the floor, an empty bottle of scotch beside him. He is dead to the world.*

MEI *hurries in.*

MEI: You are—!

She sees him on the floor.

Mr Walsh?

She gently shakes him. He doesn't stir.

Mr Walsh!!

She shakes him again. No response. She checks his breath and begins CPR. She knows what she is doing.

No, no. Please.

She is about to make a call when he groans.

Mr Walsh? What the fuck?

HARRY: Ohhh …

MEI: What are you …

She sees the empty bottle. She picks it up.

You old pisspot!

HARRY: Who are you? An angel? Have I died and gone to heaven?

MEI: No, Mr Walsh, you have drunk yourself into oblivion.

HARRY: Oh? Oblivion.

MEI: And pissed yourself by the look of it.

HARRY: Oh dear.

MEI: We better get you cleaned up.

He waves her away.

You can't …

HARRY: I like to wallow.

MEI: Yuck.

HARRY: Yuck indeed.

MEI: At least change your trousers.

HARRY: In front of you?

She helps him up.

MEI: Come on.

He staggers to his feet. She holds a towel for him.

Here.

He wobbles about trying to undo his trousers.

HARRY: You better give me a hand.

MEI: They better pay me a bonus for this!

She helps him undress and get into some dry clothes.

HARRY: Jesus! My head.

MEI: Serves you right. You silly old bugger.

Together they manage to get him changed.

HARRY: Glad I couldn't find any cigarettes.

MEI: Sit down before you fall down.

He sits, leans back and shuts his eyes. It is all coming back to him.

MEI: You going to tell me?

HARRY: No. No point. Nothing to tell.

MEI: You don't want me to take you to the shower?

He waves the question away and holds his head in his hands.

She gets to work cleaning, tidying up.

So, you weren't bullshitting. You are the Prime Minister's father!

HARRY: Congratulations.

MEI: I didn't make the connection. No-one told me.

HARRY: You thought I was just another silly old bugger …

MEI: I didn't think. I just knew you were 'Harry' in Room 404.

HARRY: Harry in Room 404—

MEI: I feel like an idiot.

HARRY: One of the lucky ones?

Pause.

MEI: Bad news?

HARRY: You could say that.

MEI: Your book?

HARRY: How'd you guess?

MEI *picks up an empty bottle.*

MEI: Someone doesn't want you talking.

HARRY: I thought you were just a carer?

MEI: You know the story.

HARRY: What are you up to?

MEI: Cleaning. Looking after you. Caring for you.

HARRY: Caring for me?

MEI: You've done your bit. You deserve to be cared for.

HARRY: That's an original thought.

MEI: I thought you knew your history.

HARRY: Isn't history dead?
MEI: You can't kill history.
HARRY: You can try.
MEI: But there should always be someone like you digging.
HARRY: And you?
MEI: I'm scratching.
HARRY: Is that right?
MEI: Scratching your back.

They laugh.

HARRY: I'd give anything to get out for a day.
MEI: Don't you have excursions?
HARRY: Oh yes. But I want to see what's really going on.
MEI: You do?
HARRY: Of course.

Beat.

MEI: You serious?
HARRY: I haven't got forever. 'Course I'm serious.
MEI: We better get you in shape then.

She drags him to his feet.

Come on!
HARRY: Steady on.
MEI: Now. Touch your toes.
HARRY: Don't be silly.
MEI: You want to see things?
HARRY: I haven't …
MEI: Go on. Try.

He stands up and bends down. He doesn't move past his knees.

HARRY: See? Arthritis. Too much sitting on my bum.
MEI: That's as far as you can stretch?
HARRY: I haven't done any exercise …
MEI: You're shitting me?
HARRY: No, I'm not.
MEI: How do you put your shoes on?
HARRY: I don't have much need for shoes. I hardly leave the room but on the odd occasion I have to, I do this.

He grabs a pair of shoes and sits on the floor. He struggles to put them on.

See?

MEI: On your feet.

He struggles to stand. She helps him.

You're a bloody invalid.

HARRY: That's why I'm here.

MEI: You're here because you're rich. Now. Let's have a crack at this. You mind?

She massages his calves.

HARRY: Not at all.

MEI: Jeez, your muscles are like jelly.

HARRY: Muscles?

MEI: You must have had good legs once.

HARRY: I was a hurdler.

MEI: We gotta get you moving, dude.

HARRY: Dude?

MEI: Yeah. So?

HARRY: Don't think anyone's ever called me 'dude'.

MEI: First time for everything. Try now.

HARRY *stretches towards his feet.*

Hey man, that's more like it.

HARRY: Man? What is it? Dude, or man?

MEI: Okay. We'll try the other shoe.

She puts it in front of him.

HARRY: I can't …

MEI: Yes you can.

He bends a little.

Keep trying.

He does.

Go on, there! Put a bit a grunt into it.

She gently pushes his back.

Hurt?

HARRY: Ow!!
MEI: Good. Keep going. We're not giving up till you get there.

> *He forces himself. He is in obvious pain. He yells.*

MEI: You should be doing the water aerobics.
HARRY: Do you ever shut up?

> *He pushes himself. She cheers him on.*

MEI: Go on. Go for it!

> *He keeps at it.*

Go Harry! Go! Go!

> *He reaches his ankles.*

Nearly, nearly …
HARRY: I can't …
MEI: Yes you can.
HARRY: Tomorrow.
MEI: Mightn't be a tomorrow.

> HARRY *groans as he pushes himself. He gets the shoe onto his toe.*

Go, go, go!

> HARRY *stretches as hard as he can. She rides him home.*

You're nearly … one last …

> HARRY *puts in one almighty effort and puts the shoe on.*

There you go.

> *High-fives.*

Wasn't that hard, was it?
HARRY: My back's killing me.
MEI: Now the laces?
HARRY: Rome wasn't …
MEI: Here. Just this once.

> *She ties it up for him.*

You can do the other yourself.
HARRY: Do I have to?

SCENE SEVEN

HARRY *is doing push ups.*
A knock on the door.

HARRY: Come in!

>TOM *enters.*
>
>*At first* HARRY *doesn't notice who it is. He thinks it is* MEI.

Ten, eleven, twelve … not bad, eh?

>*He looks up and sees it is* TOM.

Oh.

>*He collapses.*

TOM: You okay?

>HARRY *lifts his head.*

HARRY: I was.

>HARRY *struggles to his feet.* TOM *offers a hand.*

TOM: Here—
HARRY: Fuck off!
TOM: What are you—
HARRY: None of your fucking business.

>*He grabs a towel and wipes himself down.* TOM *tries to make a joke.*

TOM: You'll kill yourself—
HARRY: That'd break your heart.
TOM: I was joking.
HARRY: Yeah.

>HARRY *suddenly becomes a bit doddery. He stumbles.* TOM *tries to offer support.* HARRY *steadies himself.*

TOM: Push ups may not be—
HARRY: If I want your advice I'll ask for it.
TOM: Okay …
HARRY: What do you want?

TOM: You got my message?
HARRY: Which one?
TOM: About—
HARRY: The book?
TOM: Yes. I'm really—
HARRY: Don't give me the shits.
TOM: I am, Dad. I know how much it meant to you.
HARRY: So, you had it put down.
TOM: We asked you to edit—
HARRY: Lie?
TOM: You're the last person I need to tell about political reality.
HARRY: Arsehole.
TOM: We can't jeopardise a whole political agenda for a vanity project.
HARRY: A vanity project?
TOM: In another context ... before I became leader, perhaps ...
    We need to be disciplined. We can't behave like amateurs.
HARRY: We?
TOM: We're a family. We're seen as a family. You're the father of—
HARRY: An ambitious narcissist.
TOM: We all have to make sacrifices.
HARRY: And mine is a life's work.
TOM: You know what a lightning rod it would have been.
HARRY: That's why I wrote it.
TOM: Calling us racists? Blaming us when you should be celebrating us.
HARRY: Celebrating you for making shitloads of money while people can't afford a roof over their heads.
TOM: I'm not arguing with you.
HARRY: I bet you're not. You're on clover while half the bloody country is on its knees.

    Beat.

TOM: Listen. We are in the midst of incredibly delicate negotiations.
HARRY: What are you doing here then?
TOM: I came to offer consolation.
HARRY: You've always been duplicitous.
TOM: Please ...

HARRY: Always had an eye out for the main chance.
TOM: Whatever.
HARRY: You were worried my memoir would reflect badly on you so you stopped it.
TOM: That book's got nothing to do with me, Dad. It's your story. Your legacy. Your place in history. Why can't you be reasonable?
HARRY: Me? I'm not the one who censored—
TOM: This is bigger than both of us.
HARRY: Injustice is injustice whatever the context.
TOM: This isn't about you. For once. It's about something much bigger. It's about us. All of us. This isn't my moment. It's our moment. Ours. It's a concept you've always struggled with.
HARRY: Don't give me the shits.
TOM: In the big scheme of things, your memoir is irrelevant.

> HARRY *loses it and rushes at* TOM, *swinging wildly.* TOM *backs away, avoiding the assault as best he can. He takes some blows on the arms.* HARRY *is like a man possessed.*

Stop it! For fuck's sake ... stop it!

> *There is no stopping* HARRY. *A blow glances off* TOM*'s arm and into his nose.* TOM *reacts by pushing* HARRY *away with one arm and raising the other as if he is about to strike* HARRY.
>
> *He freezes, fist cocked.*
>
> *There is a momentary stand-off before* HARRY, *completely exhausted by this mad adrenalin rush, totters about before falling down.*
>
> TOM, *horrified at what he might be about to do, lowers his fist as he stands over his father.*
>
> TOM *can't believe what has happened.*

Jesus Christ!
I nearly hit you. I nearly hit my own fucken father.
HARRY: Why didn't you?
TOM: Oh, for god's sake!
HARRY: Worried someone might have found out?
TOM: What a fucking joke you are!
HARRY: I'm not laughing.

TOM: You've got no idea.
HARRY: Haven't I just?
TOM: Why? Why do you do this? Why can't you just …
HARRY: You bastard.
TOM: You know I wouldn't hit you. You know that. I was just … self-defence. Defending myself.

> *Beat.*

You've got to let go, Dad. Let go. It's gone. Move on. Enjoy—
HARRY: Fuck off.
TOM: We can do something.
HARRY: We?
TOM: Yes, we.
HARRY: You.
TOM: Come on board, Dad.
HARRY: You're joking.
TOM: An elder statesman. You're respected. Your generation—
HARRY: What would you …

> TOM *helps him to his feet.*

TOM: Can't we just … put it behind us. Make the peace.
Here.

> *He guides him to a chair. Puts his arm around him.* HARRY *rests his head on his arm.*

> *Beat.*

You've got a new girl?
HARRY: What's that …
TOM: We should have been told.
HARRY: She's …
TOM: Yes?
HARRY: Good. I like her.
TOM: You were always a sucker for a pretty face.
HARRY: She's a lot more than a pretty face.
TOM: Is she now?
HARRY: She didn't even know who you were.
TOM: So she told you.
HARRY: Don't you take anyone at face value?

TOM: It's alright. We've done the requisite security checks. Student.
HARRY: Oh?
TOM: At uni.
HARRY: I thought …
TOM: What?
HARRY: Nothing.
TOM: What did she—
HARRY: Nothing. She's … a blank cheque … never says a word.
TOM: Good. She can stay on till Polly comes back.
HARRY: Can we get her another job?
TOM: We?
HARRY: You.
TOM: Ahhh … not sure that's my department. I have slightly bigger fish to fry.
HARRY: Yes … but …
TOM: I'm not your enemy.
HARRY: No?
TOM: No. I stopped fighting you years ago. Or I thought I did.

Beat.

I need you, Dad.

He offers his hand.

They say blood's thicker than water.
HARRY: Do they?

SCENE EIGHT

Early morning.

It looks as though HARRY *is sleeping.*

GERRY *knocks. No movement. She opens the door and enters.*

GERRY: Harry? I know it's late. I snuck past the desk. Being connected to the boss helps.

She tiptoes in. She is carrying a bundle of old books.

We know how shattered you are. These might cheer you up. They're demolishing the old State Library. Plato's *The Republic*.

She holds it up.

Must be …

She looks inside and reads.

Wow! 'Published three-eighty'! Not this edition, of course. But first. Written. And this. *The Social Contract* … Rousseau … Harry?

Puts down the books.

I can't stay. The car's waiting. Have to get to the airport.
Might take your mind off … Harry?

She peers at the shape in the bed. Something is up.

Harry? The car's waiting. Have to get to the airport.

She goes over to him and nudges him.

She nudges him with a little more force. She discovers he isn't there but there is a dummy in his place.

The 'head' rolls off.

She picks it up.

What are you up to, Harry Walsh?

INTERVAL

ACT 2

SCENE NINE

A figure walks onstage dressed in a tattered wetsuit, flippers, board shorts and wearing a diving mask and snorkel.

The figure has just emerged from the water and is carrying a bag with a few mussels. The water is very close and we may hear tiny waves gently lapping the shore.

The figure removes the mask.

It is HARRY.

HARRY: Haven't had so much fun since Nixon resigned.

    MEI *enters.*

MEI: Jeez, you talk some shit. We haven't got all day …

    He tips the mussels out.

HARRY: Not many but …

    HARRY *picks one up and inspects it.*

Bugger.

    He tries to prise it open but it is closed tightly.

Dead.

    He tosses it away in disgust.

There used to be tons of them on that rock.

MEI: We've got to get going.

    She helps him out of the wetsuit.

HARRY: And oysters. All along the riverbank there.

    He points.

Although, you can't see it now. That was the jetty. Where that pole is sticking out. You can just see it.

MEI: You wouldn't get me in that water.

    He examines the water dripping from his hair.

HARRY: I wanted to show you the middens down there. Used to be all the way along the river bank. Right around the island.
MEI: What island?
HARRY: There used to be …
MEI: I knew it was a mistake stopping off here—
HARRY: You wouldn't deprive an old digger …
MEI: Will you shut the fuck up and get a move on?
HARRY: I used to love this place.
MEI: Good. Now …

> HARRY *bends down and ties his shoes up.*

HARRY: You wouldn't believe it. The water used to be like glass. There were days you'd be diving and you could see your flippers like you were on land. The whole coast was full of …

> *Sound of a helicopter overhead.*

MEI: Shit!

> *She drags him down.*

HARRY: You think they're looking—
MEI: Bugger. Danny said he could cover—
HARRY: Who's Danny?
MEI: My friend. Works on the desk at your Home. We haven't got much time.

> *The helicopter sound goes.*

Come on!

> *She hurries him off.*

SCENE TEN

China.

TOM *is being feted at a banquet.* GERRY *sits beside him.*

They are clapping along to a rousing version of a revolutionary song from the Cultural Revolution.

GERRY *takes a message. She leans over and whispers.*

GERRY: They still can't find him.

TOM: What?
GERRY: Keep clapping.

They clap and smile enthusiastically.

I'm sorry but right now you have to focus.
TOM: I'm worried.
GERRY: Of course you are.
TOM: He is my father.
GERRY: Right now you have to worry about them.

She nods in time with the music.

TOM: Typical.
GERRY: We'll find him.
TOM: He chooses the biggest moment in our nation's recent history to go missing.
GERRY: Show them you're loving it.

TOM makes a great show of appreciating the song.

This is make or break.
TOM: I know.

TOM whispers.

TOM: I'd like to break his fucking neck.
GERRY: You are the leader!
TOM: I am.

The revolutionary song ends to tumultuous applause.

TOM stands to make his speech.

GERRY watches.

Thank you. Thank you. That was wonderful.

We are delighted to be here.

Our countries go way a long way back. Many Chinese came to our land seeking their fortune during the gold rushes.

While some of that history is decidedly chequered, the Chinese diggers left an indelible impression on our culture. One that we are only too happy to embrace to this day. There isn't a country town that doesn't have Chinese restaurant in pride of place in the main street.

Polite applause.

We have long had ties that bond us. Chinese culture is widely respected in Australia.

Applause.

He reads.

Many Australians' first experience of a cuisine other than meat and three veg was Chinese. It certainly was in my case.

GERRY: [*aside*] You're kidding?

TOM: Chinese art is studied in Australian schools and, of course, Mandarin is widely studied in Australian schools. The historical context of the strong bonds between our two countries cannot be underestimated.

He looks to GERRY *for moral support.*

The fact that China was at the top of our list of countries to visit speaks to the importance of our relationship. These are ties that will continue to grow as our relationship continues to grow.

Applause.

This Treaty will bond us together in ways that were unimaginable a century ago.

He bows and sits.

GERRY: They lapped it up.

TOM: Did they?

GERRY: Some good grabs in there. It was good.

TOM: Thank God.

GERRY: You okay?

TOM: It would be good to be able to focus on what's important for once.

He indicates his speech.

GERRY: He won't have gone far.

TOM: We can't have him running around … 'specially with a bee in his bonnet about his bloody book.

GERRY: Calm down. You've done really well. We'll never look back once this is signed and sealed.

TOM: Once he's under lock and key!

GERRY: That too.

SCENE ELEVEN

MEI *and* HARRY *have crawled up to the top of a hill.*
They have laser binoculars. It is raining. They are cold and soaked through.

MEI: Okay?
HARRY: Yeah.
MEI: Sure?
HARRY: Apart from not being able to feel my toes.

> *Sound of the chopper. He ducks down.*

MEI: It's okay—
HARRY: But—
MEI: They can't see you …

> *She points above.*

The canopy.

> *He looks up.*

Chill, dude. That lantana and shit provides perfect protection from prying eyes.

> *The chopper leaves.*

Here.

> *She points. They both look through their binoculars. He searches the horizon whilst she looks down from where they are lying.*

HARRY: My God! What a vantage point. You can see for miles. All the way down the coast.
MEI: Down there!
HARRY: Where?
MEI: This isn't a walking tour. There!
HARRY: There?
MEI: Yes. You see the barbed wire?
HARRY: I can see what looks like power lines.
MEI: They're not power lines.
HARRY: Uh-huh.

MEI: That's barbed wire.
HARRY: Barbed wire? I see. Markers?
MEI: They're not markers. They're bits of clothing.
HARRY: Really?
MEI: See where the water is lapping?
HARRY: Yes.
MEI: Roofs.
HARRY: Roofs?
MEI: If you focus tightly, you'll see the ridges just poking out of the water.
HARRY: And that? Looks like some kind of lookout?
MEI: Sort of.
HARRY: Could have been an old whaling platform—
MEI: It wasn't built for whaling! The sea was way out there.

She points.

That was dry land. They were the huts …
HARRY: And that was the fence?
MEI: That's right.
HARRY: A barbed wire fence. With a guard tower.
MEI: Now you're getting the picture.
HARRY: Detention centre?
MEI: Refugee centre.
HARRY: Okay.
MEI: There are more of them. All the way up and down the coast, in protected areas, squirreled away where no-one is allowed to go.
HARRY: Or report on.
MEI: When the tsunami hit Papua Guinea. The villages in all the low-lying areas were flooded.
HARRY: I remember. The great exodus.
MEI: Yes.
HARRY: I thought they were re-settled …
MEI: That's what everyone thought.
HARRY: It was—
MEI: In the news?
HARRY: Well …
MEI: We all know about the news.

HARRY: Yes.

MEI: Then another one hit here.

HARRY: I wrote about that.

MEI: You did.

HARRY: I couldn't get anyone to pay any attention. I wrote about the camps. The re-settlement program. I wrote a long piece about the refugees from the Pacific being re-settled in camps like this after their villages had been flooded. I went to PNG, to Rabaul, where the sea levels had wiped out what was left after the volcano.

MEI: I know.

HARRY: You know?

MEI: Yes. I read it. Buried online. In that obscure Public Policy thing you wrote for—

HARRY: Obscure?

MEI: Sorry, Harry. Only policy nerds like me read that sorta stuff.

HARRY: We tried to get the mainstream media interested—

MEI: Of course you did.

HARRY: It was a national tragedy.

MEI: But no-one knew what really happened.

HARRY: Course they didn't.

MEI: Here.

She takes a device out of her backpack.

Check this out.

HARRY: What is it?

MEI: An eyewitness account. A surfer dude who was camping up here with his mates. They were heading for some big waves when they came up here.

She shows HARRY.

SURFER: [*voiceover*] All this was overgrown. A natural canopy. The water was already over the windows. People were standing on the rooves waving. Some were trying to climb the fences. It was like a race. The water was rising and they were trying …

MEI: [*voiceover*] To get out?

SURFER: [*voiceover*] No way. You couldn't get out and you couldn't get in. All the roads were flooded … washed away. The gates must have been locked too. The … authorities … they must have locked them when they pissed off. I raced back down as quick as I could. I tried emergency services. They wanted to know who I was and where I was. Like, *exactly* where I was. Then I twigged. They wanted to shut me up. They didn't give a fuck about the drowning refugees. I didn't know what the fuck to do. I scrambled back up here but I ... I was already too late. That water ... it had just ... it was incredible. People were ... I could see them ... it was like I was trapped here like a rabbit in a trap, watching them drown.

There was like ... kids ... trying to hang on to their parents ... men and women holding little kids ... babies ... above their heads while the waters kept raging up ... rising ... all around them. One guy ... I can't ... One guy ... I'll never forget this ... I have nightmares about it ... one guy ... the water had swallowed him up. All I could see were his arms.

His arms pointing upwards ... towards ... skywards ... holding a tiny baby. He was trying ... you know ... then he sank and ... I couldn't watch.

It was like I was stuck up here on a watch tower ... an island ... the water had ... if it kept rising, I woulda drowned too. There was no way down ... no way. There were trees and machinery and shit bobbing around like surfboards in a heavy swell. Like they were weightless or something.

MEI: [*voiceover*] And you saw ... witnessed the whole thing.

SURFER: [*voiceover*] I can't stop seeing those people. Their faces all contorted. Their bodies twisted ... impaled on the barbed wire like electrocuted birds. They'd been screaming ... I could hear their screams ... even though they were so far ... and the rain and the wind and the sea was roaring ... every now and then their voices cut through and I ... I can still hear them. I can't stop hearing them. I felt like ... I was useless. I was forced ... I watched ... witnessed ... a massacre and I didn't lift a finger.

End recording. MEI *puts device back in her backpack.*

Beat.

HARRY: This is dynamite.

MEI: It is.

HARRY: How did you ... hang on.

MEI: We have to do something.
HARRY: We?
MEI: Your son was part of the government that hushed this up.
HARRY: A backbencher.
MEI: He didn't say anything.
HARRY: He didn't know.
MEI: He didn't ask.
HARRY: You want me to—
MEI: Tell the truth? Yes. This ... this could have been avoided if anyone had bothered to keep an eye on the sea levels and done their homework. They put those people here because it was cheap, inhospitable land, out of the way that could be kept from the public gaze.
HARRY: Who are you?
MEI: It doesn't matter who I am. I am part of a resistance movement. We grew out of Extinction Rebellion.
HARRY: And you want me to betray my own son?
MEI: If that's how you want to put it.
HARRY: Hooley dooley.
MEI: 'We all have to make sacrifices'. Didn't you write that?
HARRY: And I thought ...
MEI: We can't get anywhere with the mainstream media. Our socials are censored. We need the truth to be told. You talk about 'holding them to account'. Through no fault of your own, you are back in the spotlight. They sent a helicopter out looking for you, for fuck's sake!

>HARRY *thinks this over.*

HARRY: This isn't coincidence, is it?

>MEI *shrugs.*

>If you want me to expose this, you better come clean.

>*Beat.*

MEI: We infiltrated your nursing home. You have been a target for a long time. We knew you had integrity. We knew, if we got to you, that you would come on board. We didn't know your son was going to become PM. Or that your book would be cancelled. That was a bonus.

HARRY: But you knew who he was?
MEI: Of course.

> HARRY *puts two and two together.*

HARRY: And the work-experience girl …
MEI: We knew if we could destabilise the government …
HARRY: Jesus!
MEI: All revolutions have to begin somewhere. We have to act or there will be no future. Your gen and your son's gen live for yourselves. You don't give a fuck about tomorrow.
HARRY: You want me?
MEI: We want you, Harry. We need you. And we'll make sure your book gets published, warts and all.
HARRY: You have that much power?
MEI: We will. No more compromises, Harry. No more deals. This is war.
HARRY: Really?
MEI: Really.
HARRY: What will you say …
MEI: About this?

> *He nods.*

You'll say you escaped. When the guy on duty passed out.
HARRY: I saw a chance?
MEI: You saw a chance.

> *Beat.*

HARRY: Okay. I'm in. One last hurrah.

> *They high-five.*

MEI: Let's get you back.

SCENE TWELVE

TOM *is working in his office. He is multi-tasking. He is reading a brief, underlining important points, while he is taking a call.*

TOM: Okay, okay. The first thing to do is to close it down. Suffocate it. Don't give it any air. Kill the fucken thing. How? I don't fucken know. That's your fucking job for fuck's sake!!

He takes a deep breath.

Of course I'm okay. Now. Avoid any detail. Flood them with expert opinion. Yes. Get the scientists we can rely on. I don't care where they come from, just get them. And get them talking. Yes, Zhou's good. What about a Yank? Buchanan? Good. No-one will understand a word he says. He's good. Just what we want.

And a couple of farmers. That's right. Ma and Pa Kettle. Who are they? Ma and Pa Kettle? No. I don't know them. They're not Queenslanders. They're fictional characters. I'm just trying to paint a picture … a … a metaphor …

GERRY enters. She gives him the 'thumbs up'. He rolls his eyes and signals to her that he's on a crisis call.

Get them to refute the panic merchants. Exactly. Always bring it back to the Treaty. The benefits. Housing, hospital, et cetera, et cetera. Emphasise the tax benefits. As per. Goodo.

He indicates to GERRY that the person on the other end is an idiot.

Call ends.

GERRY: He's back.
TOM: What?
GERRY: In his room.
TOM: In his room?
GERRY: Sleeping.
TOM: Oh, thank God.
GERRY: Yes.
TOM: How is he? Is he—
GERRY: Okay. Few scratches.
TOM: How did he—
GERRY: The girl found him.
TOM: The new one?
GERRY: Yes. Showed some initiative. Took it on herself to search for him.
TOM: We've got every security organisation in the country looking for him and a carer finds him?
GERRY: That's why they're called 'carers'. She turned up with him, cleaned him up, got him some food and put him to bed.

TOM: Just like that?
GERRY: Apparently spent his time interviewing the homeless. Under bridges, in parks, places they didn't think to look.
TOM: Another book?

They laugh.

GERRY: Oh God!
TOM: I'm actually relieved they found him.
GERRY: Course.
TOM: I haven't been able to stop thinking about him. I was fearing the worst. I had images of him being found on the street ... bashed ... lying in some corner in a pool of blood and shit. Even he doesn't deserve that.

Beat.

GERRY: Jesus! Can you imagine—
TOM: What?
GERRY: What the media would have made of it?

'He can't even look after his father. How can he look after the country?'

They would have had a field day.
TOM: Let alone the fucken Opposition.
GERRY: Exactly. We've dodged a bullet.
TOM: What the fuck did he think he was he doing?
GERRY: He wasn't thinking about you, that's for sure!
TOM: That surprise you?
GERRY: It's the fucken book. You know that don't you?
TOM: He could have fucked up the biggest deal this country has ever brokered.
GERRY: It will be to our advantage to make him feel wanted. Important.

Be good for your image too. Use his 'research' to make an announcement about housing. 'Housing for the Homeless'. That sort of shit. He can be our beacon. Our moral compass. They'll lap it up. He'll forget about his fucken book if he gets a bit of the limelight.

'Harry Walsh. The conscience of the nation.'
TOM: Mmm ... not bad.

GERRY: Use the Treaty money to buy up some places. Do them up. We can turn his probing into a good news story. He can investigate and identify areas of greatest need. Give him something to do. It would read well and Harry would feel like he's back in the game.
TOM: You're a genius!
GERRY: And don't you forget it!

SCENE THIRTEEN

HARRY *is working feverishly.*

MEI *rushes in.*

HARRY: Would you betray your son to save the world?
MEI: I haven't got a son.
HARRY: No.
MEI: I've got some good news though.
HARRY: I have been offered the chance to do some serious investigative journalism.
MEI: I've found a site we can broadcast on.
HARRY: Something concrete.
MEI: The shit is going to hit the fan. Big time.
HARRY: Something that could really make a difference.
MEI: Around the world.
HARRY: Make a mark.
MEI: Good, eh?
HARRY: Good? It's terrific. And I've got you to thank for it.
MEI: For what?
HARRY: For getting me off my arse.
MEI: Right?!
HARRY: Researching, asking questions, writing. It's what makes me tick.

>   *Beat.*

MEI: I see. Have they asked you to work for them?
HARRY: They have.
MEI: Wow.
HARRY: Wow, alright.
MEI: What about our story?

HARRY: You can't change the past, but you can influence the future.
MEI: You're dumping me?
HARRY: On the contrary, this could be your big chance.
MEI: My chance?
HARRY: The break you deserve.
MEI: What the fuck—
HARRY: Young legs.
MEI: Why do you talk in shorthand?
HARRY: I need young legs. Someone who can get in amongst it.
MEI: You're offering me—
HARRY: You collect the material and I'll write it up.
MEI: Your assistant?
HARRY: We might be a good team.
MEI: We already are.
HARRY: That's why I want you to work with me.
MEI: Oh my God!
HARRY: You can say goodbye to this …

He indicates her uniform.

MEI: Is this for real?
HARRY: It sure is. Paid, too.
MEI: I see.
HARRY: We are going to record and collate oral histories.
MEI: People's stories?
HARRY: Get them off the streets.
MEI: Before they drown?
HARRY: We might have a chance of preventing … having an influence.
MEI: Me? Working for—
HARRY: You can get a lot more done on the inside. Gerry—
MEI: The one who wanted to sack me?
HARRY: I've told her about you.
MEI: Great.
HARRY: She's very impressed with you.
MEI: Clearly.
HARRY: You found me.
MEI: Right.
HARRY: You brought me back.

MEI: She doesn't know—
HARRY: You gave me the kick up the bum I needed. And you opened my eyes.
MEI: What did you see?
HARRY: I can see that we have been given a heaven-sent opportunity to have an impact on the present. And I can't do it without you.
MEI: Blackmail?
HARRY: A deal with the devil.

Beat.

I know. I know how you feel. We've got to pull the story. What's it going to do?
MEI: It's going to bring them to account.
HARRY: It's not going to bring those people back, but it could jeopardise the potential to stop it happening again. It's political reality.
MEI: What a lot of shit! What about 'without fear or favour'?
HARRY: I've agonised over it. I was excited. I took the bait. Couldn't help myself but … sometimes you have to weigh up the consequences.
MEI: Compromise, you mean?
HARRY: That story will cause untold angst. The Chinese will hate it. Guilt by association. Even though Tom was a backbencher at the time he'll be damaged by it. His government will definitely be tarnished. The other mob will go in for the kill. Even though they supported the policy. It's how it works. We've got a window. A chance to make some real change. We lose this opportunity—it might be gone forever.
MEI: This was a major cover-up.
HARRY: You want a chance to do something?

Beat.

It's a great story but think of the big picture.
MEI: That's why you are offering me the job. So I'll kill it.
HARRY: No. You've got a nose for a good story. And I like you.

Beat.

Hold off for a bit. Think about it.
MEI: I already have.

SCENE FOURTEEN

TOM *is speaking to camera with* GERRY *behind him.*
It is interactive.

TOM: This Treaty with China to mine Antarctica will enable us to finally break free from the restrictions that have prevented us from moving forward as a nation. Extensive environmental studies have proved that the impact on the Antarct will be minimal but the benefits for this country will be enormous.

I'm very excited to announce that, thanks to the China Treaty, we are able to finally do something about the appalling state of housing in this country. Years of neglect by previous governments, mine included, have led to an untenable state where thousands of Australians have been forced to scrounge out an existence on the streets.

As from today, we will be buying up as many derelict and abandoned premises we can find and converting them into public housing. And we're going to make it easier for students to complete their tertiary studies. We are wiping HECS debts for everyone. We will bring in a new scheme that will make university education less reliant on HECS and overseas student fees. We will return universities to the places of learning they were meant to be.

This project is very dear to my heart as I was finally convinced to do something concrete about this by a man who is, and always has been, my conscience.

My father, Mr Harry Walsh.

HARRY *totters up to his side. This is the public, old and doddery* HARRY.

He is dressed formally. There is spontaneous applause.

HARRY *waves. He clearly enjoys the attention.*

We might have had our differences in the past, but I would like to publicly acknowledge the huge debt I owe my father.

He hands over to HARRY.

HARRY *unfolds a speech.*

HARRY: Thank you, thank you.

It is so great to see you all here and to be part of this wonderful project. Although, I have to admit, it does feel a bit odd being on this side of the microphone.

And … I won't be taking any questions!

Laughter.

You can ask him.

He reads.

My role in this project will be to finally put my journalistic skills to some practical use through investigation and research. If I can twist his arm, I might even get a book out of it!

It is good to be involved in something like this and to have the opportunity to do something useful with my time.

Thank you.

TOM: Thanks everyone.

End of digital press conference.

TOM puts his arm around HARRY. GERRY opens a bottle of champagne. She pours three glasses. She raises a glass to HARRY.

GERRY: Quite the rock star!

TOM toasts.

TOM: Welcome on board.

HARRY is visibly moved. They clink glasses.

HARRY: I don't know how you do it. All those kids sticking microphones in your face.

TOM: You were one of those kids once.

HARRY: Really? I don't remember.

TOM: They've got their job to do, and I've got mine. Besides, none of them ask the kind of uncomfortable questions you delighted in asking.

HARRY: No.

MEI: Now. We better get to work.

A call.

TOM: Here we go. Another crisis?

TOM *takes the call.*

What? Yes, yes. Put it through. It hasn't … good!

End call.

TOM *turns on* HARRY.

You bastard!

He turns on a screen. Vision of MEI. *She points to the refugee camp.*

MEI: 'This is the story the government didn't want you to know about. Down there … '

The camera pans to show the bits of clothing fluttering on the submerged fence.

' … a tragedy took place, and we are going to tell you about it.'

The camera pans to pick up HARRY *looking down at the camp.*

'This is Harry Walsh. Harry was one of this country's most respected journalists. But, perhaps of more relevance to this story he is also the Prime Minister's father.'

TOM *turns down the sound. The vision continues.*

TOM: Interviewing the homeless, were you?
HARRY: I didn't know—
TOM: You didn't know?
HARRY: We agreed—
GERRY: What is this, Harry?
TOM: What the fuck were you doing?
HARRY: She—
TOM: Yes?
HARRY: I told her—
TOM: What?
GERRY: Christ, Harry. A story like this could bring down the government. Put an end to all the things we've been working towards.
HARRY: Please … believe me.
TOM: Believe you! Why would anyone believe you? You betrayed us.
GERRY: Who is she working for?
HARRY: No-one … I … I don't know … I thought—
TOM: You thought?

HARRY: I thought she would let it go …
GERRY: She must be working for some organisation.
HARRY: She's not! She's a young girl with a social conscience.
TOM: Do you have any fucken idea what … of course you do!
HARRY: I didn't think—
TOM: You can say that again.
HARRY: I'm sorry.
TOM: You're sorry?
HARRY: You won't do anything to her, will you?
TOM: She is the least of your worries.
GERRY: You have breached the National Security Act, Harry. You could go to jail for this. Ten years.

> HARRY *nearly collapses.*

TOM: Don't try that stunt on us.
HARRY: I'm not trying anything.
TOM: Can you take him back to the home?
GERRY: Sure.
TOM: And make sure he can't get out.
GERRY: Come on.

> *She takes* HARRY*'s arm. He can barely walk.*

TOM: You always had to have the final word.
HARRY: I'm sorry—
TOM: Sure. Get rid of him.

> GERRY *leads* HARRY *out.* TOM *makes a call.*

SCENE FIFTEEN

HARRY *is in his room. Writing, researching.*
Surveillance cameras in every corner. There is a knock on the door. He looks up.

MEI *enters. She checks no-one has followed her. She whispers.*

MEI: Hi.

> *He looks up.*

HARRY: What do you want?

MEI: I had to see you.
HARRY: How did you get in?

> HARRY *points at the cameras.*

Happy?
MEI: We haven't got long …
HARRY: I'm busy.
MEI: Something's wrong.
HARRY: You never told me you were going to screen it.
MEI: It hasn't gone to air.
HARRY: What?
MEI: The story. I've searched the site. It hasn't been posted. Did you blow it?
HARRY: No.
MEI: They won't return my messages.
HARRY: What do you mean it hasn't—
MEI: It hasn't gone out. Someone has stopped it.
HARRY: Intercepted it?
MEI: Yes. Censored it.
HARRY: Thank God.
MEI: Someone tipped off National Security.
HARRY: It wasn't me.
MEI: Bullshit, Harry.
HARRY: If I knew you were going to post it, I might have, but I thought we agreed—
MEI: We didn't agree on anything. You told me to think about it. I did. For about two seconds.
HARRY: They are better than we thought.
MEI: You were the man. I studied you at uni. When I was doing political journalism. I wrote my PhD about you. You were the man who always got stories out, who broke big stories. A man who talked about 'holding firm' in the face of government interference, about journalists being committed 'unshakeably' to principle. No matter the cost.

I believed you. I knew you'd be the man to help me get this story out.

> *She takes out a piece of paper.*

This is what you said—

'As long as a journalist tells the truth, in conscience and in fairness, it is not his job to worry about the consequences. The truth is never as dangerous as a lie in the long run. I truly believe that the truth sets men free.'

I carried that piece of paper everywhere. It was my talisman.

She tears it into tiny strips and drops it on the floor.

I'm not cleaning it up either.

I've still got the story though and one day ... one day you'll see yourself when, for a brief moment, you lived up to your bullshit.

A VOICE *on a megaphone.*

VOICE: Mei Ling Young. This is National Security. You are under arrest for violating the National Anti-Terrorism Act. You will be charged with 'causing serious harm and danger to National Security'.

We would ask you to come out with your hands raised.

SCENE SIXTEEN

MEI *is in solitary confinement.*

The door is unlocked. GERRY *enters.*

GERRY: Hi.
MEI: Hi.
GERRY: I'm—
MEI: I know who you are.
GERRY: I could ask how you are but that would be—
MEI: Stupid?
GERRY: Yes.
MEI: I've got nothing to say.
GERRY: I didn't come to ...
    We had—
MEI: To make an example?
GERRY: We want to bring you back.
MEI: Back?
GERRY: We've secured the Treaty. We are serious about implementing the program.
MEI: And white-washing the past.

GERRY: Moving forward.
MEI: Of course.

> *Beat.*

GERRY: Harry's dead.
MEI: What?
GERRY: He died last night.
MEI: How?
GERRY: In his sleep.

> MEI *is upset by the news.*

MEI: That's …
GERRY: Sad?

> MEI *nods.*

Yes, it is.

> MEI *shakes her head.*

He … he's been fading … he seemed to give up … after—
MEI: After I was locked up?
GERRY: He never forgave himself.
MEI: I … I can't tell you how many times I have cursed his name. Double crossing—
GERRY: It wasn't him. National Security were on to you the moment you contacted that site. He had nothing to do with it. He was trying to protect you. He was with us when they intercepted it. He was devastated.
MEI: Why did he give up?
GERRY: He was old. Tired.
MEI: No. With the story? Why did he—
GERRY: Wouldn't your father try and protect you?
MEI: How did you know?
GERRY: There's not much we don't know.

> *Beat.*

Just as he was about to deliver the knockout blow he saw what he was doing. If anyone else was PM—
MEI: I wouldn't have—
GERRY: No. You wouldn't. But you're young.

Beat.

We want you to confess.

MEI: Confess?

GERRY: Yes. Admit that you hoodwinked him.

MEI: What?

GERRY: In exchange for a public confession, we'll make sure you can finish your PhD. And we'll find somewhere for you to live. With an allowance.

MEI: You're kidding.

GERRY: Even though you were completely misguided, you did revive him. The PM wants to acknowledge that.

MEI: Really?

GERRY: Well … Harry did make us promise. When he was dying.

Beat.

And we'd like you to—

MEI: Work for you?

GERRY: Keep us honest.

MEI: You want me to tell you where the footage is?

GERRY: You don't have to. We've got it.

MEI: How? Of course.

GERRY: Think about it.

MEI: I have. Fuck off!

GERRY: Suit yourself.

She goes to exit.

Oh, by the way, we're publishing his book.

MEI: Edited?

GERRY smiles and exits. Sound of door clanging.

SCENE SEVENTEEN

HARRY*'s funeral.*

TOM *has paused in his eulogy to show footage of* HARRY *holding an award.*

HARRY: 'Thank you. Thank you. This is much appreciated. There were times when I wondered if this book would ever be published. But … you never know, do you?

What do we do, we people who report on what happens? We shine a light on the world around us so that the rest of us can see what is being hidden.

We learn, we report, we verify, we write and we publish.

We do so without fear or favour.

We don't make the news. We tell the news.

I hope you enjoy the book.'

End footage.

TOM: That is what Harry Walsh did. Uncover the 'cover-ups'. Hold us to account.

All of us.

He exposed our flaws. Revealed what was outside the frame. Made us confront our weaknesses.

He holds up a tablet.

It's here in this a book. A memoir. My father's memoir. Sadly, he died before it was published but we will honour him and his memory by ensuring it is published posthumously. He might have left us, but his words live on to remind us of what is important.

EPILOGUE

MEI: Zhishou took pity on Yugong and spoke to the king of the Gods. They were all impressed by Yugong's sincerity, if not his practicality.

The king of the Gods asked his friend Kua'eshi, the God who was strongest, to help Yugong achieve his goal. Kua'eshi ordered his sons to move the mountains so they carried them away on their backs and placed them in the east of Shuozhou and the south of Yongzhou.

The removal of the mountains pleased everyone in the village and Yugong was feted by all and sundry.

However, after a while, heavy rains flooded the great holes left by the removal of the mountains and the water overflowed into the Han River turning the pristine waters to mud and killing all the fish.

Even though Yugong's people could make their way directly to the Han River without going around the mountains, they were no longer able to drink from the river or live off the sea life.

THE END

THE SWEETEST THING
Verity Laughton

The Sweetest Thing was first produced by Arts Radar at Belvoir Downstairs, on the Lands of the Gadigal peoples of the Eora Nation, Sydney, on 28 October 2010, with the following cast:

SARAH	Diana Glenn
FELICITY	Caroline Craig
BELLA	Lucy Wigmore
ELIZABETH	Vanessa Downing
JIMMY	Chris Morris
JOSH	Tom Conroy

Director, Sarah Goodes
Dramaturg, Lee Lewis
Set and Costume, Melissa Dale-Johnson
Lighting, Verity Hampson
Sound and Composition, Emily Maguire
Stage Manager/Assistant Director, Michael Dean

CHARACTERS

ELIZABETH. A woman in her early fifties.

BELLA. Twenty-six, thirteen and forty-three, Elizabeth's oldest daughter.

SARAH. Twenty-three, eleven, forty and twenty-two, the middle child.

FELICITY. Twenty, ten and thirty-eight, the youngest daughter and confidante of Sarah.

JIMMY. Thirty, Sarah's lover.

JOSH. Sixteen, Sarah's son.

SETTING

The play has a fluid time structure.

The setting is abstract and owes something to images associated with chaos theory, which provides an underlying metaphor for the action of the piece.

Locations are: a restaurant in Taapua, New Zealand; a cottage in Taapua; a garden in Taapua that overlooks the sea; an Australian beach in high summer; a bedroom in a house in Australia; a suburban living room in Australia; a jetty in Taapua.

SCENE 1

A corner nook of a seaside restaurant in New Zealand, some in sunlight, some in shade. Around 1990.

The mirrors in the text may be suggested rather than real.

ELIZABETH: You bought him a boat.
SARAH: We can sit over there.
ELIZABETH: I can't bear the gloom.
FELICITY: Or here, you can see the water from here.
ELIZABETH: Everyone who matters is dead.
SARAH: Thanks, Ma.
ELIZABETH: I am not your father, Sarah. I can't give you this sort of advice!
SARAH: Then don't. Don't is good. Don't.
FELICITY: Got it. A boat will depreciate. You don't spend your capital on something that will depreciate—
ELIZABETH: Here. It's sunny here.
FELICITY: Oh yes! The booth.
ELIZABETH: [*sitting*] Felicity?
FELICITY: See? Mirrors on either side. We're in a double infinity.
SARAH: [*sitting*] A *what*?
FELICITY: I can see you seeing me seeing you. Us. Here. Now. Going on for ever and ever and ever. Isn't it lovely?

> ELIZABETH *and* SARAH *look at her, look at each other.*
>
> *Beat.*

ELIZABETH: How much did the boat cost?
FELICITY: Don't even try, Elizabeth.
SARAH: And a truck. I also bought him a nice—used—pick-up truck.
FELICITY: Truck?
SARAH: Aren't you my second, sweetheart?
ELIZABETH: This isn't a duel.
SARAH: To the death. Have at you, varmint!
FELICITY: Sarah.
ELIZABETH: Three daughters. My friends are envious, you know.

SARAH: Ma, you have balls enough for all of us.
ELIZABETH: Don't be crude—
SARAH: Balls, round, soft, sort of heavy in a tender way, fit so sweet in the palm of a hand.

> FELICITY *laughs.*

ELIZABETH: I have come two thousand kilometres, Sarah.
SARAH: Yes. And with Flicka, too. Thank you, yes.
FELICITY: Bella sends her love.
SARAH: [*coolly*] Cool.

> *Beat.*

The boys okay?
ELIZABETH: The boys are beautiful. Sam's started kindy and Toby's got his first tooth.
SARAH: Cool.
FELICITY: I think I'll have the duck.
SARAH: Fuck—
ELIZABETH: Must you—
SARAH: Really? —
ELIZABETH: Swear? —
SARAH: It's wet duck.
FELICITY: What does that mean?
SARAH: It means, don't have the duck.
ELIZABETH: How long does one normally wait to be served in this establishment?
SARAH: You go to the counter.
FELICITY: I'll go. Tell me what you want, and I'll go.
SARAH: Marinara's best.
ELIZABETH: The omelette.
SARAH: Omelette?! You?
ELIZABETH: Indigestion.
SARAH: You don't want the steak?
ELIZABETH: No.
SARAH: Really?
FELICITY: Oi!
SARAH: Marinara, baby. What about you?
FELICITY: The duck.

FELICITY *leaves.*

ELIZABETH: I love her calm. I do love her calm.

SARAH: Ma? I wake in the morning and—the way the light cuts through the window? The shadows are so sharp. Fern stalks and spiral fronds and the summer's spun a spider's web and you can see it on the blind. Ma? I've never been so happy, ever!

ELIZABETH: Does Jimmy always drink as much as that?

SARAH: He was nervous.

ELIZABETH: Yes.

SARAH: Yes.

ELIZABETH: Yes.

Pause.

I was sorting the photos the other day–

SARAH: Don't.

ELIZABETH: That one of you painting the gate in your bathers, the little blue ones, with the ribbing. You were about four, those little stocky legs, the only one of the three who was stocky like that, and look at you now. And you'd been eating mud pies and your whole mouth was like—

SARAH: You always do this!

ELIZABETH: Sarah, there are men with whom to have an affair, if you must, and men to—when I think of your father—

SARAH: Don't!

ELIZABETH: You are doing this to provoke me!

Pause.

I can see Jimmy's charming—that kind of man always is—the manner—that physical competence—

SARAH: He's a magician on the boat. He's magic with an engine. With the tides. When the sun's playing tricks, when there'll be a storm, what the clouds mean, he can read the sky, Mum, he can read the stars, he looks up into the night sky and he can read the great sparkling scrawl of it—

ELIZABETH: But not a book.

SARAH: Jesus Christ!

ELIZABETH: It's the truth!

FELICITY *returns.*

FELICITY: All done. Have you made peace yet?

SARAH: Not by the hair of her chinny-chin-chin.

ELIZABETH: How much have you spent on him?!

SARAH: The whole legacy's gone, Ma. A boat, the truck, a bit of fixing of the farmhouse. And we dropped by the Fisheries to pick up the manual. Then we sat in the kitchen and Jimmy let me—he let me!—coach him till he knew the rules by rote, and he's got his skipper's ticket and I've given him a life!

Silence.

FELICITY *sits.*

FELICITY: Course, regarding mirrors you'd have to wonder if the significant thing is us sitting here observing the pattern, or if the significant thing is the pattern itself—which includes us. From the standpoint of eternity, I think you'd have to say the pattern.

SARAH: Have you got a new hobby or something?

Beat.

FELICITY: No. I mean. Yes? Sort of?

Beat.

SARAH: Look, it's nice of you to offer a distraction but I can cope with this woman, you know.

ELIZABETH: But can she cope with you, is I think what Felicity is inferring.

SARAH: If she can't, she's losing her touch.

ELIZABETH: That is a dreadful thing to say.

SARAH: I could have said—New Zealand's too far! I could have said—don't come!

Beat.

ELIZABETH: You published a poem, you said?

SARAH: Yes. In a reputable magazine. How about that?

ELIZABETH: What's it about?

SARAH: Dad.

Beat.

ELIZABETH: Why on *earth*—'*Jimmy*'!?

SARAH: You will not make me cry!

Silence.

FELICITY: [*sings*] Oh, the water is wide
    And I cannot get o'er …
SARAH: My dear, dear Flicka.
ELIZABETH: How? How have I betrayed you? Sarah?
SARAH: Keep singing, Flick.
FELICITY: [*sings*] Nor do I have
    The wings to fly
    Bring me a boat
    That will carry two
    And both will row
    My true love and I.
ELIZABETH: Frank.

SCENE 2

New Zealand.

SARAH'*s bedroom.*

JIMMY *is falling over himself. He makes his stumbling way to her bed.*

JIMMY: Fu-u-ucking cuu-u-u-unt!

   SARAH *wakes.*

The most beautiful fucking woman in the entire world and I spend my night in the fucking truck.

   SARAH *switches on a small bedside lamp.*

SARAH: Oh shit.
JIMMY: I'm alive, darlin'!
SARAH: I feel sick.
JIMMY: I met this—tree? Maybe? Shook me up. So I … stopped.
SARAH: Not the truck.
JIMMY: Not a fucking scratch you wouldn't read about it! Some buggers have such luck!

   JIMMY *falls on the bed. He notices a piece of paper.*

What's this?

SARAH: It's a poem. I was trying to write a poem.
JIMMY: Am I in it?
SARAH: Nope.
JIMMY: A grown woman spends her day—
SARAH: Night, Jimmy, spent her night —
JIMMY: Grown woman spends her night making up crap about—

He peers at the piece of paper.

—'the Dogstar'??!
SARAH: Keep your voice down!
JIMMY: [*howling*] Ow-oooo!
SARAH: Jimmy!
JIMMY: Howling for the moon! Ow-ooo!!

She laughs.

He chucks the piece of paper down.

Kiss me.
SARAH: No kisses for you, puppy.
JIMMY: It's going to be a fucking beautiful day.
SARAH: Are you still drunk?
JIMMY: Nope.

Beat.

Not very.
SARAH: I asked you. Keep it sweet, at least while Mum's here, please, please keep it sweet.
JIMMY: You're sweet.
SARAH: Stop that.
JIMMY: Fucking look at you—where'd they make hair like that? It's like a storm. Storm of sunshine.

He reaches towards her as if to touch.

So soft.
SARAH: Fuck right off.
JIMMY: I love it when you talk dirty to me.
SARAH: You're a walking cliché.
JIMMY: I'm a man.
SARAH: Now you're a raging walking cliché.

JIMMY: Some men are?

SARAH: You stink of cigarettes and grog.

JIMMY: A man doesn't need god, Sarah, when he's looking at someone like you in his bed.

SARAH: My mother's in the next room.

JIMMY: And a fine woman she'd be, your mother, yairs. Spread your legs. Under the covers. Spread your legs.

SARAH: I waited all night for you! I thought you were dead!

JIMMY: I'M ALIVE!

SARAH: I can't leave you alone for a—

JIMMY: Cliché yourself!

SARAH: Don't play games!

JIMMY: Games? Oh, I get it. You own 'em, do y', y' *words*? You got yourself a goodo game an' I'm not allowed to play. Did it give you a kick? Coachin' your cretin? Did it make you feel good? What have you ever done with your words, missy, that I haven't done with my hands?

SARAH: Don't do this.

JIMMY: I want to fuck you senseless.

SARAH: Cliché!

JIMMY: Why, so it is. I want to fuck you so you melt, so you dissolve, I want to bring the queen to her knees, I want her to beg me for release. Spread your legs.

She does.

I am inside you.

SARAH: Oh, please.

JIMMY: Lie right down.

SARAH: I am not your patsy!

JIMMY: You are so weak.

SARAH: I am not weak.

JIMMY: Then why're you lying down, baby?

SARAH: I'm dizzy.

JIMMY: Shut your eyes.

She does.

I am on my knees.

SARAH: Are you?

JIMMY: Yeah. I'm on my knees and I'm crawling—on my knees, beautiful Sarah—to make you happy, if I can, just for a minute, darlin', just for however long, if I can. If you want.

Transition to:

SCENE 2A

ELIZABETH, *alone in the adjoining bedroom in* SARAH's *house.*

As ELIZABETH *speaks, the hint of a man's shape emerges. He is something like a heavy shadow, an evocation rather than a person.*

ELIZABETH *doesn't address her words to him, but he's clearly the person she has in mind.*

ELIZABETH: I don't know why the young assume, Frank, that their elders should sleep. I don't know why they should assume, either, that we might be shocked by their passion. Do you think, Frank, that they think—that she, thinks, Sarah—thinks—that she's the first young woman to be obliterated by her passion for a particular man?

Beat.

Well.

She gets up, goes to the window.

Stars. Such a far, cold light.

She looks out the window.

So dark. This place. What would you call it? 'A rural hamlet'? No. You'd say that's affected. You'd call it a town. It's small and muddy, Frank, there's been no money for generations, it's a hotch-potch, it's like a … like an ugly home-made quilt.

Do you remember? Your Aunt Ange knitted one for a baby blanket when Bella was born, made of squares of old wool. Dreadful. I was late saying thank you to Aunt, so your mother picked me up and we had afternoon tea, me and her and Aunt Ange and the baby. How could I have been so tardy? *Noblesse oblige*, Frank, it didn't come naturally. I had to be taught.

She cries.

Frank?!

Beat.

He's a man's man. Whatever that means these days. Perhaps you'd even like him. Would you? You might. He's healthy. He's kind when it suits him. He—clearly—loves her. Nothing so fine's come his way since he was knee-high to a grasshopper. He won't see what he's stealing from her.

Beat.

Does he? Love her?

She cries.

He let her spend her inheritance to buy him a boat! You'd loathe him. He's a chancer. I can hear them!

The shadows whirl, fade.

Your words girl, Frank, and her dyslexic lover!

Bird song.

The first birds.

Another trill of song.

The first notes come in the dark.

Another, softer trill.

Is it a flightless bird, padding among soft wet twigs? Hunched over? A little grey thing?

The last trill, fading.

I always come back. I always come back to you!

Transition to:.

Adjoining bedroom.

A bird, loudly.

SARAH *sits up in bed. She listens. The sleeping* JIMMY *is alongside her.*

She listens, hard, in the new light.

SARAH: Ma?

No sound.

She sinks back beside JIMMY.

SCENE 3

Australia, twelve years before the previous scene.

SARAH, *eleven, and* FELICITY, *ten, are making a cubby on the outer edge of a limestone cave on a beach.*

SARAH: Dig back there in the cave.
FELICITY: Where, Sare?
SARAH: At the back, then we can put—this—pole in there and—
FELICITY: Should I tie it?
SARAH: You can't reach.
FELICITY: I can.
SARAH: I'll do it.
FELICITY: Bella would let me.
SARAH: Bella's helping Mum and Gran.

> FELICITY *tugs at the pole. She brings the whole structure crashing down.*

Mutiny?!

> SARAH *prepares to launch herself at* FELICITY.

I'll thrash ye black an' blue, ye varmint! Ye scurvy heap o' stink!

> *It's looking dangerous.*

FELICITY: [*singing, call-and-response*] 'I'm building—
SARAH: [*singing*]   castles in the sand!
FELICITY: [*singing*]   I'm swimming —
SARAH: [*singing*]   right across the strand—
FELICITY: [*singing*]   I'm floating—
SARAH: [*singing*]   on the surface of the sea—
BOTH: [*singing*]   And the sun is shining down on me!
SARAH: [*singing*]   I'm picking crabs up on the beach
                             I'm picking legs off for a treat—'
FELICITY: Don't spoil Dad's words!
SARAH: [*singing*]   'I'm floating on the surface of the sea—'

> *She points.* FELICITY *resists.*

Come on, ye varmint!
  [*Singing*]   'And the sun is—

BOTH: [*singing*]　　　　shining down on me!'
SARAH: Oh, you sound so lovely, Flicka. I soooo wish I could sing.
FELICITY: You can make up rhymes.
SARAH: Yes. I can. Like Dad. I can.

> FELICITY *starts drawing a hopscotch pattern on the sand.*

Me first.
FELICITY: Mum says you have to let me go first, at least sometimes.

> SARAH *throws a shell on to the first square. She starts hopping, finishes her turn.*

SARAH: You now.

> FELICITY *starts hopping.*
>
> *Then stops.*

FELICITY: You've scuffed the lines.
SARAH: You want your turn or not?!

> FELICITY *starts again.*

Stepped on a line!
FELICITY: I did not!
SARAH: You're out!
FELICITY: Not!
SARAH: Yes! I won! Sarah is best again!

> FELICITY *launches herself at* SARAH. *There's an intense struggle.* SARAH *ends up sitting on top of the flattened* FELICITY.

FELICITY: [*clearly quoting someone*] You're trouble. You're more work than the rest of us combined.
SARAH: Good grief, I'd be embarrassed if I wasn't more work than two goody-goody girlies, I'd be wracked with grief!
FELICITY: And you're the melodrama queen!
SARAH: And you're just little and dumb.
FELICITY: I can add up!

> SARAH *roars—like a tiger—at* FELICITY.

And I'm not playing tigers!
SARAH: If a tiger walked down this beach, prowled down this beach, what would you do?

FELICITY: Hide.
SARAH: In the cubby?
FELICITY: I'd go in the water.
SARAH: Tigers can swim!
FELICITY: What would you do?
SARAH: I'd use my magic power.
FELICITY: You don't *have* any magic power!
SARAH: But I do. That's how it is.
FELICITY: You don't!
SARAH: Yes, I do! If I *want*!

>Beat.

FELICITY: Bella says, Mum says I should play with my own friends. Bella says, Mum says you overpower me. Bella says, Mum says 'Bella's better with Felicity. Because Bella gives Felicity more space.'
SARAH: So what do you want? Felicity?
FELICITY: I want. To know stuff.
SARAH: What 'stuff'? Felicity?
FELICITY: Every stuff, Sarah.
SARAH: 'Tyger, tyger, burning bright
>In the forests of the night
>What immortal hand or eye
>Dare frame thy fearful symmetrie?'
FELICITY: Symmetree.
SARAH: You bend the word, Flicka, when it doesn't fit because it's more beautiful that way.
FELICITY: It should be right.
SARAH: It should be *beautiful*.

>BELLA *enters carrying a small paper bag.*

BELLA: Mum says. 'Come inside.'

>SARAH *grabs* FELICITY*'s arm and starts marching her off in the opposite direction.*

Sarah! Mum says!

>Beat.

Flicky? Granny's made hot cross / buns!

FELICITY: Buns, Sarah! *Butter!*

FELICITY detaches herself from SARAH *and exits in the direction from which* BELLA *came.*

BELLA: You gotta come now. Mum says. Sarah?

SARAH: Tim.

BELLA: You are not / Tim!

SARAH: My name is Tim Kelly, Bella, and you can call me Tim!

BELLA: You are not a boy.

SARAH: Dad calls me Tim.

She growls.

Watch out. Here's Tiger Tim. Big paddy-pad old tiger prowling down the beach so—watch out! Fearful symmetrie!

BELLA: To be a boy. You need. [*With effort*] A dick.

SARAH: You don't need a dick to piss standing up!

BELLA: Oh yuck!

SARAH starts to pull her daks down.

DON'T!

SARAH: You're pathetic.

BELLA: You're not a boy, Sarah Kelly, you can't piss standing up and you can't—

SARAH: What?

BELLA: You know—!

She makes a few tentative pelvic thrusts. They collapse with laughter. More thrusting. More laughter.

SARAH: I saw Mum and Dad once.

BELLA: You didn't.

SARAH: I did!

SARAH thrusts outrageously.

BELLA: Oh yuck!

Another giggling collapse.

SARAH: Yesterday, you know, early, early. They're in bed and I come in fast because it's—you know—holidays so I ... And—

BELLA: What'd you do?

SARAH: I cried. They were together and I shouldn't be there. So I cried.

So they stopped and I got into their bed and Mum—
BELLA: Do you hate Mum?

Beat.

Do you?
SARAH: You don't get it, do you? I tell you something, really important, to be *nice*! And you just turn it into … Stupid!
BELLA: You do hate her.
SARAH: I do not!
BELLA: You do, you know. You love Dad and you hate Mum. Poor Mum.
SARAH: Look! You never *get* it! Doesn't matter what it is, you just never get it!

Beat.

Look.

Beat.

You're really kind, Bella. You look after me. You look after Flicka. You're really kind and careful and good. I'm not like you, that's all. I'm just—not!
BELLA: Who are you like?
SARAH: I'm like—Dad.
BELLA: No. Not. Flicka's like Dad.
SARAH: I do words.
BELLA: But Flicka's the one like Dad.

She's right.

Eyes are red.
SARAH: Grrrrrrooooowwwwwlllllllll!

An enormous fight. But SARAH breaks away. She ends up gasping on the sand.

I can't breathe! Bella! I can't breathe!
BELLA: Wait! Quick! Wait! Paper bag. Uh—

She empties a small beach bag of its contents.

Lunch bag.

She holds the bag over SARAH's mouth.

Breathe. Into the bag. In. Out, Yep. That's it. In. Out. Good. Goooood. Is that better?

> SARAH *nods, relaxes.* BELLA *comforts her.*

SARAH: Why do I *do* that?
BELLA: It's not your fault. Like Mum says. You care too much and … problem.
SARAH: I think … it's never going to stop. My skin prickles and there's this—drilling—in my head. And everything's very big. And everything's very small. And I'm dizzy and … no breath!

> BELLA *waits.*

Maybe I'm crazy?
BELLA: Maybe?
SARAH: Lucky they got you and Flicka.

> BELLA *strokes* SARAH.

BELLA: I guess. Lucky.

> SARAH *extracts something from her pocket, gives it to* BELLA.

SARAH: Cocoon. Silkworm.

> *Beat.*

BELLA: Thanks.

> *Beat.*

SARAH: You're Mum's. The way you are. 'Everything in its / place.'
BELLA: 'Place.'
SARAH: And Flicka's Dad's.
BELLA: They're both so calm.
SARAH: Maybe I'm an orphan.
BELLA: [*fondly*] Drama queen.
SARAH: Why am I an orphan?

> BELLA *strokes the silkworm cocoon.*

BELLA: Do you think it's still alive?

> *Pause.*

SARAH: I'll go away. On my own. Far away. Where there's magic. And people can live like tigers. Big and mean and beautiful. And no-one cares if you're good.

SCENE 4

New Zealand.

SARAH *and* FELICITY *are dancing arm in arm, a waltz.* FELICITY *dances well,* SARAH *a bit clumsily.*

JIMMY *is unloading a pile of bricks. Alongside the bricks is a rectangular plate of iron. There may also be a spade that he has just used to level an area of the grass.*

JIMMY: Is this where you want it?

FELICITY: [*to* SARAH] One, two, three, one, two, three …

>   *Carries on through much of following conversation.*

ELIZABETH: It's your barbecue.

SARAH: [*to* FELICITY] I can't do it when you push me.

JIMMY: Mrs K, let's not kid ourselves that I'm building this thing for me.

ELIZABETH: But aren't you?

SARAH: Just show him where you want it, Ma.

JIMMY: See?

SARAH: [*to* FELICITY] That's better, Flicka. Me leading. See, it works best this way.

FELICITY: Yes, but you need to do it the other way when you're out.

SARAH: Why are you always right?!

ELIZABETH: If one *were* to choose, I think one would put it here.

FELICITY: When you can do the boring stuff, then you're allowed to have fun!! Come on. Try.

SARAH: I said. Alright!

>   *But then they laugh.*

ELIZABETH: They always got on so well as children. I felt sorry for Bella, really. She'd been so close to Sarah, then along came Felicity and everything changed.

JIMMY: Felicity's a better dancer, that's all. Missy's pissed off.

ELIZABETH: Or what about here? Is that better, do you think?

SARAH: Thank you, Jimmy, for your great support. 'What a great twirl, Sarah, I'll be proud to take you to the Thursday-night hop at the Taapua Pub.'

FELICITY: One, two, three ...
ELIZABETH: Yes. Here. It's the obvious place with the bank behind and the view to the sea.
JIMMY: You're the boss.
ELIZABETH: I hate statements like that.
JIMMY: Just calling it like it is, Mrs K.
ELIZABETH: Can you please call me Elizabeth?
SARAH: It's sign of respect, Ma, because you're such a picky old bird. No-one else tells him what to do. Try to enjoy it.

> SARAH *breaks from* FELICITY. *She comes to check the barbecue site.*

SARAH: About a metre to the right, don't you reckon?
ELIZABETH: Wha—? Oh. Yes of course, because the line of the —

> FELICITY *comes over, too.*

FELICITY: —slope. There. Yes. Mind the ants.

> JIMMY *starts hefting bricks to the desired location.*

JIMMY: Busy little buggers.
FELICITY: Remember the ant farm?
SARAH: Oh gawd. Let's not.
ELIZABETH: Frank bought Bella an ant farm and Felicity—well, Frank and Bella and Felicity, the three of them—where were you, Sarah?
SARAH: Boring little buggers.
FELICITY: Anyway. They died.
ELIZABETH: They did. Frank was away and the girls forgot, and the ants died. There was a funeral, of course, a whole lot of tortured flowers—just the heads, no stalks—and Sarah wrote the funeral oration. Oh! We did laugh.
SARAH: Come on, Flick.
ELIZABETH: Do people still waltz these days?
SARAH: Every Thursday at the Taapua Pub they do.
ELIZABETH: We danced of course, we all did, your father was a ... you went to classes, Sarah!
SARAH: Mum, I was smoking out the back.
ELIZABETH: You weren't.
SARAH: Red bra, transparent white shirt and all the fast boys drooling to light my cigarette.

ELIZABETH: I feel so naive.
SARAH: Ma … puberty —*hits*!

> FELICITY *goes to* ELIZABETH. *She smoothes back her hair.*

FELICITY: Hold still. There. All pretty again.
ELIZABETH: Sweetheart.
SARAH: But I can boogie, Mummy.
JIMMY: That's true. She can boogie, Mummy.

> ELIZABETH *laughs.*

FELICITY: Hang on. Shoe.
SARAH: Give it here.

> *He builds.*

> SARAH *fixes the strap of* FELICITY*'s shoe.*

ELIZABETH: Do you like the sea, Jim?
JIMMY: Yeah, I like the sea.
ELIZABETH: Why?
JIMMY: It's blue. I'm king.
ELIZABETH: Where are your parents?
SARAH: Stop it, Ma.
JIMMY: Back in Oz.
ELIZABETH: Where?
JIMMY: M' dad's up north, I think —
SARAH: Here, Flick!

> *She throws the shoe to* FELICITY.

JIMMY: He's been gone a while. M' brother saw him, year or so back. He's a bit of a handyman.
ELIZABETH: And your mother?
FELICITY: Shall we try boogie?
SARAH: She's in Perth. I wrote to her. In Perth.
FELICITY: Or a cup of tea. How about a nice cup of tea?
ELIZABETH: That would be lovely, dear.
FELICITY: Would you like a cup of tea, Jimmy?
JIMMY: Me mum's just me mum.
SARAH: [*to* FELICITY] He's black, no sugar, not necessary, sweet enough. There're some biscuits in the blue tin.

FELICITY *leaves.*

ELIZABETH: And your family moved around a lot. Lots of different schools, I gather.

JIMMY: What I like about the sea is that it doesn't end. It goes on and on. And a boat's like a feather on top of all that muscle. And you got to keep on—riding—that. Mrs K, my intentions towards your daughter are strictly dishonourable.

SARAH laughs.

ELIZABETH: Her father's dead.

JIMMY: She's twenty-three.

ELIZABETH: She's naive.

SARAH: She's clever!

ELIZABETH: Yes, she got an excellent degree!

SARAH leaves.

JIMMY: How about you hand us those bricks there, Mrs K?

ELIZABETH: These ones?

JIMMY: Yeah. They'll do, I reckon.

She puts a hand to her stomach.

Problem?

ELIZABETH: Indigestion.

They work. She hands him the bricks. He slots them into a firm shape of a rudimentary barbecue.

JIMMY: Sarah's told me about her dad.

ELIZABETH: I don't want to talk about Frank.

JIMMY: Got another brick there?

ELIZABETH: Not to you.

JIMMY: Thanks.

He waits.

ELIZABETH: It's easy to be sentimental after the event. Frank was in hospital four days before Sarah turned up.

JIMMY starts laying bricks again.

Sarah is an extrovert in grief as in everything else. Everything's always so intense. She's the only one thinking, or feeling, or experiencing this or that.

JIMMY: If my old man died tomorrow, I'd barely blink.
ELIZABETH: Did he hurt you?
JIMMY: [*re: scar on his forehead*] See that?
ELIZABETH: Did he hurt your mother?

Pause.

If you—ever!—hit Sarah— I will—
JIMMY: Shut the fuck up.
ELIZABETH: I'm sorry.
JIMMY: You're not!

Pause.

ELIZABETH: If we want this to work, we'll need to lay more bricks.

JIMMY holds out his hand for another brick. She passes it to him. They continue.

You always read about the big lives. But most people live quite small ones, really.

Beat.

Frank was just ... another man. I mean ... a thoughtful man ... but ... nothing special. A high school teacher, what's special about that? But he was ... unfailingly ... kind. I'd been very unhappy myself, my first marriage, well, disaster was an understatement. Frank was—he ... he loved his daughters, including Bella who was not his daughter. He loved me.
JIMMY: I've heard.
ELIZABETH: Yes.

Pause.

Are you really a good fisherman?
JIMMY: They tell me I am.
ELIZABETH: But are you?
JIMMY: If there's a school of fish within coo-ee, they find their way to me. They slip into me nets. Abracadabra!
ELIZABETH: All that silver all over the deck.
JIMMY: Yeah, that's it.

Beat.

ELIZABETH: I talk to Frank.
JIMMY: Yeah?
ELIZABETH: I talk to him all the time. I feel him with me. Sometimes I swear that I could see him— if I just turned my head, or maybe he's—just!—left the room but he'll be back any minute. But … But I can't touch—
JIMMY: Him—
ELIZABETH: No.
JIMMY: I touch her.

> FELICITY *and* SARAH *return with the tea.*

ELIZABETH: 'Two girls, both beautiful, one a gazelle.'
SARAH: Oh, Mum.
FELICITY: Our father had a thing about Yeats.
JIMMY: Who?
SARAH: [*declaiming*] 'Had I the heaven's embroidered cloths—'
FELICITY: Not now, Sarah?
SARAH: 'Enwrought with golden and silver light
The blue and the dim and the dark cloths
Of night and light and the half-light
I would spread those cloths under your feet—'
FELICITY: Here's your tea, Jim.
SARAH: 'But I, being poor, have only my dreams—'

> ELIZABETH *turns away.*

SARAH: 'I have spread my dreams under your feet … '
FELICITY: Enough!

> JIMMY *gets out a hip flask. He pours a tot into his mug of tea.* ELIZABETH *watches him.*

[*Re: tea*] Here's yours, Mum.
ELIZABETH: Thank you, dear.

> *Beat.*

SARAH: And what are you doing with your inheritance, Felicity?
FELICITY: I'm going to buy some shares, Sarah.
SARAH: That would be investing your capital, would it?
FELICITY: Yes. And I've decided to do another degree.
SARAH: That's not capital.

FELICITY: My future?
SARAH: A music degree?
FELICITY: Not this time.
SARAH: What, then?
FELICITY: Science.

> *Beat.*

To be specific: Maths.
ELIZABETH: Felicity?
SARAH: But the music— you can sing!
FELICITY: Not top-notch, Sare.
SARAH: Near enough.
FELICITY: No, as it happens, not—quite— enough.
SARAH: Maths! Why on earth would you do that?!
FELICITY: Because the world is as it is and not as it should be and there's not a career for me as a singer, not quite, and I am simply looking squarely at that fact.
SARAH: My beautiful bird.
FELICITY: Here's your tea.

> SARAH *takes the mug and holds it out to* JIMMY. *He pours a tot into it, too.*

SARAH: [*for* ELIZABETH'*s benefit*] Oh. Goody. Visky!
JIMMY: Why'd you like maths?
FELICITY: Well, it's interesting. It's ... sort of ... clean? And it's a mystery?
JIMMY: You lost me.
FELICITY: Nah, I lost me, too. I don't know. Look. Here's a shell, yes?
JIMMY: That's a shell, alright.
FELICITY: Well, there's a mathematical sequence—one plus one equals two, one plus two equals three, two plus three equals five and so on. When you plot the sequence out, it describes the shape of a shell. See—this curve here. So you wonder—what's the sequence that describes—a fern frond? What's the sequence that describes—the world?
SARAH: That's maths?
FELICITY: Yes. I like it very much.
SARAH: The mirrors and eternity. Maths.

Beat.

FELICITY: Yes.

ELIZABETH: Next year, Felicity, you will be studying ... maths ... where?

FELICITY: In Melbourne, Mum.

ELIZABETH: You've already confirmed a place?

FELICITY: Yes.

Beat.

If I do postgraduate research in chaos theory—

SARAH *laughs unbelievingly.*

Melbourne's best.

Beat.

I won't go if you don't want me to.

ELIZABETH: I very much want you to.

FELICITY: That's what I thought.

ELIZABETH *walks to the edge of the lawn, overlooking the sea. She looks out to the horizon.*

JIMMY'S *alert. He watches* ELIZABETH.

SARAH: 'Chaos'.

FELICITY: Yeah. Some of it's old news by now of course, but back to basics, I'm kind of—intrigued by—you know ... Turbulence. Not normal turbulence. Turbulence in a mathematical sense. Endless divisions on smaller and smaller scales where everything's rushing— hurtling towards the moment, then suddenly the disturbances kind of gallop catastrophically—

ELIZABETH *has a quick intake of breath.* JIMMY *is still watching her very closely.*

SARAH: Mixed metaphor.

FELICITY: —and everything changes.

SARAH: Magic.

FELICITY: No.

Beat.

Fact.

JIMMY *proffers his flask to* ELIZABETH. *She nods.*

ELIZABETH: The boat. Is it a good one?

He pours a tot in her mug.

JIMMY: She needs a strong hand.
ELIZABETH: I'll bet.
JIMMY: But with the wind behind her … she's the sweetest thing.
ELIZABETH: Bobbing on all that water.
JIMMY: Yeah.

She sips her tea.

ELIZABETH: Look. Last sun.

The sun, in a blaze of colour, begins to set.

JIMMY: Elizabeth, would you like to dance?
ELIZABETH: Here?
JIMMY: It's the last light of the day.
ELIZABETH: I haven't danced in years.
JIMMY: Now's your chance.

She turns to him. He bows. She inclines her head. He takes her in his arms. He's a beautiful dancer.

SARAH *moves back to* FELICITY.

SARAH: Jim said it's me or no-one. Ever again. His whole life.
FELICITY: There were three great theories in the twentieth century—relativity, quantum mechanics and chaos. Thinking. Is actually quite interesting.

The sun goes down.

ELIZABETH: Jimmy. Dancer.
JIMMY: [*he gets it*] 'Jimmy Dancer … ' Cancer.
ELIZABETH: Of the stomach. I don't want her to know.
JIMMY: Felicity?
ELIZABETH: Felicity knows. I know it's not fair, but it can't be helped.
JIMMY: Right.

She stops dancing.

ELIZABETH: What is essential? I thought I knew. And now I find I know nothing.

Beat.

JIMMY: You want an answer?

Beat.

ELIZABETH: No.

They resume dancing.

SCENE 5

ELIZABETH's *house, Australia, evening.*

In this scene, ELIZABETH's *daughters cannot hear her dialogue. She may be in bed or simply sitting apart from the rest of the action.*

At first sight, FELICITY *is standing and* SARAH *appears to be asleep, slumped in a chair.*

BELLA *enters. She's carrying her things.*

BELLA: She's not— [*dead*]?!

FELICITY *shakes her head.*

FELICITY: Sleeping.

BELLA: Toby's with the neighbours. Sam's with Tom's mum. I came as soon as I could.

FELICITY: It was all under control.

BELLA: I know.

SARAH *sits up.*

FELICITY: [*re:* BELLA's *things*] Want me to take them?

BELLA: Yes.

She rustles.

I brought some biscuits.

FELICITY: We've got biscuits.

FELICITY *exits.*

SARAH: And flowers. And quiches. And casseroles.

BELLA: Have you found the cat?

SARAH: Shoot the fucking cat.

BELLA: Are you okay?

SARAH: No. Are you?

BELLA: I wasn't asking about Mum.
SARAH: I don't want to talk about it, thanks.
BELLA: If you need any money—
SARAH: I'll be right.
BELLA: Right.

    Beat.

BELLA: Was it a very bad night?
SARAH: Pain's disgusting.

    Enter FELICITY.

BELLA: She could have gone to / hospital.
SARAH: Bella, she didn't want to go to hospital! That's the whole point!
FELICITY: She said, 'Where's Bella?'
SARAH: And then she said 'reliable.'
BELLA: 'Reliable.'
SARAH: It was a compliment! I think. She's a greedy girl. She wanted you here, too. She wanted all of us here. All her girls.
BELLA: You should have called.
FELICITY: [*to* BELLA] And you are reliable. You have always been.
BELLA: You both came back. You've both been here.
FELICITY: Of course we have. But you've done the hard yards day after day. Plus the kids.
BELLA: I want to know all of it.
SARAH: It started about nine thirty, the nurses came at ten, we kept on trying more, different drugs, more, different ways of delivery, rang the doctor about eleven, more different, drugs—
BELLA: I wish you'd rung.
FELICITY: At the time—in the middle of it—you can't imagine, that—
SARAH: I slept on the floor here in case she … but then the phone—
BELLA: Yes?

    In the following, ELIZABETH *speaks, maybe even moves. Her daughters don't hear her.*

ELIZABETH: Frank?

    The shadows broil. The young women are unaware of this.

FELICITY: The doctor rang at—six-thirty? He came at eight, then the day nurse came—

SARAH: We washed her, with the nurse, about half an hour ago, to make her more comfortable.
ELIZABETH: I don't think they understood, Frank, that they were washing me for death.
SARAH: Bella.
BELLA: Yes.
SARAH: Now that you're here.
BELLA: Yes.
SARAH: Bella, I need to visit Dad's grave.
FELICITY: Sarah!
SARAH: I never have.
FELICITY: Well, cop it sweet, sunshine!
SARAH: I need to visit it while it's still just his.
ELIZABETH: She's leaving me. Of all times, she's leaving me now, Frank.
BELLA: Sarah, you've had two years!
SARAH: I couldn't before.
BELLA: You don't drive.
SARAH: Flicka will drive. Please, Flick?
BELLA: What if Mum—?
SARAH: The doctor said it'd be—well, he said it can sometimes go on for days like this.
ELIZABETH: I can move my finger, Frank, towards you, darling.

    Pause.

Yes. Like that.
SARAH: We'll go, take him some flowers, say goodbye, come straight back.

    Beat.

BELLA: I think you should hurry.

    SARAH *and* FELICITY *leave.*

    BELLA *sits with* ELIZABETH.

BELLA: What should I do?
ELIZABETH: [*looking to 'Frank'*] Do?
BELLA: It's been easier, hasn't it, with us? I'm here. I get the right job, marry the right man, I have the little boys, Toby—Mum?—and Sam.

Beat.

They're easy, we live close, it makes sense. Life—unfolds—for some people.

ELIZABETH: Reliable. Keep talking, Keep me here. Frank's so close. Just a breath away.

BELLA: Remember when we went down the coast? Remember walking along the beach near Granny Kelly's shack? Remember? You loved it so. The white beach and the limestone caves all along the back. Maybe we're doing that now—walking along the beach? And it's early afternoon before it gets hot and there's a big old pelican sitting on one of the jetty stumps looking out to sea. And it's all blue sky and the waves ebbing, returning, ebbing, returning. And later, we'll wander up to the shack and have a cup of tea and a bit of a nap and I'll cook dinner? Would you like that, Mum?

ELIZABETH: Like that.

BELLA: Sarah has left that Jimmy. He trashed the boat, and she threw him out. Or they fought and he left. Or something. She didn't want me to say anything, but I thought you'd like to know.

ELIZABETH: Like to know.

BELLA: I could read to you. Would you like that?

ELIZABETH: Like that.

BELLA: What?

She shuffles among the books.

ELIZABETH: Your face is young, Frank, that's the surprise, your face isn't the one you had at the end and certainly not the face you had after the accident; it's the face you had when we were young. Surely that's a sentimental affectation on my part, wouldn't you think? What's a young man like that going to do with a middle-aged wreck like me?

Pause.

Breath … I need my … breath.

BELLA: Shall I read the Bible?

ELIZABETH: Fancy you and me, Frank, raising a Christian?

BELLA: 'Reliable.'

Beat.

This is not fair.

Beat.

They should be here.

She shuts her eyes, opens the book with them shut. She stabs at a page.

ELIZABETH: Read that. That will do.
BELLA: 'The Song of Solomon'?!

Beat.

Well ... why not?
ELIZABETH: Reliable.

BELLA *starts reading from 'The Song of Solomon'.*

BELLA: I am come into my garden, my sister, my spouse:
I have gathered my myrrh with my spice;
I have eaten my honeycomb with my honey;
I have drunk my wine with my milk ...

Transition to:

SARAH *and* FELICITY *are at Frank's grave plot. They carry flowers.*

SARAH: Dad? I brought you flowers ...

She deposits the flowers.

I couldn't come before—
FELICITY: Why couldn't you?
SARAH: He still belonged to her!

Beat.

Give him your flowers.

FELICITY *is about to react angrily but ...*

FELICITY *gives her flowers, too.*

SARAH: We rang. We helped where we could. She's not an easy woman to help. She likes her own way. Dad?

She is crying.

We tried our best, for you, for her, we tried. It's not good enough, but it'll be a better death than you had, that's all we could manage.

Beat.

FELICITY: I'm worried, Sarah.

SARAH: In a minute. Dad? I didn't tell Mum. [*To* FELICITY] And I'm not telling Bella.

FELICITY: Bella knows.

SARAH: Not this.

FELICITY: Oh, shit.

SARAH: I'm three months gone, Dad. [*To* FELICITY] And I'm keeping it.

FELICITY: Shit, shit, shit.

SARAH: It's my baby!

FELICITY: And where's Jim in this?

SARAH: He will keep faith, in his fashion.

FELICITY: To you or to the grog?

SARAH: He's a proud man! Pride's all he's got!

Pause.

I want my mum!

FELICITY: We'd better get back.

Transition to:

BELLA: I sleep, but my heart waketh:
> It is the voice of my beloved that knocketh, saying
> Open to me my sister, my love, my dove, my undefiled
> For my head is filled with dew
> And my locks with the drops of night ...

BELLA *is on one side of her mother's bed.* FELICITY *is at the other.* SARAH *is slumped at the foot of a chair.*

The shadows.

FELICITY: There's a pulse ... there's another ... it's very faint.

Pause.

Another.

ELIZABETH: Frank?

Pause.

I can't see.

> *Pause.*

Where's your hand?
FELICITY: And another.
SARAH: It's time, Flick.
FELICITY: Yes. Okay. Yes.

> FELICITY *takes her hand from the pulse at her mother's neck.*

ELIZABETH: Fingertips.

> *Pause.*

Why haven't I understood all this?
BELLA: There's a breath.
ELIZABETH: Step up?

> ELIZABETH *takes a step.*

It wasn't hard.

> *She takes another step.*

SARAH: [*whispering*] I want my mum!
FELICITY: [*gently*] Shhh, Sare.
BELLA: It's done.
ELIZABETH: Frank, I can't look back.

> *Pause.*

Frank?

> *She leaves.*

SCENE 6

Australia. A suburban living room, eighteen years later.
Enter FELICITY. *She is carrying a suitcase.*

FELICITY: Anyone in? Josh?

> *Enter* JOSH, *aged sixteen.*

JOSH: Hi, Aunt Flick.

> *Kiss.*

FELICITY: Sweetheart. Where's your mum?
JOSH: In the shower. She's stoked you're here. You can keep her company.

FELICITY: What do you mean?
JOSH: I'm off.
FELICITY: Joshua, I am your almost-parent, and I haven't seen you for two months.
JOSH: Move to Sydney, you can see me every day.
FELICITY: I'm a Melbourne type.
JOSH: I've got a gig.
FELICITY: You couldn't possibly have put it off?
JOSH: It's a paying gig!
FELICITY: No!
JOSH: Yup.
FELICITY: You're going to be a rock star!
JOSH: You want my autograph?
FELICITY: I do! Now! Quick!

He laughs.

How beautiful you are.
JOSH: Come on, cut the crap.
FELICITY: It makes me want to weep.
JOSH: For Christ's sake! [*Calling*] Mum! Sarah! The aunt's here!
SARAH: [*off*] Get her a cup of tea!
JOSH: I'm running late!
SARAH: [*off*] *Noblesse oblige,* Josh!
FELICITY: I'll get it.
JOSH: She stuffs up the meaning of that corny old phrase!
FELICITY: It's sort of an apology.

He looks at her.

JOSH: Whatever you are saying there, aunt, is wilfully obscure.

FELICITY *shrugs.*

FELICITY: Before your time.
JOSH: Well, we're used to that, eh? Most things are. A distinct lack of information!
FELICITY: Josh, that's between you and your mother.
JOSH: But—
FELICITY: Not my territory. Not.

Beat.

JOSH: I really am late. I stayed to say hello.
FELICITY: Off you go.
JOSH: Ma! I've got your keys!
FELICITY: Good luck for tonight.

He leaves. SARAH *enters.*

SARAH: Hello, my Flicka.
FELICITY: Hey, Tig.
SARAH: Grrr-owl.
FELICITY: Josh's bouncy. Is the band that good?
SARAH: It's not the band. Joshie's in love!
FELICITY: No!
SARAH: Yes! She's an older woman. Eighteen. He told me last night. I just had time to think, 'Whatever you do, don't tell her you love her,' when he said, 'I told her I loved her and she said she loves me!' She'll probably break it off tonight, and he'll be bereft.

Beat.

The light deepens.

Oh, I do like this moment.
FELICITY: Dusk?
SARAH: Yeah.
'In the gilt dusk
all's linked like lace.'
FELICITY: Yours?
SARAH: No. Dad's.
Oh! Christ! Tidy up! Bella's coming!
FELICITY: Coming here now?
SARAH: She rang just then.
FELICITY: Oh shit. I didn't tell her I was flying up. Oh shit.
SARAH: Don't swear! You know she—

BELLA *enters.*

BELLA: Hi.
SARAH: —hates it. [*To* BELLA] Hi.
FELICITY: Hi, Bella.
BELLA: Flicka.
SARAH: You want a cup of tea?

BELLA: Wine.
FELICITY: It's lovely to see you, Bella. I was going to ring.
BELLA: Clearly.

> SARAH *hands* BELLA *a glass of wine.*

Thanks. So. Flicka. How's … chaos, then?
FELICITY: Oh. Chaotic. Nah, it's not, really. It's like chaos, in fact. There's a buried pattern somewhere there.
SARAH: As in?
FELICITY: As in it depends on how you look at it. I go for the job for the chance to research, then spend all my time teaching. But does the world need my limited capacity for original thought or my considerable ability to teach?

> *Beat.*

Look. A butterfly.
SARAH: Remember the year there was a swarm in the garden at home?
FELICITY: The monarchs migrating.

> SARAH *indicates to* FELICITY *'Wine?'* FELICITY *shakes her head.* BELLA *holds out her glass for more.*

SARAH: Hundreds of them, all orange-gold over the fig tree.
FELICITY: And Mum pulled us out to see them before school.
SARAH: 'It's a miracle, my girls, you are watching a miracle!'
FELICITY: And she made us pancakes and we took them out to eat under the fig tree, watching the butterflies. I remember.

> *Beat.*

Where was Dad?
SARAH: Looking on, I guess. She was so high with it all. He'd have loved that.
BELLA: But did it mean anything?

> FELICITY *and* SARAH *look at each other.*

SARAH: Enchantment!
FELICITY: Migration patterns.
BELLA: But if your work is real, Flicka, why wasn't there a tsunami?
FELICITY: The butterfly wing in Brazil causing a tidal wave in Florida is just a figure of speech, Bella. Just an extreme example of … you

know ... 'sensitive dependence on initial conditions' ... tiny ... factor ... morphs into ... enormous ... unpredictability ... there *is* a pattern but it's—
BELLA: So it's not—
FELICITY: Not—
BELLA: True?
FELICITY: Accessible.

Beat.

It could be true. Theoretically.
BELLA: It's funny. All these years. We've been asking, 'How's chaos?' and you say, 'Oh. Fine.' ... 'Fine.'

Beat.

I tried to read that—you know—the popular book.
FELICITY: I was going to ring!
BELLA: Don't patronise me. *Chaos for Dummies*, that's what I want.
FELICITY: You don't!
BELLA: I do! Go on!

Beat.

FELICITY: I—uh— I give this lecture to high school students who come to uni to have a bit of a look-see. I say—something like, 'Until the twentieth century, science was dominated by regularity. The ... great harmonies of Euclidean geometry—the 'music of the spheres'—
BELLA: Go on.
FELICITY: But—this bit's a quote—'nature isn't regular. A cloud is not a perfect circle, a mountain is not a cone, and a bolt of lightning does not travel in a straight line.'
BELLA: I said, go on!
FELICITY: So you say—well—the interesting thing might be that very irregularity, that seeming unpredictability, and it turns out—and this was the new thing, the paradigm shift, the discovery that kicked off the field—it turns out that complexity is, in fact, not random—it's weird for sure, but it's not random—and it can't be seen directly, it can only be glimpsed through the pattern it leaves behind it, and you need computers for that.
SARAH: Maths.

BELLA: Yes?
FELICITY: Yes.
BELLA: [*goading*] Yes?!
FELICITY: And then—it turns out that once you have the eyes to look for it, you see that chaos is—everywhere—from the … ocean currents to galactic cycles, from a dripping tap to the human heart.
BELLA: The heart.
FELICITY: Yeah. None of it's easy to crunch, but I think—this is just what I think—chaos is the rule, and order is the exception to it. Order is the sustainer, maybe, but chaos is the creator … breaking, making, breaking, making—
SARAH: Magic.
BELLA: God.
FELICITY: The crack inside creation. The thing that forces change.

> *Beat.*

So I say to the kids, if you take the time, if you want to come on the journey, you will learn about things like—it's such a beautiful term!—'strange attractors'—you know that owl-eyed, butterfly-winged shape that started it all, that was the first 'strange attractor'—and you'll learn about fractals, self-similarity, phase transitions, Mandlebrot sets—that's the pretty one that describes the shape of coastlines, where you see the strange attractor reappearing and reappearing on endlessly smaller scales and it's spooky because if there is such a thing as eternity then that's the map.

> *Beat.*

BELLA: Do you see, Sarah, that your dear girl in fact has no respect for you? Or me.
SARAH: Bella, what's wrong?
BELLA: All that theory. It's only meaningful if you can relate it to a life.
SARAH: There is something wrong.
BELLA: I think—I think—all that—stuff—just comes down to—There's a moment when you say yes or no and that's the still point of all the rest of your life. And ever after, everything returns and returns to that. That's the meaning. That's it.

> *Silence.*

FELICITY: Bella?
SARAH: It's Toby.
FELICITY: But it's been nearly two years! I thought he—!
SARAH: It's Toby.
BELLA: You think it'd never happen to you, don't you, you think because you tried so hard, because Joshie is so everything, because—!
SARAH: Don't you do this! Don't!
BELLA: Toby could be anyone's kid.

    FELICITY *moves to* BELLA.

Don't touch me!
SARAH: You want another drink there, Bella?
BELLA: Yes, please.
SARAH: You want some wafers in it?

    FELICITY *fills up her teacup with wine and slugs it back.*

BELLA: Don't mock my faith!
SARAH: Why ever not? Oh, now look! There's another fucking butterfly!
BELLA: It's dead. And it's not a butterfly. It's a moth.
SARAH: Bella, whatever has happened I don't have to take that. Joshie is my best thing—
BELLA: I do not want to—!
SARAH: What else have I got? —
BELLA: I don't want to talk about your—!
SARAH: Crappy jobs and —
BELLA: Crappier relationships! —
SARAH: I wanted so *much*!
BELLA: 'Poetry'!
SARAH: Yeah. To aged care. Bit of a comedown, eh?

    Beat.

But. Whatever else I have or have not done—

    Beat.

I have done well by my boy!
BELLA: Yes!
SARAH: And you, who have so much, will not take that away from me!
[*Hurt and angry*] Jealous!
BELLA: Jealous! Of course I'm jealous! Why wouldn't I be?

Beat.

I have given my son a father, I have given him a good home, I have tailored my life to my children, I have taken care of my parents, I nursed our mother, I have kept faith with my church—!

Beat.

Mum and Dad.
FELICITY: Yes?
BELLA: It was good.
FELICITY: Yes.

Beat.

BELLA: So you think—if you do the same thing—
FELICITY: Oh, Bella.
BELLA: —behave the same way, make the same choices—
SARAH: Tom ain't Dad.
BELLA: He loves me like Dad!
SARAH: Yes. He does.

Beat.

BELLA: I must go back.

Pause.

Toby's been clean, as you know, oh—for twenty-three months. We thought it was over. Home safe. Then a few days ago he met this—mate, someone he'd cut contact with, but Toby bumped into him at—a movie. The seat next to him. Can you imagine? What are the chances of that? … Random, Flicka? You—blink—and suddenly—north, south, east, west—it stretches out in all directions and none of it's your life.

Beat.

It was only the one hit. He's been in a coma ever since. They said, today, 'Try him without the ventilator.' So—what do you do? We said, 'Yes?' He's still breathing. He still—looks like Toby. But if he does—keep breathing—the damage will be long term. I don't know what—I should want?

Beat.

After a while you can't—like them. But you still—love?— them?
   Beat.
What was he wanting? What did he *need*? What didn't I *give*?
   Beat.
Tom says—forget about you lot. After all, I've got him. But—I wanted—my family. I wanted—what *was*.
   SARAH *holds her.*
SARAH: Oh sweetheart. Sweet girl. Come, darling, come.
   A moth circles round and round the light. FELICITY *and* SARAH *watch it as* BELLA—*very quietly—sobs.*

SCENE 7

SARAH *and* JOSH *are sitting side by side.*
Sound of a boobook.

JOSH: That was savage.
SARAH: That's death for you.
JOSH: The past got guillotined.
SARAH: That's called 'significant death.' Your life's just been divided into 'Toby' and 'After Toby.'
JOSH: [*crying*] Fuck him! Stupid fucking—!
   Pause.
SARAH: Would you like a drink?
JOSH: Would it help?
SARAH: I want one.
JOSH: What if I'm genetically susceptible to addiction?
SARAH: I doubt it. You can read, Joshua. You're my words boy. You've got my brain.
JOSH: As opposed to my father's.
SARAH: Yep.
   SARAH *gets a glass of wine.*
JOSH: I get sick of it always being women, you know. All the people who can tell me what to do, who might have something decent to

say about bloody anything—are all women. So, Sam and Tobes ... Sam's almost like another generation but Toby ...

He gets a glass of wine, raises it.

You only got now, right? To do what you want.
SARAH: Joshua?

He drinks down the wine in one gulp.

JOSH: Shall we talk about my father?
SARAH: What?!
JOSH: My father. Now. I want to. Why not?
SARAH: No! Josh! Not!

He gets another glass of wine, knocks that back, too.

JOSH: Fucking tell me about my father, fuck you!
SARAH: You are swearing at me!
JOSH: If that's what it takes, why the fuck not!?

Beat.

Let's start with the simple stuff. Is he alive? Or dead?!

She looks out the window.

SARAH: Why's it so dark? When it's only five o'clock?
JOSH: It's dark because at a certain point it's time for it to be dark. Just like, at a certain point, it won't be dark because it'll be time for it to be light. Dead or alive? Coming, ready or not!
SARAH: Alive.

Beat.

JOSH: How do we know?
SARAH: We just know.
JOSH: [*very loudly, straight at her*] Ahhhhhghhhhh!

Beat.

SARAH: Joshua, we'll know when your father dies.
JOSH: How?
SARAH: We'll know because someone will find us because—
JOSH: How will—'someone'—'find us'?!—
SARAH: Someone will find us because he'll have kept something.
JOSH: Kept 'something.' Kept what? Fuckin' tell me fuckin' 'something', will you!? I don't know fuck about my father! Why not?!

SARAH: In between. All my ups and downs. Lots of different houses. But lots of good toys. A few different schools. But some really good teachers. Late nights. Crazy people. But. Your own good bed. And the dog. And that fucking pony.

JOSH: Thanks.

SARAH: Years ago. Before you were born. My mother didn't tell me she was dying. I was so hurt and so angry! But later I realised that—under the circumstances—she was actually quite honourable, actually.

JOSH: This is not about your mother, Mother. It's about my mother, Mother. Actually.

Beat.

Who. Am. I?

Pause.

SARAH: He had exceptionally good eyes.

JOSH: Eyes.

JIMMY may possibly be present, fishing quietly off the jetty, for the rest of this scene.

SARAH: Yes. Like yours. Brown eyes.

JOSH: Brown eyes.

Beat.

Come on, give it a try.

SARAH: A crappy little kitchen in a rubbish old farmhouse in Taapua.

Beat.

JOSH: Okay.

SARAH: I didn't want to tell you like this.

JOSH: Tell me like this.

SARAH: I'm pregnant, three months gone.

JOSH: Yes.

SARAH: I shouldn't be, of course.

JOSH: Of course.

SARAH: I haven't told Jim, but he knows. He always knows.

JOSH: Does he?

SARAH: Yes. It's uncanny really, because you never catch him looking, or listening, that's kind of beneath him, but it doesn't matter what it is, he always knows it. He knew when my ma was sick. She fucking told him. I don't know why. But I'm not surprised. He could—pick the moment. He'd have been a hero in a war. You can imagine men following him to oblivion. But for everything else, he's rubbish really, unless it's just doing his time, fishing, not thinking, a bender at the weekend, all that chat in the pub with these stupid fuckers so boring he can run rings around them, so … nothing. But he's a little tin god in there. They love him. He's king.

JOSH: King.

SARAH: Yeah.

Beat.

So I spent—all my dad gave me—to buy him a boat. But then he tossed in the boat. The *Karenne*. He just left her on the water … just … bobbing on the sea. He couldn't handle being alone at sea. Couldn't be king of only a castle. He had to be working with his stupid mates.

And then, because it was such a shame job to do that, such a shame, he'd been drunk for two weeks solid.

Bella had called. 'Come help Mum die, please, come.' So I went to the fisheries to sort out his debt for the new motor, but it was no dice and they sold the boat from under us. Jimmy's nowhere to be seen—he must have known that that would happen, so he needs a drink even more to drown that one, too.

So I'm waiting in the dark, in the kitchen to tell him I'm going. I'm waiting, with my suitcase, and I'm sort of fighting—you know that thing I do—fighting for my breath—and I'm thinking of all those other nights I've waited.

She cries.

How could I tell you that? How could I tell you your father did that to me?

She sobs. Quietens.

Beat.

Twice in my life I've felt, what might have been. Sitting. You know. Just inside. What is.

JOSH: My father.
SARAH: Your father.

> *Beat.*

Came in dirty. His eyes were bloodshot, and his eyelids were red and fat as hell. He looked like a bad old man.

He knew Mum was close to the end, so he didn't ask any questions, but he wouldn't have anyway. I kissed him—on the cheek—his mouth smelled of vomit—and I said 'Bye, Jim.' And he said, 'Send me a photo.' And he didn't mean Mum.

So when you were born, I sent him the photo, with the date and time and place of your birth, of me and you, with your brown eyes and your rosy skin.

He'll have kept it. Even as a baby you looked like him.

> *Sound of a mopoke.*

JOSH: What's that?
SARAH: Boobook. Big bugger bird that looks like tree.
JOSH: So he's alive.
SARAH: Yep. Somewhere.
JOSH: So I can look for him.
SARAH: I don't want you to.
JOSH: This is not about you.
SARAH: No. It's not.

> *Sound of a mopoke.*
>
> JOSH *refills their glasses.*

JOSH: Cheers, Ma.
SARAH: Cheers, Josh.
JOSH: And the other time?
SARAH: What?
JOSH: Inside—inside the moment?
SARAH: None of your business.

SCENE 8

Twenty-two-year-old SARAH *is sitting on the end of a jetty.*

JIMMY *is a short distance away, ostensibly fishing but in fact watching her closely. He is in the same spot (if that stage direction is followed) as in the previous scene.*

SARAH *turns to him.*

SARAH: You don't look creepy.
JIMMY: You don't look creepy either.
SARAH: Why are you watching me?
JIMMY: That's a hard thing to answer without sounding creepy.
SARAH: Give it a burl.
JIMMY: This isn't your first time down the jetty.
SARAH: No?
JIMMY: Every day for two weeks, isn't it?
SARAH: I suppose it is, give or take a day.
JIMMY: It's exactly two weeks and you're usually here for about an hour and a half and about twenty-five minutes in, you have a little sob, then you calm down—sort of—then you watch the sea some more, then you wander off.
SARAH: That's a bit creepy.
JIMMY: Possibly.
SARAH: Why do you watch me?
JIMMY: You want now or two weeks ago?
SARAH: Two weeks ago, it'd be really creepy, right?
JIMMY: I dunno. Is lust creepy?
SARAH: If it's indulged in a subterranean fashion, it is, surely?
JIMMY: That's a big word.
SARAH: Is it?
JIMMY: Look. Sometimes … Just … a particular combination of … flesh, bones, walk … shape, eyes, mouth …
SARAH: You're fading.
JIMMY: That was a biggish effort.
SARAH: You don't really go for the chat.
JIMMY: It was two weeks ago, anyway.

SARAH: It was a one-night stand?
JIMMY: Not … entirely.

Beat.

SARAH: Do you want to come over here?
JIMMY: I wouldn't want to be creepy.
SARAH: Well, I think I'm twenty-three minutes in now and it'd be good not to cry, just the once.

He comes over, sits next to her.

Did you catch any fish?
JIMMY: I'm squidding.
SARAH: Squid?
JIMMY: Yeah. Little round squirmy things with lots of legs and suckers.
SARAH: You usually catch a few and take them home in that bucket.
JIMMY: You been watching me, too.
SARAH: Yeah.

Pause.

JIMMY: I've been waiting all my life for you.
SARAH: Is that a hook?
JIMMY: No, it's the truth.

She cries.

JIMMY: I haven't interrupted the schedule at all!
SARAH: You're not good for much, are you?
JIMMY: Nah. Disaster, I reckon.
SARAH: But you shared the twilight. That was nice.
JIMMY: Who'd leave you?
SARAH: It's not a lover.
JIMMY: Right.
SARAH: My dad died.
JIMMY: Right.
SARAH: He died a month back in a car accident. A silly one, it didn't need to happen, it was his fault apparently, he was tired … He was nearly home.
JIMMY: I'd be your man if some bastard had messed you around—
SARAH: Oh, I'm messed around—
JIMMY: But death's a bit of a hard bugger, really.

Pause.

He gets up, goes over to his previous spot, comes back with a squid line, some bait, and a bucket.

Wanna catch a squid?
SARAH: Bizarre.

He gives her the squid line.

JIMMY: You hold it like this, that's it. Now—
SARAH: Don't you need bait?
JIMMY: They come to the lure. Jump on the hook.

She lifts a squid body up out of JIMMY'*s bucket.*

SARAH: Yuck.

She drops the creature back.

JIMMY: Everything's animal. You got to—participate—in that.
SARAH: I don't got to do anything.
JIMMY: Everything—*is*. Right?
SARAH: If you normally go round stating the obvious, I'm going to be really disappointed.
JIMMY: Bone. Is. Flesh. Is. You eat or you die. Shit. Is. Worms and stink.
SARAH: I've got it.
JIMMY: Hang on. I told you. Seeing it's you, I'm making an effort. So. You're in—*it*—whether you want to be or not. So you say, 'yes.'
SARAH: Fuck that.
JIMMY: Now I chuck this—out there—and you hold on to it. Keep your finger on the line. You never know your luck.

Pause.

Who's messed you around?
SARAH: It's no-one's fault.
JIMMY: Who?
SARAH: Dad didn't die straight up. There was—some brain thing—and so when she rang …
JIMMY: … when she rang …
SARAH: … wait.
JIMMY: Yep.

SARAH: When my mother rang, she made it sound—as if—but maybe I just didn't hear, maybe I heard what I wanted to hear, it was such a shock—

… She implied that the best thing would be for me and my sisters—I've got two sisters—to stay away, not to jeopardise his recovery, to give him complete rest.

JIMMY: She might have been right.

SARAH: No. She's smart enough, you see, but she's never right—not when there's a crisis, she's just not. I should have known that. There was no chance he'd make it, apparently, but even if there had been, we should have been there, too, don't you see? It's greed. It's primitive. She's a survivor, that's the difference between us, when push comes to shove, she takes what she needs, what she wants.

JIMMY: You've got a bite.

SARAH: He died without us! She didn't call us! She knew he was dying but she kept him to herself!

JIMMY: Wind in … slowly.

She does, then stops.

SARAH: It's loose again. Squid got away.

JIMMY: Pull it in anyway. We'll throw it right out.

She does.

Why Taapua?

SARAH: There was a lover in Christchurch. We came here once.

JIMMY: I'm paying particular attention to the word 'was'.

She laughs.

Oh, that was good!

SARAH: You're not creepy.

JIMMY: Nah, not me.

SARAH: I throw this out there?

JIMMY: Yep. Just … easy. Yep.

She does. He offers her a hip flask.

SARAH: I haven't had a drink for so long.

JIMMY: Whiskey.

SARAH: Why not?

She drinks.

Whooo!

She coughs.

JIMMY: Easy there.

She hands him back the flask. He drinks.

SARAH: This landscape's so spectacular, all that green, all those windy curly details on everything.

JIMMY: Yeah. Pretty.

SARAH: Dramatic.

JIMMY: You like that.

SARAH: Indeed I do.

JIMMY: Drama queen.

SARAH: So I'm told.

Pause.

How long have you been in Taapua?

JIMMY: I been here eighteen months or so.

SARAH: From?

JIMMY: Perth, would you believe?

SARAH: Two exiles.

Beat.

What do you do? In Taapua?

JIMMY: Oh, I worked the boats for a bit. Then I got sick of that and went on a bit of a bender, but I'm low on cash now so I might have to—uh—re-establish my credentials down the docks, I reckon.

SARAH: You drink.

JIMMY: Sometimes.

SARAH: Why?

JIMMY: It's just an itch.

SARAH: Why?

JIMMY: Fucked if I know.

SARAH: You're wounded.

JIMMY: [*angrily*] You're not?!

SARAH: I've got no *reason* to be. I've always been loved.

JIMMY: [*a bit coldly*] So?

SARAH: When I was tiny, my ma wouldn't let anyone other than her or my dad handle me. She said I got distressed.
JIMMY: Right.
SARAH: It's true!

Beat.

I was so shy. I'd follow Bella all around the neighbourhood. She was like my shield, my protector. And I think that she—and my Mum, both of them—both so loved that—tiny creature, who needed them so much. I'd follow along behind them. I'd hardly speak.
JIMMY: Been making up for it ever since.
SARAH: You're supposed to be listening.
JIMMY: Sorry.
SARAH: My Dad, but. We had these games. I was the tiger. Or I was the mean, bad, scary pirate king. It was fantastic. Like a new self. Grrooowll! Roarrr! Yo ho ho! Permission to be everything!
JIMMY: I see.
SARAH: Yeah … But the catch is, it's followed me through. That broken thing. I get these … panic attacks. Push things too far and …

She shrugs.

I'm in trouble. Really. So my ma. Watches me … and I … don't like that. So we … fight …
JIMMY: That's not exactly—uh—a story of abuse.
SARAH: No. I know. It's a small—tiny!—— trivial thing. But—
JIMMY: But?
SARAH: Well. Seems to me. There's a part you can negotiate.
JIMMY: Possibly.
SARAH: Oh, I think you can. I have to think that. But that—core thing … the bit that's broken …
JIMMY: Yep.
SARAH: Are you stuck with it? Is it going to dictate … everything?
JIMMY: You got another bite! Here.

He pulls in the squid line.

SARAH: It's quite little.
JIMMY: Here we go …

He takes the squid off the hook and slips it into the bucket.

SARAH: You do that so quickly, the whole thing happens like magic.
JIMMY: It isn't hard.
SARAH: I suppose not, if you know how.

Pause.

I like you very, very much.
JIMMY: Yes.
SARAH: I like the way you … pad across the jetty … prowl across the wood. I like that.
JIMMY: Good.
SARAH: Just then, pulling in the squid …
JIMMY: Yes?
SARAH: My mother wouldn't like you at all.
JIMMY: I can understand that.

SARAH *laughs.*

Your name is Sarah Kelly. You're staying at the Taapua Lodge. You're here alone, but you use your phone a lot. You stay in each night. You walk the beach each morning and every evening about five o'clock, you come down to the jetty and you watch the sea.
SARAH: How old am I?
JIMMY: Twenty-two?
SARAH: How old are you?
JIMMY: Thirty. I'm no catch.
SARAH: How do you cook squid?
JIMMY: Crumbed, fried, a little bit of lemon.
SARAH: Shall I buy a bottle of wine?
JIMMY: You could do that.
SARAH: Thirty.
JIMMY: I'm not going to change.
SARAH: No.

Pause.

Maybe I could make you happy.
JIMMY: There'd be no question on that.
SARAH: Maybe you could make me happy.
JIMMY: There's a chance.

SARAH: I never want to go back to Australia.
JIMMY: Alright.
SARAH: Life.
JIMMY: Yes.
SARAH: Alright, then. Yes.

THE END

THIRD PERSON
Noëlle Janaczewska

A PARTIAL AND APPROXIMATELY ACCURATE SYNOPSIS OF SHAKESPEARE'S *THE MERCHANT OF VENICE*

If you're not a Shakespeare scholar, the play is a kind of memory: we know Shylock was a Jewish money-lender; we know the phrase 'a pound of flesh', and perhaps 'the quality of mercy'; we may recall an oft-quoted speech about our common humanity, and something about a cross-dressing woman. Beyond that the details are murky. So here's a brief, partial and partisan synopsis of *The Merchant of Venice*.

Bassanio asks Antonio to lend him a large sum of money so that he can court the wealthy heiress, Portia. Antonio's finances are all at sea, but he really wants to help Bassanio. So he asks Shylock to lend him the cash for three months. The penalty for late or non-payment is a pound of flesh. To marry Portia a man must choose the correct one of three caskets in a silly game devised by her father. Luckily for her, Bassanio, the man she loves, picks the right casket. Antonio's ships sink. Shylock calls in the debt. Shylock's daughter Jessica helps herself to his money and jewellery and runs off with Lorenzo. Portia gives Bassanio the money to repay Shylock, who refuses to release Antonio from his obligation. The servant/clown Lancelot Gobbo fathers a child with a Moorish girl. Portia disguises herself as a man and defends Antonio in court. Her argument: if Shylock sheds any blood while taking his pound of flesh, he will lose everything. Shylock forgives Antonio's debt, but is stripped of his fortune and faith. *The Merchant of Venice* ends with marriages. Bassanio and Lorenzo claim they are marrying for both love and money, but neither union is worry-free.

Third Person begins in Berlin in 1946, roughly ten years after the end of *The Merchant of Venice*. Nothing else that happens in Shakespeare's play is necessarily relevant to what unfolds.

The Berlin of *Third Person* is a place in the way that Shakespeare's Venice is a place.

Third Person was first produced by Union House Theatre. It opened at the Union House theatre, Melbourne, with the following principal credits:

YAMINA/SINGER	Elyssia Koulouris
JESSEKAH	Isabella Vadiveloo
PORTIA	Sarah Fitzgerald
ANTON	Clancy Moore
CHRIS	Ronnen Liezerovitz
MISTER	Shawn Tan
MRS	Sara Tabitha Catchpole
ENSEMBLE	Liam Bellman-Sharpe, Rachael Besselink, Camilla Best, Nick Campbell, Hannah Dallas, Claudia Hong, Jai Leeworthy, Georgia Marett, Nicky Nguyen, Adam Porrett, Alex Scott, Sophie Waddy, Pallavi Waghmode, Laura Wilson

Dramaturg, Kathryn Millard
Director, Tom Gutteridge
Composer, Ashlee Clapp
Lighting & Set Designer, Nicola Andrews
Set & Costume Designer, Ellen Strasser
Sound Designer, David Porteus
AV Designer, David Hairdon

Band:
Piano, Lizzie Eng
Bassoon, Emma Morrison
Double bass, Gabrielle Castelluccio

An early draft of *Third Person* was shortlisted for the Griffin Playwriting Award.

CHARACTERS

JESSEKAH. Shylock's daughter.
PORTIA. A lawyer.
YAMINA. A café singer.
ANTON. A black-marketeer.
CHRIS. A photographer.
MISTER
MRS
SOLDIERS
RUBBLEWOMEN

Third Person has seven named characters plus an ensemble of Soldiers and Rubblewomen. Feel free to cast in favour of women and diversity.

Doubling is possible.

PRODUCTION NOTES

Third Person uses punctuation and layout to suggest delivery.

/ is an interruption or overlap.

Lines not attributed to the seven named characters begin with a '—'. These are spoken by either the Soldiers or the Rubblewomen, and can be allocated as the director and cast chose. These '—' lines can overlap, be repeated or spoken by more than one performer.

Stage directions are suggestions and possibilities rather than absolutes.

1. DECEMBER 1946

A street corner.

A knot of tinsel. 'Ausverkauft' (sold out) hand-written on cardboard.

RUBBLEWOMEN *sift through debris, passing buckets to a wheelbarrow. Dressed in a bizarre mix of rags and plundered theatrical costumes—Elizabethan, and cabaret glitz circa 1930s.*

PORTIA, *dressed in male attire, works among the* RUBBLEWOMEN.

ALLIED SOLDIERS *with several watches on their arms make a show of keeping watch.*

— The Russians got here first.
    Raised the flag over the Reichstag and
    some of us were over the moon and others
    let's wait and see because God knows we've seen enough
    and sure enough, when the dust settled
    we had a clearer picture of where we were.

Berlin.

Berlin. Cut up like a cake. The eastern portion for the Soviets and the rest for the Yanks, the Brits and the French.
    It's a sticky mix though: soldiers from middle England and American GIs, foreign observers, public officials, the red crossed, the double crossed, the Bolshies, the cameramen, the refugees and displaced with nowhere to go and no money to get there.

Much better with Hitler's buildings in ruins.
    Burnt out interiors, lift-shafts stranded
    a hole in everywhere you turn.
    The city broken up like a jigsaw—
    but the ground breathes more freely now.

The rubblewomen—look at them! Like crows and vultures. Look at them picking up the pieces.
    When they bend down you can see right up their thighs.
    They come from the theatre, those weird clothes they're wearing,
    before it was locked up, what's left, and left to a cast of rats and cut-throats.

You know, those women will take anything: wonky chairs, cracked mirrors, rotten food, anything.
    They can't bear having nothing, so they collect any old crap.
    But don't be fooled, they're not nearly as old and dried up as they look
        and of course they're not all women either.
        Hey, Pretzel-head!

PORTIA *looks up. Briefly.*

It's pilfering, shit-or-miss looting, what the rubblewomen do.
    To sell stuff commercially you have to plan and calculate
    but they just hunt and gather like primitives.
    They'd like to spit on us or chuck stones—would if I didn't have a uniform and a gun
    for some reason they're scared …

— Hey, Strudel! Show us your tits!
— What are they going to do with them?
— Depends.
— Yeah?
— You've got to offer. Something.
— You open your wallet, she opens her legs. That's the deal.
— I heard they'll do it for condensed milk.
— Fuck.
— Fuck.
— I said they not we.
— What?
— What are they going to do with the Germans? In general.
— Do with them?
— Now the war's over.
— Up to the law. Put them on trial, didn't they. The big shots / and top brass.
— I don't mean those 'them'. There are special places and laws for them. I mean the ordinary hum-a-day people.
— Well then it's a question of depth isn't it? How deep-in were they? What distance from the top? What hidden depths, what extensive and detailed knowledge did they have? And if and when they say 'I was out of my depth' how do we know if that's a real truth or a convenient truth?

Pulls forward a fellow SOLDIER.

Take Martin.

Martin here is a useless poker-player.

Snorts of laughter.

Loses big time every time, owes everybody—right? So when he comes snivelling to me and says: [*Mimicking Martin*] 'I'm out of my depth', we know he's telling the truth 'cause we've witnessed it with our own eyes and can add up the cost and know that Martin here has been—let's be polite and say a very bad boy. Right Martin?

Slaps him.

— Right.
— But these people?—Fuck knows.
— Meantime, we're all doing our bit to enlighten the locals.
— Right.
— Gotta kick the swastikas out of them.
— We're here to civilise this fucking country.
— Fact is, all this destruction is a good thing for the Germans. They can begin again, wipe the past and build afresh ...

The SOLDIERS *move off.*

One of the RUBBLEWOMEN *removes her gloves to light a cigarette. She's the only one with two intact gloves.*

— Where did you get those?
— Café in the French zone. The one with the Arab singer.

There was a foreigner with a camera, and he bought red wine / and he wanted to take—

Laughter.

— Yeah, yeah.
— No. No, he wasn't like that, he was nervous. He said there were butterflies in his stomach.

Afterwards he gave me his gloves.

— I'd kill for soap.
— Shoes.
— Soap that smells of rose petals or lilac.
— My feet will be the death of me.

— A handkerchief that hasn't been sneezed in by someone else.
— What would you know about it, you stupid, fat cow!
— Hey! There's / no need to be—
— That's what I did before. While you sat in your fancy-pants-y apartment with china teacups, I was washing snotty handkerchiefs and strangers' underwear till my knuckles was raw and bleeding. Day fucking in, day fucking out.

What do you know about hard work, about hunger—about anything!

She lashes out. PORTIA *grabs her.*

PORTIA: Ripping at each other's throats won't help. You or any of us.

The RUBBLEWOMAN *bursts into angry tears.*

— I'd eat the crows if I could catch the buggers, I'm so hungry.
— Berlin stinks.
— The only thing we've got coming out our ears is rumours and melodrama.

If only you could swap a bit of gossip for a juicy steak, eh Marta?
When was the last time you had a piece of meat? Not that rubbish stiff with salt, but proper butcher's meat?

PORTIA *initiates a game. It's one they've played before to lift the mood.*

PORTIA: My family and I just enjoyed the most delicious meal.
— What did you have?
PORTIA: Let me see … five different roasted meats and fowls. Potatoes. Carrots—
— Pea soup with parsley fresh from the garden.
— Curly sausage.
— Tomatoes, and cucumbers pickled with bay leaves.
— Fish and no bones.
— Rye bread soft as.
— Red cabbage cooked with apple and pepper.
PORTIA: Cherry tart with thick, vanilla cream.
— Strawberries.
— How about a plate of chocolate éclairs?
— Or lemon pancakes hot from the stove, running with butter?

— Christmas cake.
— Drenched in rum.
— With a big marzipan heart.
— Marta, would you care for some more wine? It's / a particularly fine vintage—

The game derails.

— Am I a bad person?
— Shh!
— Am I?
PORTIA: Why?
— Everyone looks fat to me.
PORTIA: You mean Americans?
— No, everyone. Everyone looks fat. She looks fat, you look fat. If their bones aren't poking through their skin, I think they're fat.
—That's weird.
— I know.
— Psychological.
— I know.

★

The Café Rialto.
YAMINA *is singing her own version of 'Lili Marlene'. In French.*
Her clothing is contemporary, not 1940s.

YAMINA [*singing*]
    Devant la caserne
    Quand le jour s'enfuit,
    La vieille lanterne
    Soudain s'allume et luit …

In a dark corner ANTON *is doing a black market deal with some* SOLDIERS. *Documents and money change hands.*

Flash! CHRIS *takes a photograph.*

— Hey!
— You!

— With the fucking camera.
— Yeah, you.
— We're talking to you, dickhead.
— What the fuck do you think you're doing?

    ANTON *pushes the* SOLDIERS *aside. Approaches* CHRIS.

ANTON: Nice camera. What is it? A Leica?
CHRIS: Yes.
ANTON: You're a professional then?
CHRIS: Yes.
ANTON: Anton Kaufmann.
CHRIS: Chris Norwood.

   They shake hands.

ANTON: English?
CHRIS: Yes. And you?
ANTON: Me? I move about. Here, there, everywhere.
    Business.
CHRIS: I wouldn't have thought there was much business to be had in Berlin right now.
ANTON: You'd be surprised.
YAMINA: [*singing*]
    Cette tendre histoire
    De nos chers vingt ans
    Chante en ma mémoire
    Malgré les jours, les ans …

After a while the song comes to its end. Cheers and applause.

ANTON: Pretty, isn't she? The singer.
CHRIS: Yes.
ANTON: Exotic.
CHRIS: Yes.
ANTON: I could introduce you—if you're interested? Although of course, her interest may lie elsewhere …
    Do you like girls, Chris? Or perhaps you'd prefer a blonde?
CHRIS: No, I mean, no thanks. I'm uh, I'm meeting someone.
ANTON: Of course you are.

   Beat.

So. Are you attached?

CHRIS: Uh—?

ANTON: To one of the newspapers or film outfits?

CHRIS: I'm a freelance. I go where they pay me, wherever the stories break.

October I covered Nuremberg. July it was the bombing of the King David Hotel in Jerusalem.

ANTON: Ah, Palestine. What a mess.

CHRIS: Mmm. So what's your business?

You said you travel on business.

ANTON: I have a number of interests.

CHRIS: Such as?

ANTON: Currency. Wills, bonds, matters of choice and law. Candy bars, consumer goods, credit, insurance, you-name-it my ventures are in several baskets …

CHRIS: You're a capitalist?

ANTON: What's the alternative? Communism?

CHRIS: Why not? Stand alone and it's a boiled egg. Get together you can make an omelette.

ANTON: Ah but the difference between a boiled egg and an omelette shared is still only one egg apiece.

Money is a passion, like—like collecting butterflies. Or moths.

Very good at camouflage, the moth.

CHRIS: Mmm.

ANTON: Take this for example—

Shows CHRIS *a banknote.*

CHRIS *recoils in horror.*

CHRIS: Look, I don't know / what you think I—

ANTON: No, no, no.

He laughs.

Trust me, I would never be that explicit.

Beat.

Or that cheap.

No.

I want you to examine that bill and tell me what you see.

CHRIS: It's a ten-dollar note.

ANTON: So if I were to offer you that ten dollars in payment for whatever, you'd accept it?

CHRIS: I suppose so.

ANTON: Even though it's counterfeit?

CHRIS: It's a fake?

ANTON: Show me the money, a letter of credit, a passport, and I can tell in seconds if it's real or a forgery.

CHRIS: What's the give-away?

ANTON: Hesitation. Repetition. Any forger worth his gravy corrects his copy no more than once. And with no hint of indecision.

A bit like being an immigrant, I imagine. The foreigner who makes a forgery of himself, learns to imitate his host culture.

Beat.

Could you do it?

CHRIS: Be a migrant?

ANTON: Forge.

CHRIS: Ah.

ANTON: What do you think makes the world go round, Chris?

CHRIS: I don't know—love?

ANTON: Money.

Money makes the world go round.

He kisses CHRIS. *It's a serious kiss.*

And sex makes the trip worthwhile.

YAMINA *begins a new song. Contemporary, jazzy with a North African inflection.*

The same street corner.

The RUBBLEWOMEN *and* PORTIA, *who is still in male dress, are sifting through rubbish and debris.*

— Empty houses are fair game.

I mean why shouldn't they be? You take what you need and

anything else. Half a jar of jam, scissors, a window-frame / to chop into firewood.
— She was back yesterday.
— Yeah?
— With the same questions. More or less.
PORTIA: Who?
— Some girl looking for her father.
— Join the queue.
— We're all looking for someone. Isn't that so, Marta?
— He was arrested or something.
PORTIA: This girl's father?
— That's what she said. He was in a prison camp or some such.
PORTIA: Why?
— No reason.
— That's impossible.
PORTIA: That's the law. People are always arrested for some reason.
— That's what she said.
— No reason.
PORTIA: I don't believe it.
— They found out he was a Jew.
— Shh!
PORTIA: So there was a reason.
— Shut up! That's all finished and behind us now.
PORTIA: No-one is arrested if they're innocent.
— What's the matter with you? Talking your mouth off like that?
— Haven't you seen the photographs? Some people didn't have to do anything. Just being who—what they were was cause.
PORTIA: It's about the rule of law.
— How can you say that when you know it's not true?
— Can we talk about something else?
— You lock the door, you throw away the key. And then you forget. About the key about everything.
— What door? What key?
— It's a metaphor, stupid!
— Hey, how's your foreigner with the camera? Why don't you ask if he'd like a threesome?
— You've got the wrong end of the stick.

— S and M, that's extra.
— It's not about sex—least not with me.
>   Actually I don't think he's that into girls.
— What's he after then?
— Some kind of story, I suppose. He wanted to meet Jessekah.
— Perhaps he likes brunettes?
— Or maybe they've got some English connection going? That's where she's been living, isn't it? Since.

PORTIA: Who's Jessekah?
— That girl who's looking for her father.
PORTIA: What's her surname?
— Dunno.
>   Why?
PORTIA: No reason.

> SOLDIERS *enter.*
>
> *The* RUBBLEWOMEN *go back to work.*
>
> *One of the* SOLDIERS *is humming 'Lili Marlene'. Softly.*
>
> *They're putting up a poster/s for a screening of the 1939 film* Stagecoach.

— After twelve years of Nazi rule we can't expect Germans to come up with democratic ideas overnight.
— But isn't a military government introducing democracy a kind of contradiction?
— It's just temporary. Once they've got their own show up and running we'll hand over.
— Right.
— Meanwhile we hand out Christmas packages. And organise youth groups—to keep them away from pubs and dancing.
— I like pubs.
— Course you do, Martin. We all do. That's normal. A man's gotta rinse the grit from his gullet. But this isn't about us. Not me, not you. It's about Fritz and Franz and keeping them away from the black market.
— But we skim petrol and stuff to sell.
— Redistribution. We're middlemen, oiling the wheels, making sure there's circulation. Freedom of choice for the little people.

The poster is up. The SOLDIERS *stand back and look at it.*

— *Stagecoach.*
— Cowboys and Indians.
— I like those films, they've got definition. No-one's mixed up or conflicted. None of that arty-fart-y introspection. They want to shoot the Indians, they want to screw the chick with the big bazookas.
— I just like John Wayne.
— That's only his stage name. Guess what he's really called?
— Marion. Everybody knows that. They've all got fake names, / the big stars.
— Enough with the chit-chat.
— Remind us. What are the films for?
— To help the Germans.
— By showing them Westerns?
— Yes. Dubbed into their own language by local actors.
— Why?
— People here have enough to cope with without subtitles.
— No. I mean why, what's the point?
— It's not all Lili Marlene and Beethoven you know. To deNazi the fucking Germans so they can build a better future for themselves.
— By acting like Americans? Or like Hollywood actors playing cowboys.
   It seems—what's that word?—incongruous.
— Life is incongruous.
— What's incongruous?
— You're incongruous, I'm incongruous, we're all incongruous in Berlin. And we manage it by being very careful—about what we say and what we swallow.
   So, for example, if a local says 'It appears I owe you' we focus not on the debt, but on the word 'appears'.
   It can be frustrating of course, pussy-footing around, but it can be useful when you want a bit of distance. To emphasise the appearance rather than the fact. As in 'You appear to be responsible'.

> JESSEKAH *enters. She's dressed in 'normal' and fashionable clothes. She carries a small red vanity case. She looks smart compared to the* RUBBLEWOMEN.

The SOLDIERS *whistle at her and make lewd gestures.*

JESSEKAH *ignores them.*

— Hey darling! Wanna suck on my bratwurst?
— She's smiling at you.
— Come on, it's hot and spicy and oh so big!
— Nah, she isn't.
— Is so.
— Go on talk to her.
— Ask to see her ID.
— Can't.
— Why not?
— Don't speak the lingo, do I.
— Fuck.
— Who needs words.
— Shoot her.
— What?
— Foreplay.
— I can't do that.

Beat.

How do you shoot someone flirtatiously?
— Fire into the air beside her. Give her a fright, so she comes over all weepy and grateful.
— I can't do that!
— See.

Bang! He fires his gun at JESSEKAH. *She falls down.*

— Shit!
— Shit!
— Fucking idiot!
— Now look what you've done!
— What the fuck are you playing at!
— Go on, get out of here.

The RUBBLEWOMEN *and* PORTIA *rush to* JESSEKAH'*s aid.*

The SOLDIERS *hurry off.*

— Bastard!
— Fucking pigs!
— Are you hurt?
— Did he hit you?

JESSEKAH: No, I'm alright I think.

— You're bleeding.

JESSEKAH: It's just a graze where I fell.

> *The* RUBBLEWOMEN *help her up.*

— Here, have some water.

> *She pours water into a tin cup and hands it to* JESSEKAH, *who dabs it on her graze.*
>
> *The* RUBBLEWOMEN *drift back to work.*
>
> PORTIA *lingers.*

JESSEKAH: Why are you still dressed like a man?

PORTIA: What?

JESSEKAH: Did you think I wouldn't recognise you, Portia?

PORTIA: No, I—uh, it's from when the Russians were here. You've no idea what it was like to be a woman in this town when they rolled in. Lots of us disguised ourselves or made ourselves look horrible with disease. One of the women over there used to be an actress, she made herself up into a babushka and / the Russians didn't give her a second look.

JESSEKAH: But that was last year. Why now?

    What are you hiding from?

PORTIA: This is a dangerous city. Remember that.

> *The* RUBBLEWOMEN *come over.*

— You know each other.

JESSEKAH: Yes.

— Friends?

JESSEKAH: Our paths crossed.

PORTIA: It was a long time ago.

— Before?

PORTIA: Yes.

JESSEKAH: Your house on Belmont Straße—?

PORTIA: Destroyed.
— Belmont Straße—that's old money.
PORTIA: No such thing as old money now. Money is money.
— Any progress? Finding your father?
JESSEKAH: Not yet.
PORTIA: There's not much chance. I'm sorry, but you must realise that by now.

> JESSEKAH *says nothing.*

Is it true you live in England?
JESSEKAH: Ten years. Almost.

> *A* RUBBLEWOMAN *grabs* JESSEKAH'*s hand and studies her ring.*

— Is that a turquoise?
JESSEKAH: Yes.
— I had one like that. Where did you get it?

> JESSEKAH *pulls her hand away.*

JESSEKAH: My mother gave it to my father before they were married.
I stole it from him when I ran away, and sold it. But after all that monkey business with my idiot husband, I bought it back. It meant—it means a lot to my father.
PORTIA: And what-was-his-name?— Your husband?
JESSEKAH: Was a fortune hunter.
But we all need a way to leave home, don't we?
PORTIA: What's England like?
JESSEKAH: Clouds and daffodils. / Lots of administration.
PORTIA: Are you going back?
JESSEKAH: At some point.
PORTIA: When?
JESSEKAH: When I know.
PORTIA: What?
JESSEKAH: I need to know.
PORTIA: Which is?
JESSEKAH: One thing I've learnt is dealing with human beings, you never know everything. Not even when you know everything there is to know.

PORTIA: Aren't you going to ask after Bassanio?
JESSEKAH: Okay.
PORTIA: He disappeared. Somewhere in the North Sea, more than two years ago. Autumn of '44. You remember Anton?— Of course you do. Well, he knows people who know people who know things.
>Made enquiries.
>He told me that Bass went down with his ship.
JESSEKAH: People do come back …
PORTIA: Yes, but not from the dead.

2. JANUARY 1947

The same street corner.

A dusting of snow.

ALLIED SOLDIERS *in heavy greatcoats keep a half-hearted watch.*

— It's all crunchy plaster and sour odours
>in the beer garden where brass bands filled the corners
>of the afternoon,
>and men in jackboots saluted.
>But the mirrors still echo in hallways
>and sleep is a fragile thing.

The year is a new one and it's bloody cold one, and already you can tell
>it's going to be a hard one.
>No more swans in the park.
>Lake's frozen,
>the carp are there—somewhere under the surface—
>but I'll bet you, pound to a penny, the swans made Christmas dinner.

Berlin, then.
>A murder of crows. Ugly as sin.
>Shit and ice—and yeah lice too, of the hair-on-the-head kind.
>Thing is, it's not that nice, people-skating-in-a-ring ice,
>it's grubby, melty ice, so you never know
>if you're stepping on solid ground.

Jessekah meanwhile passes from one zone to another.
　　　　Now with the idea of finding the apartment building where she lived with her father.
　　　　But the streets look nothing like themselves.

A front door.

Night. In the shadows, some SOLDIERS *on watch.*

JESSEKAH *approaches the door.*

— Eventually she strikes it lucky.
— Almost by accident, she finds the building that belonged to her father.
　　Where she played hide-and-seek as a child in the cupboard under the stairs.
— Still standing. Pockmarked with shrapnel, but otherwise unscathed.
— She hesitates. Her fingers flinch from the keyhole's breath.

　　JESSEKAH *knocks on the door.*

　　Nothing.

　　She knocks again.

　　Waits.

　　The door opens a fraction. Behind it huddle MISTER *and* MRS.

JESSEKAH: Hello?
— A couple.
— Husband and wife.
JESSEKAH: I'm Jessekah.
MISTER: Jessekah … ?
JESSEKAH: I used to live here.
MISTER: Oh.
MRS: Oh.
JESSEKAH: Yes.
MRS: Oh.
MISTER: Must be what?— Twelve, thirteen years ago.
MRS: We wouldn't have recognised you.

— They're embarrassed.
— Mister or Mrs says:
MISTER: It's such a long time you've been gone—back, before—well, we've all had our troubles these last years, haven't we?
MRS: When you ran off with that young man, you made your father very unhappy. What with the trial and everything, he was in a bad way.
MISTER: And then one day he was gone.
MRS: America.
JESSEKAH: No. No.
   He didn't go to America. That's not true.
MISTER: Well, that's what we heard. / America.
MRS: He was good to us your father, let us stay here when you lost your job, didn't he? Reduced the rent. But later—we couldn't help him, it was too precarious. With Rüdiger and Andreas in the army, and Gabi—you remember Gabi?—you used to play together as kids?—
MRS *and* MISTER: [*chanting*] One upon a time,
   The goose drank wine,
   Gabi kissed a soldier—
MRS: All those skipping games the two of you loved so much.
   She's got children of her own now, Gabi, three of them, so it was dicey, / very dicey …
MISTER: Everything was risky because of them.
JESSEKAH: Them?
MISTER: Because of the Jews.
JESSEKAH: No.
   Because of the Nazis.
MRS: You have to remember the circumstances. We suffered too—
MISTER: Oh, we suffered a lot. I don't know where you were, but Berlin was no picnic. Ordinary decent folk like us, who / just wanted to live our lives—
MRS: We lost our youngest in North Africa. A sister in the bombing. My father died—
MISTER: Heart attack.
JESSEKAH: In his bed, then?
MISTER: Yes, but he's dead just the same. Death is death, Jessekah.
— Then she asks the question they'd been dreading.

— Seriously dreading.
— Mister and Mrs.
JESSEKAH: What about this building? My father's building?
— They said:
— We / sorted that out.
MISTER: We sorted that out.
MRS: It wasn't easy, nothing was easy, but we managed to buy it. For us, and for Gabi and her kids.

    The third flat we rent out—to foreigners mostly, well, they're the only ones who've got any cash / these days—
MISTER: We've got an Englishman there at the moment, a photographer.

    Can't wrap ourselves up in the grudges of the past, can we?
MRS: Rüdiger and his family have the fourth apartment.
JESSEKAH: What about the furniture?
MISTER: All included.
JESSEKAH: The books, the Venetian glass? Hand-woven Persian rugs?
MISTER: Included.
JESSEKAH: I don't understand. How can you buy a building from someone who isn't there?
MISTER: We had legal advice from a proper lawyer. It's all above board.
MRS: Not any old lawyer either. One with a ritzy office on Belmont Straße.
MISTER: We've got the necessary paperwork. We can show you the contract if you like.
JESSEKAH: Yes, thank you. I would like.

    MRS *leaves.*

— She wants to ask them:
— How much did you pay?
— A four-apartment building for the price of what?— A dog kennel?
— But instead she says:
JESSEKAH: Perhaps you did try to help my father—your good neighbour. I hope that's true. But your good neighbour was also a good bargain, wasn't he? For you.
MISTER: Don't be like that, Jessekah. Of course it wasn't expensive, but it was difficult to manage and we had to pay a small fortune in taxes and lawyers.

We're fair people. Fair-minded, honest, ordinary people. Surely it's better for us to have the building, rather than others? We knew you, it's not like strangers. Why don't you come back another evening and see for yourself. We've hardly changed hardly a thing.
— And on he went.
— Chit-chattering away.
— Gabi had taken the kids to the country—
— The air-raids were terrible—
— But now this chaos—
— Allied soldiers, bootleggers—
— So-called refugees pouring in regardless.

  MRS *returns to the door.*

— Mrs can't find the contract.
— But everything's in order.
— The law is on their side.

  Lights shift.

— As for Portia—
— She's heading for a rendezvous at the Café Rialto.

The Café Rialto.
PORTIA *enters. No longer disguised, but still ambiguously dressed.*
Before she joins ANTON *she blows* YAMINA *a kiss.*
YAMINA, *again dressed in contemporary attire, blows a kiss back.*
CHRIS *is at one of the other tables buying drinks for a couple of the* RUBBLEWOMEN.

PORTIA: I need a cup of tea. Something bright and fragrant. Darjeeling perhaps. Or Chinese with jasmine blossom floating in it.

  ANTON *laughs.*

ANTON: Unless you want to drink the muck swept off the floor, this is a safer bet.

  Pours her a glass of vodka.

  So.

PORTIA: So?
ANTON: My future here is, shall we say, uncertain.
PORTIA: Not necessarily.
ANTON: I want to emigrate to America.
PORTIA: Ah.
ANTON: For the future.
PORTIA: The future.
ANTON: It's time to trade in this European sensibility, this neurotic, self-questioning mind-fuck.
PORTIA: Trade it in for what?
ANTON: Freedom. The oxygen of Wall Street—
PORTIA: I used to believe in abstracts like freedom.
    Once / upon a time.
ANTON: There's no future in the past.
PORTIA: Ignoring it is like running from your own shadow.
ANTON: I prefer dealing with tangibles. A lead pipe, hard cash, a Mercedes-Benz, under-the-radar cigarettes. Consumer choice. That's what we need, not pay-back and promises and a filthy tide of displaced persons.
PORTIA: How deep in were you?
ANTON: After a fire does everyone have to be either a fireman or an arsonist?
PORTIA: How deep?
ANTON: Enough to count. You?
PORTIA: No-one cares about a woman's politics—they assume we change them like shoes. Clients come to my office and address me as if I'm the typist, not a lawyer.
    Even my father who wanted me to be richly left, left me those ridiculous caskets and a knot of obligations I couldn't untie.
    Beat.
Those wretched caskets!
    Anyone who knows their fairytales know the princess is never in gold.
    Never.
    If you want the princess you pick tin or cardboard, whatever is dull and utilitarian.

Beat.

Have you read any Freud?

ANTON: Another Jew.

PORTIA takes a book from her pocket and opens it.

PORTIA: Here's what Freud says about Bassanio.

[*Reading*] ' … what he finds to say in glorification of lead as against gold and silver is little and has a forced ring. If in psychoanalytic practice we were confronted with such a speech, we should suspect that there were concealed motives behind the unsatisfying reasons produced.'

She snaps shut the book. Hurls it across the café.

Walk into the light.

Open your eyes.

No wonder I ended up with Bass. Married to a man who was more in love with himself than me!

Beat.

He was calculating and he made scenes, but—

I loved him.

Long beat.

A quick glance at YAMINA.

At least I thought I did …

ANTON: Men act devoted because women expect it. Usually we don't think you're that hot. And we get obsessed with other men all the time.

Portia?

Pours her another drink.

I need you to sign some uh, paperwork.

PORTIA: Paperwork?

ANTON: Official stuff, permissions, et cetera. The documents I need to leave the country.

He pulls a wad of papers from his briefcase.

PORTIA *flicks through them.*

PORTIA: Who's William Newman?

ANTON *shows her a passport.*

But this is—it's you, isn't it? How / did you—?

ANTON: A rather luscious photographer.

He looks over at CHRIS.

CHRIS *interprets* ANTON*'s glance as an invitation to join him. He gets up.*

ANTON *laughs and turns back to* PORTIA.

CHRIS *sits down again.*

And delightfully naïve in the ways of the unofficial marketplace.

PORTIA: Ah.

ANTON: For a price of course.

PORTIA: Of course.

ANTON: The world isn't black and white. Sometimes you have to work with shades of grey.

PORTIA: Is that what they are?

YAMINA *makes for the stage. Her hand casually brushes* PORTIA*'s neck as she passes.*

She sings another contemporary jazzy number with a North African flavour.

PORTIA *signs the papers.*

The same street corner.

The dusting of snow.

The RUBBLEWOMEN *continue their clean-up. They're playing another game.*

— When I was young—
— When I was young I had stars in my eyes.
— When I was young the red flag seemed glorious.
— I thought teachers had the answers.
— I knew my place.
— Was a law unto myself.

— When I was young I thought I could earn a living as an actor.
— I dreamt of travelling across the desert on a camel.
— Thought all my friends should meet each other.
— Thought the present was infinite.
— Thought I'd find love in one person.
— Thought fat people were a blot on society.
— Thought everyone wanted the same things.
— If I lost hope in one place, I'd find it in another.
— When I was young I knew I was right.
— I knew better.
— Money didn't buy happiness.
— Revolution was the key.
— You and your bloody revolution! Why don't you hop over to the Russian zone and find your way back to each other?

> PORTIA *enters. Yawning.*

— Here comes her ladyship.
— Rough night?
— Your friend was here looking for you?
PORTIA: Friend—?
— Jessekah.
— With her little red case. Wonder what / she keeps in it …
— What's the matter?
PORTIA: Nothing.
— You look like someone just crapped in your borscht.
PORTIA: Like you said. Too much booze from the bottom of the barrel.
— Me. I'd like to fill my face with mulberries.
— Eat too many and you'll turn into a bird—isn't that a proverb?
— Curse, more like.

> JESSEKAH *enters. Unobtrusively, during this exchange. Carrying her red vanity case.*

— What type of bird?
— Dunno.
— Mmm, maybe a swallow.
— A seagull.
PORTIA: I think it's a lark.

JESSEKAH: Do you? I'm thinking more a cuckoo. Making your home in another bird's nest.

> *Beat.*

> I found the apartment building. It's bigger than I remember.
> > There are weeds sprouting in the cracks
> > And loose tiles on the roof
> > But otherwise—
> > I know what you did.

PORTIA: A skylark. I meant a skylark.

JESSEKAH: I can forgive you my father's trial, just about, because I was stupid with love.

PORTIA: I went into court to save Anton's skin and / prevent a terrible cruelty.

JESSEKAH: But I can't forgive you this new treachery. That building was all my father had left.
> It was my home.
> Until you came along / with your loopholes and—

PORTIA: What are you talking about?

JESSEKAH: That couple. You helped them steal my father's property.

PORTIA: Not steal.

JESSEKAH: Near as.
> And worse, you made it appear legit.

PORTIA: It was legit. I did what the law allowed. To the letter.
> If it wasn't me, it would have been another lawyer.

JESSEKAH: Oh please! That's such a pathetic excuse.

PORTIA: It was my job and I did it and that's the truth. Pure and simple.

JESSEKAH: No, it's something you say to give a reason for an act that hasn't got one. Or when the reason isn't reasonable.
> Why?

> PORTIA *says nothing.*

That question requires an answer.

PORTIA: And in the absence of an answer?

JESSEKAH: The question remains. And so does the answer, even if it takes you a long time to find it.

PORTIA: I believe in the law.

JESSEKAH: Even when it's obviously biased?

PORTIA: Even.

    CHRIS *enters with his camera.*

    He starts taking photos of the RUBBLEWOMEN. *Then he notices* JESSEKAH.

CHRIS: Haven't I seen you somewhere?

JESSEKAH: I don't / think so.

CHRIS: Yes. You came to the house where I'm living. It was dark. Past curfew actually. I saw you from the upstairs window. I'm in Number three.

JESSEKAH: I used to live in your building.

CHRIS: Before—?

JESSEKAH: Forever ago.

CHRIS: Ah.

    He extends his hand.

I'm Chris Norwood by the way.

    JESSEKAH *shakes his hand.*

And you're—?

— Hey, loverboy.
— Over here!
— We haven't got all day.
— I've got something to show you.
— Over here!

    CHRIS *goes back to photographing the* RUBBLEWOMEN.

— Typical crows. Go on, buzz off!
— Shouldn't they be in Africa or somewhere south for winter?
— God knows.
— [*Chanting*] The hunter drew back his arrow and bow
    Took aim at a big fat carrion crow
    Shot wide and wide and missed his mark
    Shot / his wife right through the heart.
— I remember that rhyme.
— We used to skip to it as kids.
— I like crows. Everybody hates them. But they're only what they're supposed to be.

Throws up her arms and acts like a bird.

I'm a crow—no, that's not it. I'm an actress! SQUAAAAAAAAAK! SQUAAAAAAAAAAAAK!

The RUBBLEWOMEN *laugh.*

JESSEKAH: They'll go back, won't they?

PORTIA: Who will?

JESSEKAH: The middlemen and uniforms. All the blind eyes. All the financiers and mid-rank politicals with their dirty little thoughts will return to what they were doing before.

PORTIA: Maybe.

JESSEKAH: Especially the financiers.

JESSEKAH leaves.

CHRIS *continues photographing the* RUBBLEWOMEN.

Go to a series of freeze-frames, either live tableaux or projected images.

3. FEBRUARY 1947

The same street corner.

Snow.

ALLIED SOLDIERS, *wrapped up against the cold, try to keep warm.*

— Good bloke, good interrogator, never sick
    not even drink-slowed.
    Quite the opposite.
    Always up for it, bash the buggers with a steel bar
    where it doesn't show.
    Push a bastard's head back and pour water down his nose to make him gag
    because he's bored that day.
    Once he drilled a hole in some poor sod's buttocks—same. Felt like it, so he did.
    Twenty-three and he thought he could do whatever, like God.
    Well he's gone—
    Where? Fuck knows. Reassigned, top secret somewhere—
    or dead in a ditch, crows scooping out his eyes.

Tell you what
    can't say I'm a hundred per cent sorry he's out of the picture.
    Bad all round when you go too far.
    The odd bruise—fine.
    Broken rib—grey area.
    'Cause you've gotta keep in mind our reason
    the reason we're here
    is to win over the locals.

Coldest February on record they say
    as if we wouldn't realise standing out in it!
    The wind is fucking Arctic
    and out in the Baltic even the sea is frozen.

Probably why it's so quiet at the moment
    just background
    no inadvertent photographer
    no rubblewomen flashing their thighs.
    Plenty of whispers though. They've ferreted a former Nazi boss
    into that building across the street.
    Then there's the butcher with his party affiliation, the deserter
with his desserts—
    any number of others with this or that past ...

The Café Rialto.

ANTON *is drinking alone.*

PORTIA, *still somewhat ambivalently dressed, storms in. Waving a bank statement.*

PORTIA: Three thousand! Three thousand he's swiped from my account.
    You told me he was dead.
ANTON: Did I?
PORTIA: You told me he drowned in the North Sea.
ANTON: Mmm.
PORTIA: You did.
ANTON: I'm hopeless when it comes to shipping.

PORTIA: Where is he?

ANTON: Wish I knew.

PORTIA: He didn't concoct this on his own. It takes financial nous to shift money across national borders—

ANTON: No. It's incredibly easy when you have the contacts and networks.

PORTIA: Swiss banks, I suppose?

ANTON *shrugs*.

It takes brains to disappear. And you know, and I know, Bassanio was somewhat challenged in that department.

ANTON: True, alas.

Anyone can die, same as anyone can murder. The clever thing is to know how to make people disappear.

PORTIA: You helped him.

You invented his death. You forged him a new identity. And then you taught him to cheat.

ANTON: Guilty as charged.

And now he's flipped on the both of us.

PORTIA: You were friends, were you intimate friends?

ANTON: Yes.

PORTIA: Lovers?

ANTON: Yes.

PORTIA: When did you last see him?

ANTON: I don't recall.

PORTIA: Translation: I'm not telling.

ANTON: He was leaving.

PORTIA: Was it a casual affair?

ANTON: Not on my part.

PORTIA: But on his?

ANTON: I thought—I assumed he felt the same way. Evidently I was wrong.

'I'll love you as long as I can,' he said. And I thought: No-one can promise more.

The war wasn't rolling in our direction by then. He suggested we wipe the slate and begin anew.

Only problem—typical Bass—he didn't have the funds.

Don't worry, I told him. I'll organise the necessary paperwork and backhanders.

Beat.

He waxed lyrical about us moving to the country, and growing vegetables and old together, and I almost believed him.

Beat.

I wanted money to do what it cannot.
Buy what it cannot.

PORTIA: Cowards and swine can be handsome. As I've learnt to my cost.

Beat.

What do you think makes the world go round?

ANTON: Depends how you spin it.

PORTIA: I reckon it's war makes the world go round. Not love. Not money. But war.

ANTON: What do you want?

PORTIA: Repayment. Three-thousand.
The principal.
The rest—
the rest is a sorry business. He married me for my inheritance. It hit me before the confetti hit the ground.

Beat.

No more husband. No more home, not even a lover who comes by the hour.
Now I'm solo, but once—once
I was passionate.
And I was passionate
about the law. I thought it was a beautiful thing.
I was passionate
about burrowing into the places where people are vulnerable, and helping them find an escape clause.
I was passionate
about seeing people who took risks with other people's savings get more than they bargained for.

I was passionate and I put in hours upon hours.

I embraced jurisprudence. One cannot comprehend a society's legal system until one knows some moral truths about the justifications for the practices in that society.

Beat.

And then—and then the compass swung. I found myself on the wrong side

of a bad law, the evidence was mounting. I realised …

I realised

the law is a street fight. It's a battleground. There's nothing beautiful about it. It's self-serving and capricious. Sometimes the right side loses. Often everyone loses.

Justice is a whore, and the quality of mercy is well and truly stuffed.

YAMINA *enters. Acknowledges* PORTIA.

Music begins.

PORTIA *takes her bank statement and tears it into tiny pieces. Tosses it up into the air like confetti.*

Waves goodbye to YAMINA *and leaves.*

Lights shift to spotlight YAMINA.

Music swells.

YAMINA *gestures to stop the music.*

YAMINA: I'm not going to sing this time. I'm going to show you some pictures instead.

She takes out her iPad.

Some cities are boring. Like a hole in a slab of Swiss cheese. Some are held together by a river—without the river the city would be smudge. There's Berlin which brings together the incompatibles of power and melancholy. There are cities that have closed in on themselves—Al-Jaza'ir where I was born is an example of this.

She shows images and graphics/animations from her iPad. Nothing too literal or illustrative.

We moved to Paris when I was five.

We were migrants with a small M. An M that tried to make itself as small and inconspicuous as possible.

Before immigration became this hot-button issue.

Mum wanted to go to Switzerland because it had mountains, chocolate and neutrality.

But France is a land where the soup is rich and creamy, and that's where we ended up.

We arrived in Paris with nineteen plastic bags, and Dad went straight to the Red Cross—

to get a list of the most frequently occurring accidents and viruses in France.

He came home and instructed us never to stand on a ladder, because ladder-related incidents accounted for eighty per cent of home accidents.

More images and/or graphics and animation.

Paris is surrounded

by a grey urban ring that encircles its museum heart.

These suburbs are much the same.

I imagined French architects gathering in some posh club to sign an agreement that they would never build anything to compete with the beauty of the centre.

Our neighbourhood was likewise. Concrete, edgy, and close to the car factory. Oh and it had a tiny park with bad public art, which was somehow supposed to *Heal the World* and make us feel better about living in such a shithole.

Michael Jackson. *Heal the World*. Remember the video with all the photogenic African kids?

Poverty porn.

Brilliant.

Not.

Actually I loathe those 'We are the World', 'Do They Know it's Christmas?', let's-help-the-poor-brown-people songs.

Hey, superannuated rockers! Ever stop to think you might owe the world more than a schmaltzy pop song?

If you can believe what you read in Wikipedia—which of course you can't always—in Sri Lanka the Yellow Pages are called the Rainbow Pages. Works for me.

Laughs.

Our first year in France, Dad worked at Citroën, and Mum took out an ad in Yellow Pages.

Being listed showed she was serious,

but if you don't fit under one of the headings, it's like you don't exist.

Beat.

I won't bore you with school, which was plenty boring enough.

My eldest brother left a.s.a.p. to work in a factory, which—far as I could see—produced mostly soot.

More images and/or graphics and animation.

There are bare-skin cities like Sydney or LA, and covered-up cities—have you ever noticed that? And it's not all down to climate.

Then there are that handful of guidebook cities—Vienna, Kyoto, Venice.

Paris too, I guess.

But Venice was where I went after I stumbled out of high school. An aunt who lived there got me a job in the hotel where she worked

and I worked shifts in unventilated cellars.

Thing is, Venice hardly manufactures or sells anything except its history to tourists.

Met a guy, another import like me. Lancelot. Yeah, totally pathetic name. He was personal assistant to some rich bloke. Dogsbody, more like.

Long story short: I was young. I was lonely. I was naïve. I got pregnant. Big deal.

Beat.

Look, he was a clown, no way on earth was I going to marry him and become—what? A family of dogsbodies?

No way.

Children don't wait and neither does life.

I moved back to Paris

to a nineteenth-century basement where I spent my days staring at trainers, boots, and stilettos as they hurried past on the footpath outside my window.

I got to know a lot about shoes.

Laughs.

I'm raising my son on my own. I don't want problems. Mum said: put a ring on your finger and pretend.

I refused.

This is France with its laws and famous people: Monet, Coco Chanel, Frantz Fanon.

Starts showing images of suitcases.

People leave for lots of reasons. And all of us end up annoying the communities where we end up. Civilised countries don't admit this of course. They find their own reasons to hide behind. The environment, housing, traffic, different values, blah, blah, blah.

What it often comes down to is baggage.

A picture of a battered leather suitcase, circa 1940s.

This is romantic baggage. Old, reliable. Seen a few adventures and has the scars to prove it. Down the Nile, up the Rhine, whatever.

Pictures of ordinary, modern suitcases and hold-alls.

These are your modern standards.

My ancestors were travellers and merchants who had geography at their fingertips.

No surprise I like suitcases, then.

A picture of a very, very expensive suitcase.

Here's a model with an expensive name
    and gold initials
    for what it's worth.

Now a photo of an unremarkable bag.

This bag's mine. Flea-market special.
    X-rayed by a thousand airport eyes because
    that M I mentioned before, that small case M,
    is now a capital M. Muslim.

Not sun-baked soil and goats leaping from the edge
but high alert, do not pass Go, stop the boats, and all the rest of the halal-aballoo.
And on that note—

Puts away her iPad.

We're going back to the past.

Steps up to the microphone.

Music please!

Music begins.

This time she sings a classic 1940s number.

Night. Snow.
The same front door.
In the shadows, SOLDIERS *make a show of keeping watch.*
One of them whistles 'Lili Marlene'.

— What's that smell?
— Nausea.
— Yeah, nausea.
— Vomit.
— Puke.
— Sick.
— I asked a simple question, I don't need a bloody thesaurus.
So come on, own up. Who's the guilty party?

No-one says anything.

Someone here is an up-chucker—maybe several someones.

Still no response.

That's the key issue, nail on the head, isn't it? No-one wants to put their hand up and say
it was me
I owe you
an apology. Or more than that—
Martin?

— Okay, it was me. Sorry. It was that Russian gutrot. Tasted like pig-piss, knew I should've said something—stop would have been a good word, but you pass the point of no return and then you pass out / and then you—

Mimes vomiting.

— Peace is always messy. No-one want to stick around and police it.

It's rah-rah 'We've won the war' now let's get the fuck out of here.

But who do we think is going to run the country?
— Same people who saluted Hitler and torched Jewish shops.
— Hence John Wayne.
— John / Wayne—what's he—?
— Our Soviet brothers are hammer fisted, no subtlety. Their notion of entertainment is a lecture called 'Karl Marx and Historical Materialism.'
— Yawn.
— We, on the other hand, favour camouflage. *Stagecoach* and cowboys galloping over the sunset.
— Geronimo!
— Not so fast. Problem now is, we can't tell them apart.

Who's seen the light, and who's merely acting.
— So what? We're equal opportunity, treat the buggers the same. Make them all pay.
— Won't that backfire? Radicalise run-of-the-millers who might otherwise be on-side?
— Eggs and omelettes, eggs and omelettes.
— Don't mention—Oh fuck!

He throws up.

— When a man's gotta spew, a man's gotta spew.
— Have you noticed the shifts
    in pronouns among the locals?
— Pronouns?
— Pronouns. First up, 'we' became I, as in I wasn't a supporter, I didn't torture, I was a hapless bystander standing by.

Plural to singular. And 'us' was scarce as hen's teeth—or real coffee.

It's all about distance, you see, and how you stretch the elastic that binds. So now 'we' has gone by the wayside, and it's he, she and they instead of me.

The third person has taken over.

— He's the one who did it.
— True.
— He's the one who did the bad thing to the Jew's daughter and so forth, letting her bleed into the snow.
— There was no snow.
— There was a lot of snow and she bled splots onto it.
— Superficial.
— He shot her and ran off.
— Correction. We all ran off.
— Shut up!
— Here she comes.
— Enter Jessekah.

>   JESSEKAH *enters with her red case.*

— See. Not even limping.

>   *She knocks on the door.*
>
>   *Nothing.*
>
>   *She tries to peer through the keyhole.*

— They've blocked up their keyhole.
— Mister and Mrs.

>   *Knocks again.*
>
>   *The door opens. Behind it stand* MISTER *and* MRS.

MRS: Oh, it's you.
JESSEKAH: Yes, it's me.
MISTER: You're back …
— No-one speaks.
— Silence.
— In the silence, Jessekah remembers.
    Patchy, mossed, forgotten childhood stuff.
— Her father waving goodbye, off on a business trip to Frankfurt.
— Birch trees muffled by night and fog.

MRS: Possession is nine-tenths of the law and the law is on our side, whether you like it or not.
MISTER: They're not going to change the law now.
MRS: No.
MISTER: If you want to buy it back, we can talk with our lawyer. Only you'll have to expect some readjustment—times are still hard, prices are soaring because of the shortages, we knew you when you were a little girl / and you and Gabi …
JESSEKAH: Yes, times change. Prices go up. But explain how either of those facts justifies theft. Because that's what we're / talking about here.
MISTER *and* MRS: No, no, no, no, no.
MRS: It became the property of the state.
MISTER: We didn't know where you were …
MRS: Your father was gone …
MISTER: Our sons were away—and Gabi—
    You have to think things out, Jessekah, not look at everything from one point of view.
— Then they hit on nostalgia.
— Nostalgia.
— Desperate.
— Attempt to change the subject.
— This, that, anything.
— What does Jessekah think about the influx of American films? Young people seem to like them. But / they're not sure—
— Mister and Mrs are concerned.
— They don't want to see their own literary and musical traditions overwhelmed by American culture.
— Jessekah isn't buying it.
JESSEKAH: You might at least have the decency to offer me the difference.
MRS: The difference?
JESSEKAH: Between the real value of this building and the peanuts you paid for it. Instead you want to sell me my own property for as much as you can get.
MISTER: All we've done has been correct.
MRS: Perfectly correct.

MISTER: And everything we've told you.
  We haven't been like lots of other people and engaged in sharp practice. It was all done according to the rules.
MRS: But what's done is done and paid for and signed.
MISTER: It's over now and you got through it in the end, and that's the main thing.
— Again no-one speaks.
— Silence.
— A space where Jessekah imagines the delicate bone structure of a hand. Pictures the survivors picking nettles.
— She sees the shadow of some ferns in the hallway.
— Sees rats and blood-clots and all the flies in the world.
JESSEKAH: May I come in?
— Silence.
— Again.
JESSEKAH: May I come in?
MRS: Well ...
JESSEKAH: I'm going back to England tomorrow.
MRS: I don't know if—

Turns to MISTER.

  What do you think?
JESSEKAH: One last look.
  Please.
MISTER: [*to* MRS] What harm can it do?
  Come in.

They open wide the door.

JESSEKAH *crosses the threshold.*

— Jessekah puts her case on the table.
— They stand there in the hallway.
— Mister and Mrs.
— And Jessekah.

JESSEKAH *opens her case and takes out a gun.*

She shoots first MISTER, *then* MRS. *So fast there's no time for them to say a word. Barely even time for then to register surprise.*

MISTER *and* MRS *fall into the floor.*

JESSEKAH *fires another bullet point blank into each of their hearts.*

She puts the gun back into her red vanity case.

— Then she took the front door key.
— It was her father's. She recognised its silver ring.
— That was all she took.
 Her father's key.

Lights shift.

The focus is JESSEKAH.

She could almost be giving evidence in tribunal or court of law.

JESSEKAH: Such a night.
 The moon in its sling of cloud.
 The altered view, the stars twitching—

Beat.

Those people had plenty of good luck all though everything.
 I'm their bad luck
 I'm the faulty ladder, the falling flowerpot, the unexploded bomb.
 I didn't go there that first time with any notion of—I just wanted to see the house again.
 I'd been wandering about Berlin, in the chaos and shit, and then to see that self-satisfied pair—
 inaccessible to the tiniest crumb of shame or doubt—or sense of debt.
 That was their real bad luck: what they stood for and who I was in that particular moment.

My original plan was to set fire to the house and watch it go up in flames.
 But two things stopped me. The person in the third apartment—he has nothing to do with this.
 And there wasn't any petrol to be had for love or money.

They bled out on the carpet. On my father's Persian carpet in my father's house where my relatives and ancestors made promises and swore and lit candles and sang us to sleep.

Their death was quick and easy. The kind denied those packed onto trains. The kind denied my father. You could say I saved those despicable people from old age and the pain of remorse.

My father didn't just up and leave one morning for America. I don't believe any of the words they threw at me.

I think they sat there stewing in their little apartment thinking: What a big house for a single man, and a Jew.

Shows a passport and documents.

I found these.

Under a loose floorboard that no-one else knew about. Only my father and myself. A passport and exit papers in a false name—but with my father's photo.

He was planning to leave, but never did.

Beat.

I'm not afraid of the consequences, the law or whatever.

Beat.

But …

Beat.

But I am afraid …

Long beat.

Who am I that can hate so much?

Beat.

I find myself
   wondering about—
   is it possible
   to know why people acted as they did?

The state of their souls as they did what they did. With two hands, with arms and feet, with organs, senses, passions, flesh and blood.

The distant sound of a passing train.

And when the crows come down from their loud flight
   and there's no wind to carry away the stories
   will we remain forever haunted by those death trains clattering across the back gardens of suburban Germany?

From far away comes the echo of music.

Somewhere in the future YAMINA *is singing in Arabic. Pianissimo at first.*

PORTIA *enters.* YAMINA *holds out her hand to her.*

THE END

PERFECT STRANGER
Hilary Bell

Perfect Stranger was commissioned by Yale Repertory Theatre and first produced by the University of Tasmania at the School of Creative Arts and Media, on the Lands of the Kanamaluka peoples, Launceston, on 8 October 2020, with the following cast and creatives:

RUTH	Amelia Bartlett, Sally Drummond, Sakura Walker, Kiarna Haas
GEORGE, KOJO	Matt Harris
MURRAY, MIGUEL, BRENDAN, DUANE	Kyle Ennis
OWEN, RICHARD	Kurtis Maher-Johnson
SKYE, JANICE	Lilly Amos
ROBERTO, JESSE	Freddy Brown
BOY	Joel King
DAVID, DEAN, FATHER	Daniel Story
SUSAN, GILDA	Erin Maloy
ADAM, KURT	Owen Spanswick
SLEEPWALKER	Hazel Butchart
GRACE	Kiralee Brundritt-Howell
DONKEY	Alexander Chatwin-Dalgleish
GRAVEDIGGER	Paige Kruger
DAWN	Ashley Eyles

Director, Ben Winspear
Assistant director, Tansy Gorman
Designer, Ralph Myers
Vision, Kyle Enniss, Kurtis Maher–Johnson
Costume, Amelia Bartlett, Freddy Brown, Daniel Story
Lighting, Nathan Enniss, Kiarna Haas
Set, Lilly Amos
Sound, Matt Harris, Joel King
Props, Sally Drummond, Erin Maloy
Marketing, Kurtis Maher–Johnson, Sakura Walker
Technical officer, Chris Jackson

CHARACTERS

RUTH. Around 30.
HENRY
DONKEY*
GRACE
MARIE*
BARRY
ROBERTO
MIGUEL
OWEN
SKYE
BRENDAN
NADIA
HORTENSE*
LEONIE
ROD*
OLIVE
RICHARD
TAXI DRIVER*
ANTHONY
DEAN
KIM*
GILDA
DAWN
LEE*
GRAVEDIGGER
NURSE
WOMAN (TAXI DRIVER'S WIFE)
MOTHER (GRAVEDIGGER'S)

CASTING

There is no upper limit for cast-size. As well as the characters listed below there are crowds, commuters, passers-by. The minimum, with doubling, is around eight.

Ruth is around 30. The ages and races of all other characters are either suggested in the text, or at the director's discretion. Asterisks indicate flexibility around gender.

ACTION

The action of the play unfolds over a day, and revolves around different locations in a city.

The time is, for all intents and purposes, the present.

Ruth is in every scene, indicated or otherwise.

PRODUCTION NOTE

Scenes should flow without interruption. Necessary is a sense of constant movement, with occasional moments of stillness.

A song appears in the script, 'Whither Must I Wander', by Vaughan Williams and Robert Louis Stevenson.

ACT I

I.

Breakwater, sunrise.
HENRY, *eighties, stands looking out.*
Several beats. Then he's resolved.
He throws his wallet and phone into the water.
He starts filling his pockets with rocks.
RUTH *pulls herself out of the water.*

RUTH: Good morning!

> *He stares.*

What a glorious day. The sun's barely up but you can already feel it's going to be hot, I'll be dry in seconds.

Sorry, did I give you a shock? Are you not used to seeing people haul themselves out of the water fully dressed?

> *She laughs.*

There was nobody here when I arrived, it was still dark. I was a bit naughty, I parked in the emergency zone because I thought I'd only be a minute. Just to paddle, you know, get my feet wet, but somehow—this happened.

> *No response.*

Have you ever gone swimming in the dark?
No?
It's a strange feeling, it's like you're dreaming. You can't tell how far you've gone because you can't get your bearings. The night sky and black water merge and you forget yourself: it never even occurred to me that it could be dangerous—you know: boats, or sharks, a rip. Full of toxic sludge, no doubt, but I'll live.

And you? What are you doing out and about so early, watching the sunrise?

He stares.

... Well, I don't want to get a parking ticket. Nice meeting you.
HENRY: Is it you?
RUTH: Sorry?
HENRY: Your dress.
RUTH: It's fine, it'll dry in no time.
HENRY: It's me, Henry.
RUTH: Really? That's my son's name. Hello Henry, I'm Ruth.
HENRY: You came back.
RUTH: Um, I was here a couple of weeks ago, if that's what you mean? This is his favourite spot, he loves playing on the rocks. Maybe you've seen us here.
HENRY: Why?
RUTH: Why what?
HENRY: Why have you come?
RUTH: Well ... I had a concert last night, it's always hard to sleep afterwards, all the adrenaline—and then it was so hot. I tossed and turned and finally thought stuff it, drove down here hoping for a breeze. Left my husband snoring away, our little boy tucked in with his robot. They won't even know I was gone, it's barely even—
  Oh, what? Look at that, my watch has stopped.
HENRY: Why now, why are you doing this?
RUTH: Piece of junk, so much for being waterproof. You don't have the time, do you? I'm guessing round six?
HENRY: Am I wrong, is this wrong?
RUTH: Sorry, what?
HENRY: Don't try to talk me out of it.
RUTH: Oh gosh, don't cry. Here you are on this beautiful day, by the water, the sun's shining, how could anything be wrong?
HENRY: I don't know what to do.
RUTH: Maybe a swim would cheer you up? There's nobody around, go in your undies. I feel amazing—though it could be the adventure: it was exciting, creeping out of the house, swimming in the dark, nobody in the entire world knowing where I am. Even if Martin rang my phone's in the car, I'm incommunicado.
HENRY: That's what I want, to be free.

RUTH: Me too, I wish I could float free for a bit longer, but life calls: breakfast to make, lunches to pack and all the rest. It was lovely talking to you.
HENRY: Will you wait for me?
RUTH: No time to wait, sorry, but if you want a lift?

—

Hang on, where's my car?

Don't tell me it's been towed … Oh for god's sake. I can't believe it.

My wallet's in there, my keys, phone—I can't even call Martin to pick me up.

This is ridiculous. Could I use yours?
HENRY: My phone? I—
RUTH: Wait, he just got a new number, I don't know it. I don't know anybody's numbers any more. Shit, what am I going to do?
HENRY: Stay with me, till it's done.
RUTH: Seriously, am I supposed to walk? That'll take hours! They'll wake up and I won't be there and they'll freak. This is a disaster. My in-laws are coming from Germany, I'm supposed to collect them from the airport, and tonight I've got a rehearsal for the recording next week.
HENRY: It's alright, you're not real, I know that, the eyes playing tricks. A mirage, like in the desert during the war, seeing that lake, conjuring up what we wanted to see.
RUTH: Martin will have to make the lunches, walk the dog …
HENRY: The mind in extremis.
RUTH: I'm not real? Why would you say that?
HENRY: Are you?
RUTH: Of course I am, as real as you are—feel.

She extends an arm.

Instead, he gingerly approaches and takes her face in his hands.

She laughs, surprised.

HENRY: You are. I'm sorry. I thought you were somebody else, someone who's not here.
RUTH: What you just did? That's what I do to my son when I need him to take a deep breath and calm down. Thank you: I've just realised

I'm completely overreacting. I mean, really, so what if I don't get back in time? There are taxis at the airport. There's all afternoon to rehearse. Martin is capable of walking the dog. I'm always so wound up, I forget that I'm not at the centre of everything.

HENRY: You can go.

RUTH: Losing the car, and my phone, perhaps it's a sign. Stop and smell the roses, right? Get off the ride for a moment, look around at the world. It won't stop turning without us.

HENRY: No.

RUTH: Okay universe, I'm listening. I'll walk home—but I won't run. [*To* HENRY] And you, enjoy this lovely day.

She leaves.

He takes two more handfuls of rocks, and he steps towards the water.

II.

Street mall.

There is no-one else in sight but a moth-eaten, sagging DONKEY. *The person in the suit is bent over, their front legs elevated on scuffed hooves. The costume includes a hand-made donkey head. They are completely motionless. There's a paper cup before them.*

RUTH: Hello, little donkey.
    Pretty quiet round here, everyone's still in bed.
    Sorry, I don't have any change. But can I give you a pat?

It nods slightly, causing a little bell around its neck to tinkle. She laughs, charmed.

I'll come by later with my little boy, he'd love to meet you. Don't go anywhere, okay?

III.

Traffic lights.

GRACE, *in army fatigues with a duffel bag and a bottle in a paper bag.*

GRACE: Hey.

RUTH: Hey to you too.

GRACE: Want some?
RUTH: What is it?
GRACE: Beer, what else?
RUTH: What else indeed? Sure.
GRACE: What are you doing, jogging or something?
RUTH: Enjoying the morning.
GRACE: It's like forty degrees, you enjoy getting fried to a crisp?
RUTH: I don't know why we're waiting, it's not like there's any traffic.

Awkward silence.

Are you off somewhere?
GRACE: Just got back.
RUTH: Welcome home.
GRACE: Yeah, right.
RUTH: You look tired.
GRACE: No way, I'm wired, man. If what you're saying is I haven't been to bed: yes, you are correct.
RUTH: Partying all night?
GRACE: No I was not partying all night. Psyching myself up for this is what I was doing. I've got a meeting in ten minutes.
RUTH: Sounds important.
GRACE: It is. It's with my ex.
RUTH: Aha, boy trouble.
GRACE: It's not 'trouble', not yet anyway. He got demoted. He's a cop—he was heading for superintendent, now he's directing traffic. Sexual harassment, can't say I was surprised. I would've stuck by him but he breaks it off, for my sake he says, spare me the shame; what he doesn't tell me is he's met someone else.
RUTH: Maybe—
GRACE: Maybe what?
RUTH: … it's just as well?
GRACE: Why?
RUTH: I mean, sexual harassment.
GRACE: What would you know?
RUTH: Nothing.
GRACE: What are you doing?
RUTH: There are no cars.

GRACE: There are cameras.
RUTH: I think they might be broken.
GRACE: 'Don't walk' means don't walk.
RUTH: Well, I hope your meeting / goes—
GRACE: The things I've seen, things I've been up against, I'm sorry but I'm not off defending my country to come home to this shit. I'm going to get him back, don't you worry, she's not staying in the picture.

> *The lights change.* RUTH *escapes.*

RUTH: Good luck!

> GRACE *calls after her.*

GRACE: And if she digs her heels in, I've still got my service rifle. But hopefully it won't come to that.

IV.

Bench.

MARIE *is sitting.*

RUTH: Mind if I join you?

> MARIE *stares at her.*

Is that okay?

> MARIE *shifts over, astonished.* RUTH *tilts her face to the sun.*

That feels good. The simple things, right?

I just had an intense encounter at the lights. Takes all sorts, I guess.

Do you live around here?

MARIE: —
RUTH: I'm west of the city, it'll be even hotter there.
MARIE: I don't go out.
RUTH: You're out now.
MARIE: Not for long.
RUTH: Yeah, I'm indoors way too much. Actually, my doctor said I've got an occupational Vitamin D deficiency from spending all day in a rehearsal room. The whole orchestra, everyone's on supplements.

Do you have an indoor job?

MARIE: I don't work.

RUTH: Lucky you! Make the most of it, it's a perfect day for a swim. As you can see, I've / already—

MARIE: You don't know who I am.

RUTH: No, should I?

—

Are you famous?

God, I'm sorry, I'm terrible at recognising people.

MARIE: No, thank you.

RUTH: Who are you? I'm really embarrassed now.

MARIE: What's your instrument?

RUTH: Oh no you don't.

MARIE: I haven't had a normal conversation in a while.

RUTH: But who am I having a conversation with? What do I tell my in-laws when I say I met a celebrity?

MARIE: Please don't.

RUTH: Can we do a selfie? Oh, I haven't got my phone.

BARRY rolls his coffee cart on.

Hello over there, look who I found! Would you mind taking our photo?

BARRY double-takes, then turns his back as he sets up his cart.

MARIE leaves.

Where'd she go? Who was that?

BARRY: Eh?

RUTH: Did you know her?

BARRY: I know who she is.

RUTH: And?

BARRY: Serious?

RUTH: Yeah, I'm serious!

BARRY: That was her.

RUTH: Who?

BARRY: You know, the screamer.

RUTH: Who?

BARRY: The one screaming at the bloke with the pram.

RUTH: What bloke? When?
BARRY: On the bus, it's everywhere. You haven't seen?
RUTH: Screaming? Why?
BARRY: I don't know, some stupid shit like him pushing in. Everyone hated on her. Lost her job, had to move, change schools, the whole drama. You been under a rock or something?
RUTH: I must've missed it.
BARRY: Don't know how.
RUTH: God, I feel bad now.
BARRY: This fucken city makes people crazy.
RUTH: Doesn't it?
BARRY: Stand on this corner a couple of hours, making coffees …
RUTH: Smells great.
BARRY: … the things you see.
RUTH: Country boy, are you?
BARRY: How'd you guess?
RUTH: You've got a farmer's physique.
BARRY: Mining.
RUTH: A miner. And now you're a barista.
BARRY: That's right. What can I get you?
RUTH: My car just got towed, with my wallet in it.
BARRY: Bit ordinary.
RUTH: I'll say.
BARRY: What do you want? On the house.
RUTH: Oh—no.
BARRY: Coffee?
RUTH: No, really.
BARRY: Tea?
RUTH: Coffee, but you so don't have to.
BARRY: I don't, but I want to. Milk and sugar?
RUTH: You don't do cappuccinos, do you?
BARRY: No.
RUTH: Actually, cancel that, coffee's bad on an empty stomach.

    BARRY *smiles*.

BARRY: Righto, a breakfast roll to go with it?
RUTH: I couldn't.

BARRY: My good deed for the day. The works?
RUTH: With onion instead of bacon, if that's okay.
BARRY: That is indeed okay.
RUTH: Scrumptious.
BARRY: Thank you. Oh, the roll.
RUTH: Ha, funny too.
BARRY: Been for a dip, have you?
RUTH: I couldn't resist.
BARRY: Don't blame you. We had a billabong behind our place, a day like this we thought nothing of jumping in, jeans and all.
RUTH: So you don't like the city?
BARRY: I'm outta here soon as I've got enough cash.
RUTH: What's wrong with it?
BARRY: Bloody lonely, isn't it.
RUTH: Is it?
BARRY: Worst thing about this place? The women.
RUTH: Why?
BARRY: Turn up their noses when you try to talk to them.
RUTH: I didn't.
BARRY: I noticed that.
    Sauce?
RUTH: And mustard, if you've got it.
BARRY: They're either too good for you, or they're like that lot.
RUTH: Who?
BARRY: Them, over by the wall.
RUTH: … Everyone's got to make a living.
BARRY: Not like that they don't.
    There you go: one roll, one coffee.
RUTH: That is so nice of you.
BARRY: Barry.
RUTH: Barry. It's been a pleasure.
BARRY: Where are you going?
RUTH: Somewhere out of the sun.
BARRY: Stick around, keep me company.
RUTH: You'll have customers soon.
BARRY: Doesn't get busy till eight.
RUTH: I think I'll find some shade.

BARRY: What are you doing tonight?
RUTH: Tonight?
BARRY: I'll cook you up some tea.
RUTH: Oh …
BARRY: You think that roll's good, wait till you taste my chops.
RUTH: I don't eat meat.
BARRY: Fine, no chops. I'm in a boarding house—probably better if I come to you.
RUTH: That's such a sweet offer …
BARRY: Nah, too easy. Where do you live?
RUTH: A long way from here.
BARRY: I'll need an address.
RUTH: With my husband, actually.
BARRY: Husband?
RUTH: Yes, and son.

Pause.

BARRY: You prick-tease.
RUTH: I beg your pardon?
BARRY: That's a new one, hit on a man for a free feed.

BARRY indicates the wall.

Even they wouldn't stoop that low.
RUTH: That's not very fair.
BARRY: Don't you tell me what's fair. You flutter your eyelashes and talk about my physique …
RUTH: Please stop following me.
BARRY: … come on all chatty,
RUTH: Here, have it.
BARRY: I'm not touching it now.

She dumps the roll and leaves.

V.

Street.

ROBERTO *and* MIGUEL, *Chilean migrant workers, hurry along beside her.*

MIGUEL *has a paper napkin.*

ROBERTO: A lo mejor ella sabe dónde está. Enséñale la dirección. (*Maybe she knows where it is. Show her the address.*)
MIGUEL: Señorita, disculpe: do you know here?
RUTH: What?
ROBERTO: Habla español?
RUTH: I can't understand you.
ROBERTO: Es una obra de construcción, vamos a trabajar ahí. (*It's a building site, we're supposed to start work.*)
RUTH: What is that, an address? No I don't know it.
ROBERTO: Cuéntale de los hijos, que vamos a traer a nuestras familias. (*Tell her about the kids, bringing our wives over.*)
MIGUEL: We need the work, bring family here.
ROBERTO: Si llegamos tarde no nos darán el trabajo. (*We can't be late or we won't get the job.*)
MIGUEL: We cannot be late; just look.
RUTH: Sorry.

VI.

Public toilets.

OWEN *is stripped to the waist, washing.*

OWEN: Oh goodness, I thought this was the gents', pardon me.
RUTH: It's both.
OWEN: Ladies *and* gents?
RUTH: Unisex.
OWEN: Whatever next?
RUTH: Would you mind checking outside?
OWEN: Who am I looking for?
RUTH: A man in an apron.

OWEN: No men in aprons. All clear.
RUTH: Thanks.
OWEN: Is everything alright?
RUTH: This guy suddenly got really aggressive.
OWEN: There are quite a few lost souls around.
RUTH: I didn't ask for anything, he offered.
OWEN: Can't let it get you down.
RUTH: I was just making conversation, that's not flirting. It really stressed me out.
OWEN: Maybe you should turn right around and go back to bed.
RUTH: I'm not letting him ruin my day. This is my time, to enjoy myself.
OWEN: Atta girl.
RUTH: But I might just wait here a minute.
OWEN: I'm not a vagrant, by the way. If you're wondering.
    I came down yesterday, eleven hours on the train for a job interview, only to find I got the day wrong! Can you believe it? I couldn't afford a hotel, so there was nothing for it but to walk around all night.
RUTH: God, sounds awful.
OWEN: It's alright, I've had my wash and here I am, bright-eyed and bushy-tailed. How do I look, are my pants wrinkled?
RUTH: No.
OWEN: Is this the fashion now? Not too high? My friend who's in menswear back home said it's all the rage with youngsters.
RUTH: I'm sure you'll be fine.
OWEN: I'm very nervous, actually. If I don't get it I'll be completely devastated. I haven't had a job in seven years, you can't imagine.
RUTH: I'd have thought—
OWEN: What?
RUTH: I mean, you know, you're not thinking about retiring?
OWEN: No, oh don't even say it. I need to work, I need this.
RUTH: What's the job?
OWEN: Right there, across the street.
RUTH: Where, the kindergarten?
OWEN: Yep.
RUTH: Doing what?
OWEN: Looking after children! What else?

RUTH: Have you done it before?
OWEN: Come on, how hard can it be?
RUTH: I'm guessing you never had kids.
OWEN: Never had the pleasure of meeting the right lady. No, I'm a career man. Next stop: kindy teacher!
RUTH: But if you've had no experience—
OWEN: With children? No. With job interviews? Plenty! That's all I've done for seven years. Taken trains to different cities. Brought my own sandwich and waited across the road so I can walk in right on time. Punctuality, that's the first thing they look for. Tell the gal behind the desk she looks pretty, give her a little wink. They'll pick someone they want to see every day, right? Human psychology. Doesn't matter what it is: deck hand, security guard, flight attendant (and I've gone for all of them)—it comes down to the same thing. Hasn't paid off yet, but this time it will: I have a good feeling.
RUTH: What will you do if you don't get it?
OWEN: I don't let myself think negative thoughts. I won't even contemplate that possibility. Listen to this: I gave up my lease so I can move here. That's thinking positive!
RUTH: My son's in kindy.
OWEN: Not that one?
RUTH: No, it's on the corner of our street.
OWEN: Convenient. Can you give me some tips?
RUTH: His dad'll be dropping him off in about an hour, putting his lunchbox in the fridge.
OWEN: Lunch in the fridge, got it.
RUTH: There are pegs for their bags; they have to wear hats outside.
OWEN: Very sensible. What else?
RUTH: Sometimes they cry when you leave.
 Henry always cries when I leave.
 I need to go.
OWEN: Time waits for no man, or woman.
RUTH: I'll surprise them.
OWEN: Ooh, they'll love that.
RUTH: If I get a cab I'll be home in time to take him myself. What is it now?
OWEN: You've got a watch there.

RUTH: It doesn't work.
OWEN: It's quarter to eight, nearly show-time.
RUTH: Yep, I'll make it. Wait, damn, I've got no money.
OWEN: Hit me up once I've got the job.
RUTH: How do I pay for a taxi?
OWEN: There's a pawnbroker's down the street.
RUTH: A what?
OWEN: Sell something. You've never done that before?
RUTH: God, no.
OWEN: No shame in that.
RUTH: What would I sell? A broken watch?
OWEN: You've got a ring.

    RUTH *laughs*.

RUTH: Martin'd kill me.
OWEN: You're doing it to get home to him, it's romantic. You can buy it back.
RUTH: Pawn my wedding ring?
OWEN: Every problem has a solution, my dear. If you want to get there in time …
RUTH: I suppose. We'll be laughing about this over dinner tonight.

    She leaves.

OWEN: Hey, wish me luck!

VII.

Pawnbroker's.

SKYE *is examining the ring.*

RUTH: I can't believe I'm doing this. If anyone saw me in here I'd never live it down. Just to be clear, I can get it back, right?
SKYE: Twenty bucks.
RUTH: Twenty, for a wedding ring? Are you joking?

    SKYE *shakes a box.*

SKYE: All wedding rings.
RUTH: That won't even cover my cab fare.
SKYE: Buy a train ticket.

RUTH: The train'll take forever, I need to get home now. Please, can't you just give me fifty?
SKYE: Fifty. Ha.
RUTH: Twenty dollars for a gold ring, it's absurd.
SKYE: Not if you're desperate.
RUTH: I am desperate!
SKYE: What about your watch?
RUTH: It's broken.
SKYE: What do you mean?
RUTH: The hands don't move.
SKYE: Why are you wearing a broken watch?
RUTH: It only just stopped working.
SKYE: Show me. It stopped at twelve.
RUTH: Whatever. If my ring's only worth twenty—
SKYE: It's all rusted up.
RUTH: It was fine yesterday.
SKYE: Look at the crown, covered in rust.
RUTH: Is that the thing you wind?
SKYE: You wouldn't be able to wind it without getting all that crap off, and maybe even then. What are you going to do with it?
RUTH: I don't know, throw it out.
SKYE: Can I have it?
RUTH: Who's going to buy a rusty watch?
SKYE: Not for the shop, for me.
RUTH: Sure, how much?
SKYE: I'm asking will you give it to me.
RUTH: Give it? For nothing?
SKYE: You don't want it.
RUTH: Well yes, but you do and I need cash.
SKYE: I know, love, I wish I could help you. But you can help me.
RUTH: Thirty dollars, on top of the ring.
SKYE: I haven't got it.
RUTH: Take it from the till.
SKYE: That's the boss's, I'll lose my job.
RUTH: It's a good watch. If you got it fixed—
SKYE: I don't want it fixed.
RUTH: You want it like this?

SKYE: Why do you care? I thought you were in a hurry to go home, take your twenty and get the train. Just let me have it.
RUTH: How much've you got?
SKYE: Nothing, I gave my daughter all the cash I had.
RUTH: Well, I'm sorry.
SKYE: Where are you going?
RUTH: I'll try somewhere else.
SKYE: No wait, let me see what I can do.

She rifles through her handbag.

Lemme see lemme see ... you wear lipstick? No? I've got some nicotine patches, I've got, um, oh these sunglasses would look great on you, my handbag, take my bag, just have it—
RUTH: No thanks.
SKYE: Wait! Please wait. Okay I'll tell you. I write poems.
RUTH: So?
SKYE: I wrote a poem about a stopped clock, and I'm the clock. I'm like, frozen. Like the rest of the world's moving forward and I'm stuck. How am I suddenly fifty? Where has my life gone? You're young, you don't know that feeling—
RUTH: No I / don't.
SKYE: It's because of the pot. Every day since I was fourteen, first thing in the morning I light up. Got married, had the kids, but it's all been like in a fog, like there's glass between me and everyone else. And you want to know the worst part? It never bothered me. I couldn't reach them and I didn't care.

Darling I don't want to live like that any more, I have to wake up before it's all over.

Your broken watch beside the bed, when I reach for my lighter and instead I grab that, it'll help me. It might even save me. Do you understand?
RUTH: And what do I get?
SKYE: I can tell you my poem. I'm begging you now.
RUTH: It's fine.
SKYE: 'My hands are stuck,
　My face is blank,
　/ Silent is the—'

RUTH: I'll take the twenty.
SKYE: Damn you.
>Get out of here.
>There's your money. Damn you to hell.

VIII.

Outside the pawnbroker's.
RUTH *stands on the street, rattled.*
BRENDAN *approaches.*

BRENDAN: 'Scuse me, can you spare any change?
>RUTH *signals 'no'.*

>I hate asking, if you told me a month ago I'd be doing this I would've said fuck off. Sorry miss, my mum hates me swearing.
>That's her over there, and my sister. We did a runner a few nights ago. I'm supposed to be doing my HSC, guess I should be happy eh.
>They're too shy to ask, so they make me do it. Reckon I'm the cutest-looking.
>—
>—
>What about you, what do you reckon?
>—
>—
>Because maybe there's something I can do. Some thing I can do, for you.
>—
>Mum's smiling, see?
>My idea, not hers.
>Anyone touches my sister I'll kill him.

RUTH: Please go away.
BRENDAN: Sorry miss. I didn't mean any disrespect.

IX.

Park.

Playground.

NADIA: You are not allowed in playground.
RUTH: I'm going to the train station.
NADIA: See sign?
RUTH: I know, I'm just taking a shortcut through the park.
NADIA: Only if you got child.
RUTH: I have a child.
NADIA: What child?
RUTH: Not here, at home. Where's the gate?
NADIA: I got two. Also at home, in Ukraine. My auntie got them. But she does not love them, she only does it because I pay her.
RUTH: Then go back to them. How do I get out of here?
NADIA: I cannot make money there. I got to work here, send it home. You know when I saw them last? Two year ago.
RUTH: Sorry to hear it.
NADIA: Five year old, and three year old.
RUTH: Right.
NADIA: That is why I am in playground. I am not allowed to be here too, but I need to ask ladies can I work for them. You got nanny?
RUTH: No, and I don't need one thanks.
NADIA: I work cheap. Small money, wait longer to see my babies, but I got no choice. What can you pay?
RUTH: I'm just trying to find the gate.
NADIA: Look, I will do you favour. Give me food and place to sleep, I work for free for one month. After that, you pay. Boy or girl?
RUTH: Sign up with an agency.
NADIA: I got no visa.
RUTH: Go back home, at least you'll be together.
NADIA: I cannot buy ticket, I got no passport, I got nothing.
RUTH: Then I'm sorry, I don't know.
NADIA: I will love your child. I will love her like she is my own. She will be so happy with me, so safe. Think about it, okay? I am here every day, please come back soon.

X.

Train station.
RUTH *waits on the platform.*
Commuters mill around.
HORTENSE *addresses them.*

HORTENSE: How many of you people ever lose your job the same week the bank forecloses on your house?
   Any of you?
   Anyone here know what it's like to be kicked out of your own home, everything you own piled up on the street? Your kids' bicycles, your private stuff there for all to see? Clothes, your plates and pillows?
   —
   But who needs bicycles when the government's taken your kids?
   [*To* RUTH] I'm asking you, who needs them?
RUTH: No-one.
HORTENSE: That's right, no-one.
   A man was preaching here in this station yesterday, he told me God would provide, he would be my home and my family. Well God didn't provide. I'm here to tell you there is nobody out there, nothing, no-one to stop you stepping in front of the next train. You all have a pleasant journey home, I hope it's still there.

XI.

Train.
RUTH *is sitting beside* LEONIE, *a woman looking at a children's picture book. Her brother* ROD *is busy texting and mostly ignores* LEONIE, *who addresses* RUTH *in a monotone.*

LEONIE: This is Fairyland, see? Look how beautiful.
   RUTH *tries to ignore her.*
Out of thin air they make you a special feast, see all the nice food? But it's glamour.

You know what that means?
If you eat it or if you drink anything, they gotcha.
ROD: Don't bother the lady.
LEONIE: [*to* RUTH] I'm not bothering you, I'm telling you. You bite into a cake and it turns to shit. Their meat is corpses. You swallow ale and it's ashes. One day in Fairyland is years and years and years.

The train goes through a tunnel, LEONIE *shouting above the racket.*

Don't touch it, don't eat a single thing or you'll never leave, they'll never let you go!

XII.

House.

RUTH *comes in. She falls into a chair.*

Exhausted, relieved.

After a few moments:

RUTH: It's me.
I'm home.
God, what a morning.
Sorry I wasn't here, I'll explain.
How was Henry, did he cry?
—
Marty? Are you back yet?
—
Hello!

OLIVE, *twenty, in her pyjamas, with a toothbrush.*

OLIVE: Oh, hi.

RUTH *stares.*

You must be Dad's friend.
—
There's toast and stuff if you're hungry.
RUTH: Who are you?
OLIVE: Sorry I'm Olive, Richard's my dad. Hello. And you're … ?
RUTH: Who's Richard?

OLIVE: ... You stayed over, right?
RUTH: What are you doing here?
OLIVE: I live here, did he not say?
RUTH: Why are you in my house?
OLIVE: —

—

Dad?
RUTH: Where's Martin?
Where's my cello, where are our things?
OLIVE: Dad!

RICHARD appears.

She's lost her cello.
RICHARD: Who's this?
OLIVE: Don't you know her?
RICHARD: Excuse me—
RUTH: What's happening, what's happening?
OLIVE: Isn't she Felicity? I / thought—
RICHARD: How did she get in?
OLIVE: She was just here, oh my God.
RICHARD: Okay let's calm down.
RUTH: I need you, please, to tell me what you're doing in my house.
RICHARD: I think you're confused.
RUTH: Where's my husband?
OLIVE: Dad, call the police.
RUTH: Did he put you up to this?
RICHARD: I don't know him, he doesn't live here.
RUTH: Is he punishing me for being gone?
RICHARD: Your husband, why don't we find him for you?
RUTH: Yes, yes.
RICHARD: We'll sort this out, okay? What's his number?
RUTH: It's— in my phone, I don't know, I can't remember, 0424— 0434— I don't know it, I don't know!
RICHARD: Why don't we call the hospital, then?
OLIVE: Call the police.
RUTH: What about Henry, is he with Martin? Because if he's not with Martin—

She starts having a panic attack.

RICHARD: Listen, you need to wait outside and somebody will come, you can't stay in here.
RUTH: Where are they, where have they gone?
RICHARD: Christ, alright, alright—
OLIVE: She's crazy, get her out of our house.

>RUTH *lunges at her.*

RUTH: What have you done with them?

>OLIVE *screams.*

RICHARD: Get your hands off her, get out.

>*He pushes* RUTH *out, slamming the door against her.*

>OLIVE *shakes and cowers.* RICHARD *holds her, as* RUTH *hammers on the door.*

Sweetheart, it's okay, shh. I'm here, I love you, you're alright, I'm not going anywhere, I'll always be here. Hold my hand. You're safe, we're safe.

XIII.

Suburban street corner.
RUTH *looks around her.*
Sounds of bird song.
A lawn mower.
A garbage truck.
Kids splashing in a distant pool.
RUTH *buckles at the knees.*

IVX.

Taxi.
The radio is on an easy-listening station, playing a tinny version of The Three Degrees' 'When Will I See You Again'.

TAXI DRIVER: Alright back there?

>RUTH *says nothing.*

Saw you in the nick of time, you gave me quite a scare. What were you sitting in the middle of the street for? Bit silly.

She is silent.

I'm heading back to the depot, I can drop you somewhere along the way if you like. No charge.

They drive in silence, just the radio.

RUTH: Where are the children?
TAXI DRIVER: Come again?
RUTH: The kindergarten's gone.
TAXI DRIVER: Used to be a kindy, did there?
RUTH: Where are they?
TAXI DRIVER: How long are we talking? Maybe they grew up.
RUTH: I don't know where my son is.
TAXI DRIVER: You've lost your son … ?
RUTH: This can't be happening, it's a nightmare, or I've fallen into somebody else's dream and I'm trapped. I'm being sucked into a bog, a black wet swamp, the more I struggle and thrash the deeper I sink, the tighter it grips till I'm choking on mud, ears and nostrils packed with sludge, that's how it feels, filling my eyes, there's no light, the cold ooze swallows me up and I'm gone, life above carrying on, Martin thinking I left him, Henry forgetting me but I'm here, I'm right here, I'm—where? Lost, among losers, deadbeats, psychos, the sad, hungry, desperate, while demons taunt us with their smug, belongingness, devils and demons, in a hellish replica of the sweet world I loved and lived in just yesterday. *Devils*, yes of course because this is hell. I'm in hell.
TAXI DRIVER: I wouldn't know about any of that.
RUTH: She said damn you to hell, and that's where I am.
    Take me to the city.
TAXI DRIVER: The city? Bit out of my way.
RUTH: It's urgent.

XV.

Pawnbroker's.

RUTH *throws down the watch.*

RUTH: Have it, take it.
SKYE: Yes can I help you?
RUTH: Don't you remember me?
SKYE: I remember.
RUTH: Take the watch, it's yours.
SKYE: It's busted.
RUTH: That's why you wanted it!
SKYE: Maybe I don't need it now.
RUTH: I want you to have it.
SKYE: Why?
RUTH: And the rest of the twenty, here, all yours. I'm sorry I was selfish, that was wrong of me, please, I'll do anything to help you, anything.
SKYE: You've changed your tune.
RUTH: You cursed me.
SKYE: You're giving me too much credit.
RUTH: I want my life back, I wish it was yesterday.
SKYE: I wish I was thirteen years old, before everything went to shit.

Beat.

RUTH: Wind it back.
SKYE: Eh?
RUTH: What if we wind back the watch?
SKYE: What'll that solve?
RUTH: Make it yesterday, make it forty years ago, change the time to before any of this happened. Don't laugh, that's what we both want, isn't it worth trying?

Pause.

SKYE: No way this was working yesterday, it's totally rusted up.
RUTH: Can't you get it off?
SKYE: Even if I could, it might not wind, probably the inside's corroded.
RUTH: Can you try?

SKYE *works.*

Did you ever dream you were old, and that your life was behind you?

SKYE: I am old.

RUTH: Maybe you're not, maybe you're asleep. You could be a thirteen-year-old girl, dreaming she works in this shop, only dreaming she's wasted her life. Maybe you'll wake up to find your whole future's ahead of you.

SKYE: Don't.

RUTH: It's possible.

SKYE: Is it?

Do you think?

RUTH: I've dreamed you up too, and the woman on the train, those people in my house—

SKYE: Actually the rust's coming off pretty easy.

RUTH: And we're about to wake up and find everything's how it was before.

SKYE: Look at that, like new.

RUTH: Now what?

SKYE: We wind it and fix the time.

You want to do it?

RUTH: No, you.

SKYE: [*laughs*] Why am I scared?

RUTH: Go on.

SKYE: I don't want to.

RUTH *takes it.*

SKYE *snatches it back. She starts to wind it.*

She is instantly reduced to a pile of ashes.

RUTH *stares. The watch lies amongst the ashes. She takes it and leaves.*

ACT II

I.

Breakwater.

Lunchtime passers-by press around police tape.

ANTHONY, *a policeman, has a takeaway coffee.*

RUTH: Officer, I need you to help me.
ANTHONY: Stand back from the tape please, gentlemen.
RUTH: Something's happened.
ANTHONY: Keep walking folks, thank you.
RUTH: Constable?
ANTHONY: Where'd you come from? Ma'am, you'll have to move away. This is a crime scene.
RUTH: A crime scene? I was here this morning, what happened?
ANTHONY: Use the other footpath, people, you all need to cross to the other side of the road!
RUTH: Is somebody hurt? Was it an old man, was he swimming?
ANTHONY: We're just trying to do our job and keep everyone safe.
RUTH: I need the police.
ANTHONY: Ring triple O.
RUTH: Just listen to me. I think I killed someone.
ANTHONY: —
RUTH: I don't know what happened, I can't explain it.
ANTHONY: Somebody's dead, are they?
RUTH: Just now, a few minutes ago.
ANTHONY: How?
RUTH: I gave this watch to the woman in the pawn shop and told her to wind it because it had stopped. She started winding it and—
ANTHONY: And?
RUTH: She turned into ashes. A pile of ashes.
ANTHONY: —
RUTH: Have you ever come across something like that before?

ANTHONY: No.

RUTH: I swear I didn't know that would happen, it's not my fault is it?

ANTHONY: Oh I wouldn't think so.

RUTH: I'll take you there, I'll show you the ashes if they haven't blown away.

ANTHONY: I'm pretty busy right now.

RUTH: Can you send someone else?

ANTHONY: There's a church over there, nice and cool, why don't you get out of the sun?

RUTH: But I don't know what to do now, she was my only hope, maybe the police can get her back.

ANTHONY: Ma'am, you're lucky you're crazy or you'd be in trouble.

He gives her his cup.

I haven't drunk any, now get lost.

II.

Road near pawn shop.

KYM, *a cyclist, speeds past, nearly knocking* RUTH *down. She leaps back.*

The DONKEY *waits to cross. She's an elderly woman, carrying her donkey head under her arm.*

RUTH: Did you see that? If I hadn't moved he'd have hit me.

The DONKEY *looks straight ahead.*

You saw, he could've killed me. Hello?

Without looking at RUTH *she drops a coin in Ruth's coffee cup and crosses.*

What the fuck? How dare you?

A moment.

RUTH *is quiet.*

Then she pours out the liquid and keeps the coin.

She peers in the pawn shop window.

DEAN *walks by without acknowledging her.*

Hello, excuse me, sir? This shop was open before, I was just in there.

He stops.

If you passed this way earlier maybe you saw somebody go in, or come out?

... Why are you smiling?

DEAN: I know you.
RUTH: —
DEAN: Dean.
RUTH: You know me.
DEAN: Yeah I'm positive we've met.
RUTH: Where?
DEAN: Hang on ... Okay, are you on TV? Maybe that's why you look familiar.
RUTH: No.
DEAN: I once did that to this totally gorgeous model, went up and said hi thinking I knew her but it's because I'd seen her in some magazine, mortifying! You're not a model, by any chance?
RUTH: No.
DEAN: I bet you're a dancer, are you?
RUTH: How do you know me, from where?
DEAN: Hmm.
RUTH: Think.
DEAN: I'm thinking.
RUTH: Where do you live?
DEAN: That'd be telling.
RUTH: Could it be the kindergarten, do you have a child?
DEAN: I might.
RUTH: Do you or don't you?
DEAN: I / —
RUTH: A dog, is it the dog park?
DEAN: No I don't.
RUTH: It must be the orchestra then, are you a musician? Or do you work backstage, we might've met at the concert / hall—
DEAN: No.
RUTH: Then where?

DEAN: My mistake.
RUTH: No, come on, think harder.
DEAN: Sorry.
RUTH: You can't just walk off, try to remember!
DEAN: It's a line.
RUTH: A what?
DEAN: A line.
RUTH: —
DEAN: I'll leave you be.
RUTH: But you said you knew me.
DEAN: Let go please.
RUTH: How could you do that?
DEAN: Let go of my arm.
RUTH: I thought it's all going to be alright, somebody knows me,
DEAN: Don't force me.
RUTH: … but you've made it worse!

    DEAN *twists her arm hard.*

III.

Church.

RUTH *nurses her arm.*

GILDA *is flipping through a magazine.*

RUTH: Is there a priest here?
GILDA: A what?
RUTH: A priest.
GILDA: He's busy—don't worry, you're safe. There's a christening at three, we'll be kicked out soon enough. You're here for the free meal, I assume? You're too late. You're not missing much, I'd rather go hungry myself.
RUTH: I'm not hungry.
GILDA: But if you are, there are more desirable options than standing on a line with a lot of pungent people holding out your plate.
RUTH: Can I sit for a moment?
GILDA: Gallery openings, for instance. Good wine, plenty of tapas. Thursdays I meet the girls for brunch and when the bill arrives I'm

in the powder room. One meal a day is plenty if you care about your figure. Go ahead, sit.

Even if I still had my kitchen, who wants to cook? It's lonely eating solo. My Qantas Club card lets me shower in the Lounge, which I never leave before checking the magazines for perfume sachets, it's amazing what people overlook. And who needs a bed when one can luxuriate on red leather under a fox fur? Just as long as I get my beauty sleep.

RUTH: You've got nowhere to live?

GILDA: Certainly I do, didn't you notice the white Jag at the bottom of the steps? I know, you're not allowed to park in front of a church, but it doesn't matter how many tickets I get, how will they find me?

You need to make an effort, dear, you look ghastly.

It's because I take care of myself that nobody knows. My children haven't guessed. Why tell them? It's only until the alimony comes through, I've waited this long I can wait a bit longer. No point needlessly humiliating oneself.

I haven't used this one, dab it on—you'll feel so much better.

She gives RUTH *a magazine.*

The christening party, here comes the family, time to make ourselves scarce. Out, go, hurry up.

IV.

Street.

ROBERTO *and* MIGUEL *pass, laughing as they joke in Chilean.*

RUTH *raises her hand in greeting, they don't recognise her but nod politely.*

V.

Clinic.

DAWN *is regaling the other receptionist,* LEE, *with her story.*

RUTH *waits passively to be noticed.*

DAWN: They thought there was no way I was going to pull through but I was still breathing, so they put me in a nursing home where they could monitor me. They thought if I ever did wake up I was going to have severe brain damage.

LEE: How long were you there for?

DAWN: Nine years.

LEE: What? Asleep the whole time?

DAWN: Coma.

LEE: No way.

DAWN: True.

LEE: Then what happened?

DAWN: See that lady out there, waxing the floors? That's Cheryl. She worked at the home, cleaning the wards. One day I opened my eyes and there she was, standing beside my bed. She said, 'Good morning, Sleeping Beauty'.

LEE: Aw, sweet.

DAWN: We got jobs here so we could be near each other all the time.

LEE: Do you remember anything?

DAWN: I was told my husband beat me almost to death.

LEE: Oh, Dawn.

DAWN: Yeah.

LEE: And he stole nine years of your life.

DAWN: He did, yes, but when I woke up everything had changed. Ronnie had died of cirrhosis. The wasteland opposite my flat is a community garden. I can walk down the street holding Cheryl's hand and no-one bats an eyelid. All these wonderful things and I didn't have to lift a finger, I just woke up and found myself in a beautiful new world.

She notices RUTH.

Hello there. Have you filled in a form?

RUTH *hands it over.* DAWN *glances at it.*

You think you may be dead.

RUTH *nods.*

Darling, I've been dead. You're walking around, aren't you?

LEE: You look a bit peaky, maybe you just need something to eat?

DAWN: We had a little birthday party earlier, there's cake.

LEE: There are some lunch meats left, ham, beef.

DAWN: A cheeky glass of ale?
RUTH: What year is it?
DAWN: I beg your pardon?
RUTH: What century?
DAWN: You just sit down and I'll bring you some nice cake.

    RUTH *flees.*

VI.

A wordless transition, as RUTH *makes her way through singing human traffic to the edge of town. As she travels, she begins to accept an unthinkable possibility. The* STRANGERS *sing.*

STRANGERS: Home no more home to me, whither must I wander?
    Hunger my driver, I go where I must.
    Cold blows the winter wind over hill and heather;
    Thick drives the rain and my roof is in the dust.
    Loved of wise men was the shade of my roof-tree.
    The true word of welcome was spoken in the door—
    Dear days of old with the faces in the firelight,
    Kind folks of old, you come again no more.

VI.

Cemetery.

RUTH *is at the gate.*

RUTH: Let me in.
GRAVEDIGGER: I'm starting to lock up.
RUTH: I need to know if somebody's here.
GRAVEDIGGER: Gates close at sunset.
RUTH: It's important.
GRAVEDIGGER: The records are in my office, other side of the cemetery.
    I don't have time to get over there and back.
RUTH: It isn't sunset yet. Please.
GRAVEDIGGER: —
    Alright. Give me a few details, maybe I can direct you. But you won't be able to hang out for long.

RUTH: That's alright.
GRAVEDIGGER: What denomination?
RUTH: He's not religious—wasn't, he might've converted.
GRAVEDIGGER: Non-denomination, okay, well then he could be in this area here. How recently did he die?

    A year? Ten? Fifty?
RUTH: I don't know.
GRAVEDIGGER: You've got no idea?
RUTH: No.
GRAVEDIGGER: Is this person related to you?
RUTH: Yes.
GRAVEDIGGER: But you don't know when he died.
RUTH: No.
GRAVEDIGGER: … Okay. This is our old section, might as well start here. What name are we looking for?
RUTH: Vedder.
GRAVEDIGGER: Could you speak up?
RUTH: Martin Vedder.
GRAVEDIGGER: Vedder … rings a bell. Was he the type to go in for a monument?
RUTH: Not then, he might have changed.
GRAVEDIGGER: Doesn't sound like you knew him too well.
RUTH: People change over time.
GRAVEDIGGER: Vedder, Vedder … The names on these old ones are hard to read, what with the weather and weeds. We do our best but they're a low priority—few people coming to pay their respects, they're dying off themselves.

    …
    Though there is one old guy, he visits every Tuesday. Set your watch by him. Nicely turned out, lovely white hair, fresh flowers. Likes a chat. He was here yesterday, see the lilies?

    RUTH *examines the marker.*

There goes the sun, I'm sorry but I'll need to lock the gates. Wish I could've been more help.
RUTH: This is it.

GRAVEDIGGER: That's your fella? With the lilies?
RUTH: Yes.
GRAVEDIGGER: Stroke of luck.

He reads the marker.

Looks like he died a long time ago—you weren't even born.

She tries to stand. He steadies her.

Bit of a shock, is it?

Take your time, I can wait.
RUTH: Yes.

I thought it might be this.

Alright.

Well.

He was my student. He's nine years older than me so that was always funny.

He did magic. He brought me an apple, apple for the teacher, and when I cut it open there was a ring inside, I still don't know how he did it.

He admitted he didn't care about learning the cello, it was me. Even after we got married I'd catch him looking, and smiling.

I cheated on him, on tour in Poland, he hugged me and kissed my tears away. It's early days, he said, we've got our whole life together.

And now he's gone. Everyone's gone.
GRAVEDIGGER: You're still here.
RUTH: I don't want to be.
GRAVEDIGGER: Well, you are; so am I. So's the guy with the flowers.
RUTH: Who?
GRAVEDIGGER: White hair and flowers. They were close, apparently, him and his dad. He's the son. Meaning, I suppose, you're related.
RUTH: Henry?

ACT III

I.

Hospital.

HENRY *is in bed in the darkened room.*

RUTH *stands in the doorway.*

RUTH: Henry.
 Are you awake?
HENRY: I don't want anything.
RUTH: Can I come in?
HENRY: I'm not hungry, I'm not thirsty, I don't need a piss, I'm refusing my medication. You can go.
RUTH: I don't work here.
HENRY: Strangers wandering around the wards now, wonderful.
RUTH: I'm not a stranger.
HENRY: What do you want?
RUTH: You.

He switches on the light, peers at her.

 Do you know me?
HENRY: …
RUTH: Henry?

 HENRY *scoffs.*

HENRY: It's you.
RUTH: You do? You remember me?
HENRY: This morning. Yeah of course, it all adds up now, it was you went for the coppers, wasn't it?
RUTH: No.
HENRY: You saved an old bugger's life, done your good deed for the day.
RUTH: The stones, I didn't realise.
HENRY: What did you think I was doing, collecting fossils?
RUTH: I wasn't paying attention.

HENRY: I know, you were too wrapped up in yourself. But later when the penny finally dropped, did you come back? A man is teetering on the edge of the world, trying to find the guts to hurl himself into the darkness—and you don't have some shred of concern, or even curiosity? You don't want to ask why?
RUTH: The penny didn't drop, I didn't call the police.
HENRY: [*laughing*] You forgot the whole thing, even better.
RUTH: But I'm here now.
HENRY: And what do you want?
RUTH: I've come to look after you.
HENRY: To look after me.
RUTH: I found you, when I thought everything was lost.
HENRY: Why would you want to look after me?
RUTH: It's true, I walked away and didn't think about you again. But when I understood it was you— … And now that I see you, here, like this, it's even more urgent.
HENRY: Oh, I see. Do I get a say in it?
RUTH: You don't need to do anything, nothing except let me.
HENRY: And you are …?
RUTH: I'm going to tell you but not yet.
HENRY: Because?
RUTH: Because you won't believe me, and I need you to believe me.
HENRY: Listen, I don't have the patience for this. I'm a tired, sick old man who doesn't want to live any longer, and I'd like you to go away.
RUTH: I'm not leaving you.
HENRY: Then I'll call for the nurse and have you thrown out.
RUTH: No, don't do that.
HENRY: Okay, I'll pull these bloody tubes out and do it myself.
RUTH: Let me just sit with you while you sleep. Don't send me away.
HENRY: I'm not going to sleep, soon as I've got the strength I'm walking out of this joint.
RUTH: Why? To go where?
HENRY: Back to the breakwater, to try again.
RUTH: No.
HENRY: And if I fail I'll try again, and again till I succeed.
RUTH: But you don't need to, I'm here now.

HENRY: I'm nothing to you.

RUTH: You're the only reason I have to live. I will, I'll tell you why but not yet.

HENRY: I'm sorry, but you're not my responsibility.

RUTH: No, you're mine. Whatever drove you to do that this morning, I'll fix it. Whatever's making you suffer, I'll take it away. All I want in the world is your happiness and I'll do anything for it, give everything.

HENRY: Anything? Help me pull the plug.

RUTH: Don't talk like that. The time we have left, it's ours to fill together, with whatever it is that makes you want to get out of bed in the morning, I don't know—dogs, crosswords and bushwalks, music, company: washing the dishes every night side by side. We can make a good life.

HENRY: You still haven't asked me why. You're so desperate to save me but you don't seem to care why I did it.

RUTH: No, I—

HENRY: I'm dying, mate.

RUTH: Dying? What?

HENRY: My throat'll go first. It's closing up, every day there's less air, it's harder speak, painful to swallow. You talk about washing the dishes: for dinner I'll be pumping liquid goop through a hole in my stomach. Soon enough I won't be able to breathe at all. Can you imagine suffocating, with no voice to call for help? I'm not waiting around for that, it's terrifying. I don't sleep at night for the sheer horror of it. I've done everything I wanted with my life and whatever I didn't do, it's okay. I'm not scared of death, only of dying like that. Death—I'm ready, I'm longing for it, I'm here with open arms.

RUTH: You won't have to call for help, because I'll be beside you.

HENRY: Oh God, why will nobody listen to me?

RUTH: Shh, my love.

She takes his face in her hands. Alarmed, he bats her away.

HENRY: What are you doing?

RUTH: It'll be like when you were a baby. Open your eyes, and I'll be there watching over you.

HENRY: Who are you?

RUTH: I've come back.

HENRY: Nurse.

RUTH: I would never abandon you and Daddy, there's nothing in the whole world I love more than my two boys, my darlings, my treasures. You know that, don't you?

HENRY: Nurse!

RUTH: Sweetheart, you need me, and I need you.

    The NURSE *runs in.*

NURSE: What in heaven's name? How'd you get past the desk, did nobody see you? You're not allowed in the ward.

RUTH: Henry I'm begging you, don't send me away.

NURSE: Don't give me any trouble, missy.

HENRY: Get her out.

RUTH: Where? Where will I go?

NURSE: The train station's right across the road.

RUTH: No, Henry! No!

    The NURSE *wrestles* RUTH *out the door.*

II.

Road.

KIM, *the cyclist, speeds past, this time knocking* RUTH *down. Nobody notices.*

III.

Train station.

While BRENDAN *busks,* RUTH, *skinned hands and bloody knees, approaches the few solo commuters; they look right through her.*

RUTH: Pardon me. I got knocked over, he didn't see me.

    She tries someone else.

The hospital won't let me in, is there somewhere I can go?

    She tries someone else.

I'm sorry to bother you but I haven't—
I can't—
I'm—
I— ...

She retreats. BRENDAN *sings.*

BRENDAN: Now, when day dawns on the brow of the moorland,
Lone stands the house, and the chimney-stone is cold.
Lone let it stand, now the friends are all departed,
The kind hearts, the true hearts, that loved the place of old.

She puts her coin in his hat; he doesn't register her.

Spring shall come, come again, calling up the moorfowl,
Spring shall bring the sun and rain, bring the bees and flowers;
Red shall the heather bloom over hill and valley;
Soft flow the stream through the even-flowing hours.

RUTH *takes out the watch and stares at it.*

Fair the day shine as it shone on my childhood—
Fair shine the day on the house with open door;
Birds come and cry there and twitter in the chimney—
But I go forever and come again no more.

She becomes increasingly agitated over the watch.

BRENDAN *approaches all but* RUTH.

Please show your appreciation. Thank you.

A train arrives.

All board it, leaving RUTH *alone.*

She is trembling violently, about to wind the watch, when the NURSE *arrives.*

NURSE: Shite, was that the eleven-sixteen?
Bloody hell, how long till the next one, do you know?
RUTH: Are you asking me?
NURSE: Nobody else here, is there? Great, it'll be half an hour.
RUTH: Then you can see me?
NURSE: Oh, it's you—hello again. I hope I wasn't too rough, usually the orderlies take care of that kind of thing but we're short-staffed. You're not looking for a job, I suppose?

RUTH: You gave me bruises.
NURSE: I am sorry, don't know my own strength.
RUTH: Nobody else can see me.
NURSE: What happened to your knees?
RUTH: A cyclist.
NURSE: You've been in the wars tonight, haven't you? You want disinfectant on that. Let me see what I've got, might as well do something useful while I'm waiting? Water and a hanky, good, there'll be band-aids somewhere …

As she tends RUTH*'s wounds:*

RUTH: I'm falling.
NURSE: Stings a bit, eh? Big breath.
RUTH: I'm never going to stop falling.
NURSE: Squeeze my shoulder, nice and tight. Don't look at the blood.
RUTH: I was standing on the rim of a bottomless abyss and I didn't know it, my back was to it, all I saw were the ordinary things of my life: annoying sometimes, frustrating, but mine—I thrived on them, they were great reservoirs of joy, replenished daily and accepted as my due. And then I must've stumbled backwards, or been pushed, I don't know, but I fell. I'm still falling. There's nobody to catch me, and anyway I'm unreachable. I'm dropping like a stone into vast black silence. I've been robbed of all I am and all I loved, stripped and gutted, and I'll never stop falling.
NURSE: Nonsense, you've got your whole life ahead of you.
RUTH: No, oh God, don't say that.
NURSE: You start again. Tell you a secret? I ran away from home. Said I was going to buy a pack of ciggies and kept driving. Changed my name, changed countries, got away. Don't tell, yeah?
RUTH: I can't get a foothold.
NURSE: Big strong girl like you, you'd make a great orderly.
RUTH: I want Henry.
NURSE: He only wants one thing, poor bugger.
RUTH: I was meant to be home before he woke up.
NURSE: Let him go.
RUTH: But I never got to say goodbye to him. Not then, or this morning, or now.

Beat.

NURSE: There's a back entrance for staff.
Here, take my ID, go and see your man.
RUTH: He'll throw me out.
NURSE: I don't think so, he'll have just had his morphine: captive audience.

IV.

Hospital.

HENRY *is hallucinating.*

RUTH: Are you awake?
HENRY: Who's there?
RUTH: I came back.
HENRY: Dad promised you would.
RUTH: Yes.
HENRY: That's my favourite dress, Mum.
RUTH: That's right, it is.
HENRY: Where did you go?
RUTH: Nowhere, for a swim.
HENRY: A swim? Without me?
RUTH: I'm sorry.
HENRY: At our rocks?
RUTH: I couldn't get home.
HENRY: Me and Dad missed you.
RUTH: I would never leave you, my darling.
HENRY: Did you bring me anything?
RUTH: Like what?
HENRY: You know, like when you go on tour.
RUTH: A present?
HENRY: You brought me a present?
RUTH: Yes, I did.
HENRY: Can I see?

Pause.

RUTH: Close your eyes and put out your hands.
—
It's something you want, a present that you want very much.

HENRY: What?
RUTH: You'll see.
　　Ready?
HENRY: Ready.
RUTH: You can look.
HENRY: A watch, wow!
RUTH: It was mine, now it's yours.
HENRY: Can I wear it?
RUTH: Of course.
HENRY: Can you teach me how to tell the time?
RUTH: Yes.
HENRY: Are they the hands? They're not moving, why isn't it ticking?
RUTH: You have to wind it up.
HENRY: Can you do it?
RUTH: I think you should. You're big enough to do it yourself.
HENRY: I'm going to wind it!
RUTH: There's just one rule: wait until I go. Okay?
HENRY: Okay.
　　Can you go?
RUTH: Don't you want me to tuck you in?
HENRY: Dad already did.
RUTH: What about a story?
HENRY: No thanks.
RUTH: One story?
HENRY: I want to wind my watch.
RUTH: My angel.
HENRY: You can go.
RUTH: Count to twenty.
HENRY: Okay, goodnight.
RUTH: One cuddle?

She holds his face in her hands.

HENRY: I'm counting to twenty. Sweet dreams, Mum, see you tomorrow!

　　RUTH *leaves.*

V.

Bus stop.
RUTH *sits under the fluorescent light and cries her heart out.*
OWEN *joins her. He has leftover food.*

OWEN: Oh goodness, what's wrong? Did you miss your bus?

    She is lost in her grief.

I've got a tissue somewhere …

—

    Wait a minute, I remember you, the lady from this morning, the unisex bathroom. There I was, oh dear, washing my pits for all the world to see. And here we are again. Isn't life funny? Guess what: I got the job! I talked about the hats, the pegs, the lunches in the fridge, they were very impressed. Human psychology, what did I tell you?

    We got on so well they took me out for a Chinese meal. Way too much food, even for this porky pig, but I hate to waste anything. Not only that …

    He opens his wallet.

… they paid me a week in advance!

    I found a hostel, I'm treating myself to a clean bed and a shower before I go home tomorrow for my things. There's a ladies' dorm, if you want to come. You helped me get the job, after all.

    This is still piping hot.

    He offers his hand. She stands.

VI.

Hospital grounds.

Morning.

The GRAVEDIGGER *wheels a chair with his elderly* MOTHER *into the sun.*

A WOMAN *with a newborn is waiting for someone. He arrives, it's the* TAXI DRIVER.

RUTH, *in orderly's uniform, serves each pair from a tea trolley.*
She glances shyly at the newborn, the WOMAN *lets her see.*
The NURSE *brings her a long-handled dustpan.*

NURSE: Here you go, Ruth. The old gentleman's room. Sadly, as of last night he's no longer with us. There's a bit of sweeping-up to do, love.

RUTH: Thank you.

    The GRAVEDIGGER, NURSE *and* TAXI DRIVER *watch her leave.*

VII.

Breakwater.

Sunset.

RUTH *stands, looking out.*

She takes from her uniform pocket a plastic bag of ashes.

She scatters them onto the water.

END

PORN.CAKE
Vanessa Bates

For Lucy Skilbeck

PORN.CAKE was first produced by the Malthouse Theatre at the Beckett Theatre, on the lands of the Wurundjeri Woi Wurrung peoples of the Kulin Nation, Melbourne, on 15 April 2011, with the following cast and creatives:

ANT	Travis McMahon
ANNIE	Christen O'Leary
BILL	Luke Elliot
BELLA	Heather Bolton

Director, Pamela Rabe
Set Design and Costume Design, Christina Smith
Lighting Design, Rachel Burke
Sound Design, Darrin Verhagen

Hiccup:

The spasmodic contraction of the diaphragm that repeats several times per minute. In humans, the abrupt rush of air into the lungs causes the epiglottis to close, creating the 'hic'.

In medicine it is known as synchronous diaphragmatic flutter (SDF), or singultus, from the Latin, *singult*: 'the act of catching one's breath while sobbing.'

The term 'hiccup' is also used to describe a small and unrepeated aberration in an otherwise consistent pattern. (*Wikipedia*)

CHARACTERS

ANNIE
ANT
BELLA
BILL

NOTES

All characters are in their late thirties or forties. Annie and Ant are a couple. Bella and Bill are a couple.

Each character to some extent reveals or develops some repetitive physical gesture. These may become quite non-naturalistic, or remain small yet insistent. I have written some of these in but I actually think actors will find their own tic within the characters.

Where a / occurs in a line, the next line starts. When the / is in the middle of a line, the next line will overlap. When a / occurs at the end of a line, the next line starts immediately with no pause or beat in between.

Some lines start or end with (words within brackets). The line or fragment within is not necessarily to be said out loud, but is there to give sense/completion to the line.

1.0 DEVIATING

BELLA: A long time ago.
There was this child
this girl
in my mind she's blonde but that's
that's
that's not necessarily right.
But actually.
Thinking about it,
the times and the
the whole Englishness of the
thing
the story
I expect that she was.
Blonde.
This girl, blonde girl, is walking in her garden
chatting to herself
singing no doubt, and also laughing
about this and that
because she's
she's
she's a very jolly sort.

Happiness.
A very simple, clear minded sort of happiness.

She's wearing
a *Charlie's Angels'* t-shirt and unbecoming shorts.
No.
Polyester pantsuit and purple headband to match.
No.
Sandals. Cotton frock. Hair tied in, bunches? Ponytails?
No. Piggy tails.
She has freckles. And rather-too-round cheeks.
Which makes you think of milk in bottles, doesn't it?

A pause as she scans the audience.

No? Fine.
   Well that's what it makes *me* think of.
   Her name was
   Is
   was
   Sheila.

   A very
   old fashioned sort of name.
   The sort of name you'd expect.
   In an Enid Blyton story.
   And, she's walking in her garden
   and yes, I do think it would have been filled with flowers:
   bluebells and snowdrops and crocuses
   yes
   and the sun *is* shining, yes.

   Beat.

and she stops a moment
   feels
   perhaps
   uneasy.
   Feels
   something
   coming.
   This,
   This
   this
   thing building inside her
   and she remembers,
   recognises,
   knows
   this thing that is coming
   but she also knows she's powerless to prevent it
   her mouth gaping, gagging, gasping
   like a goldfish,
   And there's another and another
   and another.

Uncontrollable.

And also in reasonably quick succession and at regular intervals.

And that's when Sheila says: *Oh dear, I've got the hee-cups.*

Because that's what she calls hiccups, see.
Hee-
Cups.
She giggles in between
which makes the hiccups worse
but who hasn't
giggled
at an inappropriate moment,

god, I know I have.

So. She's
standing there,
giggling and hiccupping
and saying in her piping clear girlish voice:
I wish I could get rid of these hee-cups!

And that's,
that's
that's
when *it* happens,
not unexpectedly,
there appears: a tiny little man.
A tiny
little man.
No bigger than her puppy,
the one I'm not going to tell you about because it's irrelevant.

A Tiny
Little
Man
dressed in brightly coloured things.
Oh,
coat I expect
and trousers
and hat

and waistcoat is what I'm seeing in *my* mind,
and Sheila in her cotton frock
which I've decided is white
with
delicate candy pink stripes.

He's a fairy,
of course.
A fairy
Like Tinkerbell.
But male.

He looks up at her and makes a face
like when you're trying to smile
but actually
things are going
really
shit
and he says:
Oh Sheila, do you mean it, do you really want to get rid of your hee-cups?

And once she's over the surprise of seeing a fairy
and hearing him call her name,
which is only a few seconds or so,
she smiles down at him.
It may seem quick to you,
a few seconds or so, but we must remember
things like that happened a lot more often,
in Sheila's times.
Much more common.
We must remember.

Sheila smiles at the tiny little fairy man
and says:
Yes, yes I do want to get rid of my hee-cups, can you help?

And he says: *Oh yes, thank goodness, one of the naughty pixies broke all the crockery this morning and I've asked all round and nobody has any to spare and I have a very important tea party coming up in half an hour, so if I could use your hee-cups, just for a couple of hours, I would be ever so grateful.*

Oh dear.
Misunderstanding.
Hee-cups: humorous mispronunciation of the repetitive and uncontrollable spasmodic contraction of the diaphragm.
Teacups: vessels for drinking tea.
Her fault obviously,
calling them *hee-cups*
she knows the proper pronunciation
she's not *stupid*,
she's just playing with language
but
unfortunately
when you deviate from the expected,
sometimes,
bad things do happen.

She says to him:
I'm so sorry but you can't use these hee-cups.

And the tiny little fairy man is
devastated
his little face screws up
and his little eyes shine with tiny little tears
and his little nose starts to stream with tiny little balls of snot
and he sobs and gulps and begs her:
Please, please, you don't understand, all the most important fairies in fairyland have been invited, I can't have them drinking tea straight out of the teapot. I've even made a very special cake for everyone to share, oh Sheila, Sheila, I must have your hee-cups, please!

When I say 'bad things do happen'
I should explain
This is not a moment of physical violence,
it's not one of those scenes
where the child is ... brutally abused
and

and

and probably murdered. I realise it may have looked like this, the set-up with the girl seemingly alone in the garden,

ambiguous,

some might have expected

or even wanted

A bloody and terrifying yet entertaining little fiction that nonetheless resonates with our primal fears.

This is not that.

This is just

A tiny heart

breaking.

We'll never know his side of the story, the stakes, the risk, the tragedy.

There's just this moment, this humiliating *moment*, this godawful begging ...

That's when Sheila has her brainwave.

Which is another thing about those kids

in those days

apart from being compassionate

and empathetic

and imaginative,

kids back then were really fucking *smart.*

And so she says:

Don't cry, don't cry

of course you can have my hee-cups, I'll just run and get them.

And Sheila ducks off to her playroom

gathers up her toy tea sets,

all the little cups and saucers she can find,

and she brings them back to the garden

lays them all down at the feet of the tiny little fairy man who drops

to his tiny little fairy knees and sobs with gratitude:

I'll have them back by five today.

And with a puff of smoke, he, and all the teacups have vanished.

And so have Sheila's hiccups.
What with all the excitement, I expect.

My mother used to make us breathe into a paper bag.
When we got the hiccups I mean
Not all the time,

and I remember
a friend at uni
used to swear by drinking a glass of water
backwards.

This was
the same friend who told me years later
she used to
masturbate in the university toilets.
the library toilets in particular
but also the ones just next to the cafeteria.
She just
got into the habit she said,
and she liked reading the notices on the back of the door as she was …

She gestures.

Auditions and SRC elections and also meetings for Young Liberals.
She never joined
but she said, at the time, she did seriously consider it.

At five on the dot, Sheila finds
all the little cups and saucers,
washed and
neatly stacked
There's even a weeny slice of cake
left for her on one of the plates.
Without thinking she just wolfs it down,
and *this* is where kids *today* would come up trumps,
she wolfs it down
without stopping to think
that it could be
laced with arsenic

or potassium cyanide
or even just ... powdered glass.

Luckily
it's just cake.

And it's utterly delicious.

I mean it's just

Heaven

Beat.

She never sees that tiny little fairy man again.
But she never forgets.

Beat.

It's not in the original story
but
I've always felt that Sheila, no matter how much she tried, never again
had a piece of cake
as intensely lovely as that piece the tiny little fairy man left her in gratitude
for lending him her hee-cups.

So, while it would have been a wonderful experience,
it also left her wanting
something she knew she would never have again.

Pause.

She wouldn't know that immediately of course.
You don't.
It's just a sort of
creeping realisation
years later.

She touches her mouth.

I don't think Sheila would have been quite so jolly after that.
She may have had some
quite significant psychological problems as an adult.
She may even be dead now,

this was a long time ago after all,
and what with alcoholism
and as an adult being shunted into public housing
and forced to live in a quite dangerous part of town;
a lone drunk woman's
a very easy target.
At night.
On a darkened street.
Especially one that talks about fairies.

She looks hard at the audience.

I'm not trying to say …

I'm not trying to say … this is real
It's just …
I have been thinking about it.
A lot.
That, and my friend who used to get herself off in the university toilets.

When she told me, we laughed, of course.
Or at least, she laughed.
And I said:
You must have been very quiet.

But in my mind I was saying:
All that time I was there too.
You must remember.
All that time.

Because, you know, we were girls. We went to the toilets together.

I was washing
and rewashing my hands,
combing
and recombing my hair,
painting
and repainting my eyeliner and

You let me. Wait.
You let me
wait for you.

I spent so long
holding your books
thinking
you suffered from irritable bowel syndrome.
Waiting for you to flush.

And now of course I realise
all that time, it's gone,
it was a complete fucking
waste

And I could kill you.

Pause. BELLA *touches her mouth in a rhythmic fashion.*

2.0 ESTABLISHING

A loud intrusive beeping noise.

We see a table with four chairs. ANT *is sitting at the table.*

He takes his mobile phone out of his pocket and places it beside him.

ANNIE *enters and puts a luscious, slightly unreal-looking cake in front of* ANT.

She sits in one of the chairs. She's a little bit excited because this is some cake.

Pause.

ANT *picks up his mobile phone, stares at it, turns away a little.*

ANNIE: What's that?
ANT: It's a message.
ANNIE: I know, I meant who's it from?

> *He is staring at the phone, smiling to himself.*
>
> *She watches him. Slightly disappointed at the interruption.*
>
> *He looks up.*

ANT: Sorry, it's a work thing. Great-looking cake.

> *He clocks it.*
>
> That's not my.

ANNIE: No.

ANT: Not yet. Because.
ANNIE: No.
ANT: I'm still. People say I look.
ANNIE: They do. You are. Still.
ANT: Okay.

> *Beat.*

Great-looking cake.

> *Phone beeps. He turns to it.*
>
> *She cuts two slices from the cake, waits further before she takes one and begins to eat ... Phone beeps.*
>
> *He keeps texting.*
>
> *She keeps eating.*

ANNIE: Would you like to have sex with me?
ANT: Where did that come from?
ANNIE: I meant. It's ... hypothetical.
ANT: Oh, right.
ANNIE: Have some cake. It's Jamie Oliver.

> *He takes a slice, eats. Smiles kindly at her. She looks away.*

ANT: Time ...

> *She looks at him, interested in potential pearl of wisdom to be imparted.*

... Passes.

> *She's disappointed. More beeping. He picks up the phone. Reads the message.*

Ha!

> *Beat.*

Ha.

> *Beat.*

Ha ...

> *She watches as he starts to text back.*

ANNIE: You know, in my ...

Hand to her mouth, stops herself.

ANT: [*as he's texting*] I'm not very fast … Sorry.

Finishes. Phone down.

He reaches for the slice of cake. More beeping. Cake down, phone up.

Sorry. It's rude, I know, I know … ha.

He's looking at his phone as he says this. Laughs quietly.

Sorry I just need to. Just quickly … this. Ha!

He starts to text back. She stares at him.

ANNIE: I thought … we were having cake.
ANT: We are. Aren't we?

He looks up, registering her tone.

ANT: I thought this was just cake.
ANNIE: It *is* just cake.

But of course it isn't and they both know it.

Pause. She cuts herself another slice.

They eat cake.

They look away.

ANT: You're an attractive woman. Still.
ANNIE: I never needed to hear that before. It doesn't make me feel better. What's on your mind these days? I gave you a shopping list and you came back with a jar of horseradish. I worry about you. I worry about us. Sometimes it's like you're not even listening to me. I could be anywhere. [*Abruptly, inarticulate rage*] You … fucker. [*Calmer*] Do you love me?

He doesn't hear this. He looks up, she smiles.

ANT: Great cake.

She nods, a little sadly.

ANNIE: I never needed to hear that before.
ANT: Cake is the new porn.
ANNIE: Clicking beetles are the new hope.

He points at the cake.

ANT: Did you say ... Jamie?

She nods. He helps himself to more. She wipes crumbs from her face. They don't look at each other.

ANNIE: I just don't know when things became ... so complicated.

Lighting change.

2.1 EVOLVING

Table reset.

Loud intrusive beeping.

BILL *sitting at table. Takes his mobile phone out of his pocket, places it beside him.*

BELLA *briskly enters and puts a luscious, slightly unreal-looking cake in front of him and then sits at the table.*

BILL *picks up his mobile phone, stares at it, turns away a little.* BELLA *is irritated.*

BELLA: What's that?
BILL: It's a message.
BELLA: I know, I meant who's it from?

He is staring at the phone, smiling to himself, shaking his head a little.

She watches him, increasingly pissed off.

He looks up.

BILL: Sorry. It's a work thing.

He clocks it.

Great-looking cake.

He goes back to texting.

She waits a little before she cuts two slices from the cake, waits further before she takes one and begins to eat ...

He keeps texting. She keeps eating.

Around the time she finishes her slice, he stops and looks up. Smiles apologetically.

BELLA: [*with effort*] Would you like to have sex with me?
BILL: [*startled*] Where did that come from?
BELLA: It's hypothetical. Obviously.
BILL: [*relieved*] Oh, right.
BELLA: What I'm really asking is: do you think I'm attractive?
BILL: Yes.

> *Beat.*

I think you're still attractive.

> *She clocks this.*

BELLA: You think I'm *still* attractive.
BILL: [*carefully*] I think you're an attractive woman. Still.

> *Pause.*

BELLA: I just don't know anymore.

> *Beat.*

Have some cake. It's Jamie Oliver.

> *He takes a slice. Smiles kindly at her.*

BILL: Time passes. Things change.

> *She gives him the laser stare.*

BELLA: Things *have* changed.

> *More beeping. He picks up the phone. Reads the message.*

BILL: Ha!
BELLA: Ha?
BILL: Sorry …

> *Starts to text back.*

BELLA: You know, in my …

> *Suddenly clasps her hands to her mouth.*

… Jesus Fuck!

> *He looks up at her.*

I was about to say 'In my day … ' That's what my mother used to say. And my grandmother.
BILL: So?

BELLA: So. Next I'll be saving bits of string.

> BILL *texting*.

BILL: Hang on.

> *Pause, looks up.*

Sorry, I'm not very fast. Do you know we're the generation that missed out on the evolved thumb.

> *Texting.*

You know, they believe ... youth of today ... because of all the ...

> *Waves his thumbs at her, i.e. 'texting'. He finishes his text.*

BELLA: Evolved thumbs, I know about evolved thumbs. I told *you* about evolved thumbs.

BILL: No you didn't.

BELLA: Yes I *did*.

BILL: I read it.

BELLA: Where?

BILL: Online.

BELLA: When?

BILL: Just recently.

BELLA: Well then. No. It couldn't have been. I told you a while ago. A long while ago. People have had evolved thumbs for years. Several generations have missed out on the evolved thumb.

BILL: Fine. You probably *did* tell me.

BELLA: I probably did.

BILL: Sorry.

> *He reaches for the slice of cake. More beeping. He puts the cake down.*

Sorry.

> *He looks at the messages. Laughs abruptly, she is startled.*

Sorry I just need to.

> *He starts to text back. Snorting with laughter. She stares hard at him.*

BELLA: You said it was work.

BILL: It is work.

Finishes texting. Puts the phone back down.

BELLA: I thought we were having cake.

BILL: We are.

BELLA: [*to herself*] Waste of ingredients.

BILL: I'm sorry. It's just. I thought this was just … cake.

BELLA: It *is* just cake.

But of course it isn't and they both know it. She cuts herself another slice. They steal sideways looks at each other. They eat cake.

Cake is the new porn.

BILL: Infidelity is the new cake.

BELLA: Google is the new infidelity.

BILL: Love is the new Google.

BELLA: Confusion is the new love.

BILL: Hope is the new confusion.

BELLA: Clicking beetles are the new hope.

A pause. They finish their slices of cake.

BILL: I might have a bit more. Did you say this was Jamie?

He helps himself. She wipes crumbs from her face. She watches him eat.

BELLA: I just don't know when things became so …

He suddenly looks up at her. In this moment she hates him.

It doesn't matter.

Lighting change.

2.2 ATTRACTING

Reset.

Loud beeping.

ANT *sitting at the table. Takes his mobile phone out of his pocket and places it beside him.*

ANNIE *enters and puts a luscious, slightly unreal-looking cake in front of him. Stands beside the table.*

He picks up his mobile phone, stares at it, turns away a little.

ANNIE: [*briskly*] What's that?
ANT: [*briskly*] Message.
ANNIE: Who's it from?

> *He's texting. She adjusts the cake a little.*

ANNIE: What's that?
ANT: Message.
ANNIE: Who's it from?

> *He is staring at the phone, smiling to himself, shaking his head a little.*
>
> *She picks an imaginary hair off the cake.*
>
> *He looks up.*

ANT: Sorry. Work thing. Great cake.
ANNIE: Sex?
ANT: What?

> *She sits down.*

ANNIE: It's hypothetical.
ANT: It's evolved thumbs.
ANNIE: It's cake!

> *She cuts a slice from the cake. Loud beeping.*

What's that?
ANT: It's a message.
ANNIE: Who's it from?

> *More beeping. He picks up the phone. Reads the message. Snorts.*

ANT: Ha!

> *Starts to text back.*

ANNIE: You know, in my …

> *Suddenly grabs at her cheeks and makes a strange animal-like noise.*
>
> *He looks up at her. Startled.*

What I'm really asking is: do you think I'm attractive?

> *More animal noises. Threatening.*

ANT: Yes, I think you're still attractive.

ANNIE: You think I'm *still* attractive.
ANT: That's what you meant, wasn't it?
ANNIE: I don't know anymore. Have some cake? It's Jamie Oliver.

He takes a slice as he texts, waves the phone.

ANT: I'm not very fast. We're the generation …
ANNIE: [*suddenly*] Evolved thumbs.
ANT: Sorry.

More beeping. He picks up his phone and looks at it.

ANNIE: What's that?
ANT: It's a message.
ANNIE: Who's it from?
ANT: Sorry, it's a work thing. Great-looking cake.

He starts to text.

ANNIE: I thought we were having cake.
ANT: I'm sorry. It's just. I thought this was just … cake.
ANNIE: Yes it is, it *is* just cake. Still.

She cuts herself another slice. They eat cake.

Attraction never—
ANT: Communication never—
ANNIE: Never ever ever. Now and forever. Cake.

They eat cake and say the following fast:

Cake is the new porn. —
ANT: Infidelity is the new / cake.
ANNIE: Google is the new / infidelity.
ANT: Love is the new / Google.
ANNIE: Confusion is the new / love.
ANT: Hope is the new confusion.
ANNIE: Clicking beetles are the new hope.

She makes her animal noise but it's no longer threatening.

ANT: Great-looking cake.

She wipes crumbs from her face into a pile. She obsessively gathers up all the scraps of cake she can find and puts them in front of him in a pile. He watches her. Finally she sits back in her seat.

His phone starts beeping. He picks it up.

ANNIE: I just don't know when things became so … Jamie.

Lighting change.

2.3 DEFINING

Reset.

Loud intrusive beeping.

ANT *sitting at a table. Takes his mobile phone out of his pocket and places it beside him.*

ANNIE *enters and puts a luscious, slightly unreal-looking cake in front of him.*

Stands upstage, stretching her hands and rubbing at her wrists as if she has strained them in someway. Repetitive movement.

Beeping. He holds it up.

ANT: It is a message.
    It is a work thing.
ANNIE: It is hypothetical.
ANT: It is evolved thumbs.
ANNIE: It is Jamie Oliver.
ANT: It is attractive.
ANNIE: It is something my mother used to say.

    Pause.

  It's porn.
ANT: It's infidelity.
ANNIE: It's Google.
ANT: It's love.
ANNIE: It's confusion.
ANT: It's hope.
ANNIE: And it's also Clicking beetles.
ANT: Great-looking baked sweet flour-based food, shaped portion of ground, block, thick layer, something divided up …
ANNIE: Thanks.

She removes a tiny, imaginary crumb of cake from the corner of her mouth. Examines it closely.

I just don't know when things became so cake.

Lighting change.

3.0 DOUBLING

Reset.

Loud intrusive beeping.

BILL *sits at the table. Takes his mobile phone out of his pocket and places it beside him.*

BELLA *enters and puts a luscious, slightly unreal-looking cake in front of him and then sits opposite. Picks up a whopping big knife.*

Beeping.

BILL *picks up his mobile phone, stares at it, turns away a little.*

BELLA: [*smiling*] What's that?
BILL: It's a message.
BELLA: Who's it from?
BILL: Sorry.

She abruptly hacks the cake in half. She picks up one half.

BELLA: Would you like to have cake with me?
BILL: What?
BELLA: Do you think I'm attractive? Still?
BILL: Still I think you're attractive still.
BELLA: You still think I'm still.
BILL: Still!

He takes the other half, eats voraciously. She watches him as she nibbles, delicately.

BELLA: Things have changed.

More beeping. He puts down the cake, picks up the phone. Reads the message.

BILL: Ha!
BELLA: Ha! ha!

He looks at her, startled.

She gives an anguished moan.

Don't tell me about evolved thumbs.

More beeping. She moans again.

He looks at the message.

BELLA: [*loudly, as if she thinks he's hard of hearing*] I Thought We Were Having Cake.

BILL: [*ditto*] I Thought This Was ... Cake.

BELLA: [*ditto, plus maybe he's an alien*] It Is Cake.

He puts down the phone. They eat their halves of the cake.

BILL: Cake never used to be like this.
BELLA: New porn.
BILL: New infidelity.
BELLA: New Google.
BILL: New love.
BELLA: New confusion.
BILL: New hope.
BELLA: Clicking beetles.
BILL: Great-looking cake. Did you say this was porn?

He reaches over and wipes crumbs from her face. Tender. She grabs his hand, holds it to her face.

BELLA: It's complicated.

Lighting change.

4.0 CARING

Separate space.

ANNIE: [*seems friendly enough*] Look.

I do care for you, I do.

I am here for you. I am completely focused on you.

Take a moment to realise that, to enjoy that. Another human being, me, is completely focused.

On you.

And on your body.
And all the aches and pains and stresses and worries.

No matter how ... stupid,
how boring,
how tedious I find them, no matter how dull I find *you*, how trivial and insignificant I find your sad little stories, how horrible and pointless I find your stupid, boring, tedious little life,

I am here for you.

Your naturopath.

I don't mollycoddle people.

I don't tell people things just because they want to hear them and I don't back off from things they *don't* want to hear either.

If it's my opinion that they're lazy and lack dietary discipline, I will tell them.

If it's my opinion that they're suffering from cancer and will die within the month, I will tell them.

If it's my opinion that they need to examine their core values and contribute more for the kitty, and while they're at it, clean the bathroom a little more often than, say, once a year, I will tell them that too.

I ... did ... tell them that. Sex is not an acceptable substitute for rent or chores.

Some people think I'm too hard on my clients.

People I went to college with say, people with a lot of family money.

They think I'm a harsh sort of practitioner.

Some practitioners do like to sugarcoat. I'm not one of them, sugar kills.

Literally, sugar is responsible for several debilitating conditions, type 2 diabetes being just one.

I look into my clients' eyes. I feel their pulse.
I consult about diet, exercise levels, stress levels.
Do they indulge in alcohol? Salt? Gluten? Sugar?
Do they have unprotected sex? With their flatmate?
With random men they meet at parties?

Okay we all did sometimes, even me, but I had the discipline to get myself back on track. I can control my diet.

I can.

I don't always say no to alcohol, I'm not a wowser or a party pooper. I'm not your wife. Or your mother.

I can still drink martinis and manhattans, just like the smart people, until I feel numb and dizzy and career wildly about the room laughing and tearing at people's shirts, men's shirts, in an effort to assess their heartbeat.

I always aimed for skin-on-skin contact and it was particularly funny if I had a cold ear, which I ensured by getting the milk out of the fridge and pressing it to the side of my head. That is as close as I have ever come to dairy.

Ha.

It's quite an amusing and effective come-on actually, I usually found after a bit of skin-on-skin assessment late night at parties I didn't find myself sleeping alone.

If you know what I'm saying.

That was my choice and I really didn't need so-called 'friends' ringing me afterwards to express 'concern' about my 'alarming behaviour' and accusing me of seducing their pathetic, floppy-dicked, obviously commitment-phobe husbands to be.

My point is, I let myself indulge, imbibe, binge if you will, and then, just like that, I stopped.

It's like putting a restraining order on myself.

But that was me.

That's not you.

That's not many people. Sadly.

I can advise, I can strongly advise, but I'm not your mother. I think I've made that point already.

I massage people, therapeutic massage, and I have a part-time job at a clinic. Quite nice, run by a girl who, frankly, is a pretty poor naturopath herself, I certainly couldn't recommend her with a clear conscience.

She's younger than me, quite a bit younger, so she doesn't quite have the experience I'm afraid.

Her parents paid for the clinic actually.

This girl, she offered me the massage gig, and I thought look, she needs me, I respond to need. I can't help it, it's my calling. I respond to need.

It's actually a bit far from home for me.

It's quite a drive, actually, and on a Sunday, when people are just poodling along, it really does, God why do people assume that just because they've got the weekend off, everyone does? Huge assumption. Me holiday, you holiday.

No. Wrong. Some of us are busy saving people's lives.

What happened was, I was driving to work and it was Sunday so of course there were slow drivers everywhere and I was a teensy bit late. I was stressed, yes, I was missing my green tea and also I'd run out of goji juice which meant I was going to be late for my first appointment. It was the first one of the morning so that meant I also had to open up and check the answering machine and all that.

Actually the truth is, I had been eating gluten that week and gluten does affect me, I should just give it up for good.

The old lady next door brought me over a cake for my birthday.

Ant was away, visiting his sister, so I tried to only take half but she was very persistent, you only turn forty once, blah blah blah. I didn't want to offend her. So all week I had this … cake, Jamie Oliver's lemon drizzle cake actually, just sitting there in my fridge.

Her husband has Alzheimer's, very sad, but I suppose it … keeps her busy.

She makes a cake for me every year, old lady, isn't that lovely of her? She *is* lovely. It's not her fault her cakes are just, well pure poison really, she uses sugar, she uses butter, she uses wheat flour—not even wholemeal.

She basically peddles death, and I let her because, well, because I'm caring and thoughtful.

Slight pause.

Funny, these people, it doesn't occur to her, to them, that maybe, maybe, all their insisting and forcing things *upon* people, it might be dangerous, no, they don't take that into account at all. I might have diabetes or coeliacs, there could be a thousand reasons I don't want to eat her fucking cake and it really annoys me that she couldn't just take no for an answer.

And so I eat a whole cake in a week.

And you can imagine.

So I'm running late and there's this guy in a car in front of me and I can't get round him. There's only two lanes and it's unbroken lines and there are just enough cars whizzing in the opposite direction to stop me trying to overtake him. I flash my lights, I beep my horn and he just drives in his own sweet time and it makes me absolutely furious.

From the back he reminds me … of this man I used to live with, this flatmate, a long time ago. The one that married one of my so-called friends.

He just has the same sort of … smug set to his shoulders, that sort of 'you missed out' look to him.

Pause.

His hair smelled of green-apple shampoo. Do you remember that? Some of you? Green-apple shampoo?

Pause.

So, now, I'm yelling, I'm gesturing, and giving him the finger and calling him names at the top of my voice, well it's not like he can hear me, although we're close enough for him to see me in the rear view mirror yelling of course and it probably doesn't take a genius to read my lips and work out what I'm saying: F U C K I N G C U N T.

And finally, finally, there's a chance to overtake him and I just screech around him and give him the laser death stare and I get to the clinic with three scabby minutes to spare and I rush to unlock and check the answer machine and water the lucky bamboo and refill the oil burner and throw a clean towel over the massage table and the doorbell goes.

So, I mentally cleanse myself and rub my third eye and shake my head chakra and take a few drops of rescue remedy so that I'm present.

I'm in the moment.

I'm ready.

I go out to meet my client. *Hello, how are you this morning, I'm your massage therapist today.*

There's this silence, he's not saying anything, which is weird, usually they start dribbling on about their recently diagnosed disease or death of their child or how they've been unfairly dismissed at work and they're soooo stressed and in need of massage but not too hard please ... and then he says ... *You drive a white Barina.*

I smile at him like, okay, is that your issue or what, but then he says:

Didn't I see you just now, on the road. You drive a white Barina. You were driving behind me. Yelling things.

So I say: *Look ... I was stressing about getting to work on time, I'm sure you understand, we're really busy on Sundays ... I'm sorry.*

And he just turns around and walks out.

And I feel terrible. It sort of hits me, right here.

She touches her stomach.

In my mind I see myself, the way he would have seen me, the look on my face and the violence in my gestures.

And the projection of hate through the windscreen at him, this man, this ...

damaged, needy man, who was coming to me

for help.

For professional care.

Beat.

Because, they feel frightened, men.

Vulnerable. And fragile.

They seek out comfort, at difficult times, the night before their wedding say ... their wedding to my ... so-called friend.

I understand that. He needed me.

And of course I ... respond to need.
Afterwards, we had a bath together.
I washed his hair.

Pause.

I say: *We're really busy on Sundays. I'm sorry.*

I'm sorry.

And he turns, that man, my client, very dismissive, very arrogant, he walks out of the clinic and I'm left feeling really, really ...

She thinks about it.

... angry.
Because now I have to work that anger out.

I have to spend my time and my energy releasing all that anger before my next needy hurty client comes in, otherwise they will get a really, really, shit massage.

And see: I'm not entirely sure I can get rid of all that negativity by ten-fifteen.

It's the main reason I have decided to give up working here, it's not the AVO it's all the negative energy.

It wouldn't occur to that man that the next person to walk in that door is going to suffer. Badly.
Because of him.
Him and his stupid fucking driving.
And his green-apple shampoo hair.

And no, no, actually I bet his hair would really *stink*, it would smell like *turds*, he wouldn't bother to wash it just for a massage, he probably hasn't bothered to shower or even, even ... wipe his arse properly after his morning shit—

She suddenly retches.

God, just the thought ...

She recovers.

That's something I've learned. In my forty plus years. People can be selfish like that.

Lighting change.

5.0 FLASHING

Reset.

ANT, BILL *and* ANNIE *are sitting at the table.*

Loud intrusive beeping.

ANT *takes his mobile phone out of his pocket and places it beside him. Starts to do thumb warm-up exercises but stops as ...*

BELLA *enters and puts a luscious, slightly unreal-looking cake in front of him and then sits.*

ANT *picks up his mobile phone, stares at it. Puts it down. Stares at her.*

ANT: Great-looking.
BELLA: Would you like?
ANT: What?
BELLA: Do you?
ANT: Attractive.
BELLA: You think?
ANT: Attractive.
BOTH: Still.

>*More beeping. He picks up the phone. Reads the message.*

ANT: [*an exhalation*] Haaaaaaa!

>*Puts the phone down.*

BELLA: Evolved thumbs.
ANT: Sorry.

>*More beeping.*

Sorry. Sorry.
BELLA: It *is* cake.

>*Pause. She stands up. She picks up the knife, grips it in her fist. Threatening.*

It's hypothetical.

>*He suddenly grabs the knife hand, tussles, like an arm wrestle, it looks dangerous at first but as they lower their hands, it becomes the kind of dual cake-cutting pose couples often use at weddings.*

As they say the following words, a camera flash goes off and they grin grotesquely. The poses verge towards the pornographic.

ANT: New Porn.

Flash.

BELLA: New Cake.

Flash.

ANT: New Infidelity.

Flash.

BELLA: New Google.

Flash.

ANT: New Love.

Flash.

BELLA: New Confusion.

Flash.

ANT: New Hope.

Flash.

BELLA: New clicking beetles.

Flashing cameras go apeshit. They each grab a handful of cake and stuff it in the other's mouth. Cheers, clinking glasses. They kiss. They climb onto the table and go for it.

Lighting change.

6.0 SWAPPING

No reset.

All four sitting at the table. Remnants of previous scene.

Loud beeping.

BILL *takes out his mobile phone and sets it on the table.* ANNIE *smiles at him.*

ANNIE: Would you like to have cake with me?
BILL: You're attractive.

ANNIE: I'm Jamie Oliver.
BILL: So many things have changed.
>Porn for instance. And cake.
>And infidelity, that seems to have changed.

>*Beat.*

And Google.
ANNIE: Yes! And love. And confusion. And hope.

>*Pause. She seems smitten.*

BILL: Clicking beetles remain the same.
ANNIE: Still beetles. Still … click.

>*He undoes his shirt. She puts her ear to his chest. She has the world's tiniest orgasm.*

>BILL *points at what is left of the cake.*

BILL: Did we say this was porn?
ANNIE: I think a few people have said … oh.

>*She watches, slightly disgusted and slightly attracted, as he picks up the plate and lasciviously eats crumbs.*

BILL: [*Mr Sex-on-a-Stick*] When did things become so Nigella?

>*Lighting change.*

6.1 HICCUPPING

ANNIE, BELLA, ANT *and* BILL *all on stage. May be standing or sitting.*
Intrusive beeping noise.

They respond to the beeping in a series of repetitive movements and tics. These begin in unison but throughout the scene they break away into their own separate routines.

They leave the stage.

A stage manager comes in with a cake. Puts it on the table. Ensures the table looks reset. Leaves.

Lighting change.

7.0 VACATE

Reset.

The cake on the table.

Nobody else around.

Loud beeping.

A mobile phone is on the table. It shudders and writhes a little. It doesn't matter if no-one sees this. After a while it stops.

There may possibly be some loud vomiting sounds which start here and continue sporadically through BILL*'s speech till they stop.*

BILL: Ladies and gentlemen we're just going to hold for a sec. One of the, one of the other … we have a um, intolerance for gluten issue, in the cast. We didn't, it wasn't something that came up at the auditions, it was a tech run discovery actually, so we're just waiting on the … the stage manager is going to let me know when …

He looks to the side.

… not yet? Okay.

Personally I think the whole food intolerance slash allergy thing has got completely out of hand. Just my opinion.

I don't know how many dinner parties, restaurants, people's homes et cetera, *eating events* I've attended, have been ruined by someone not being able to eat something or being forced to eat something they don't want to eat.

I mean that's what it comes down to, you just don't want to eat it. And whether you express that by saying 'I'd rather not eat that' or by spewing on the table, it's the same thing.

The mistake people make, a common mistake, is when they first meet and realise that they are perfect except for one teeny tiny thing, for example: the whole … oh he won't eat olives, that's okay, I can change that, thing.

He won't eat olives.

Somehow, you convince yourself: I'll gradually introduce them. I'll chop them finely and put them in his sausages. I'll crush them and rub them into my hair. I'll scatter them like rosebuds on our bedlinen. Eventually we'll be eating tapenade together.

No. We won't. Right from the beginning, I hated olives. And you knew that. I didn't hide that. For better or for worse. I hate olives.

So don't get shitty now. Because you've had, what, nearly twenty years? To get used to it.

He looks to the side.

Okay we're good.

He smiles, exits.

Lighting change.

8.0 CONFESSING

Reset. (The beginning of things.)

ANT *sits at the table.*

ANNIE, *standing behind, is massaging* ANT*'s shoulders.*

ANNIE: Is that good?
ANT: That's good. That's great.
ANNIE: You're so (stressed). Is it a work thing?
ANT: It's … (I don't know …)

She does the animal mating noise.

No … (not here.)

She makes the animal mating noise again.

Annie.

She does the noise but stops as BELLA *and* BILL *enter.* BELLA *has a cake.*

ANNIE: Oh! A cake.
ANT: I couldn't.
BELLA: (But) It's Nigella.
ANNIE: It looks gorgeous but we're so (stuffed).
BILL: Bella spent ages …
BELLA: It's alright Bill. [*It's not.*] Annie might be … are you still … (gluten-free?)

> ANNIE *bows to the pressure.*

ANNIE: Just a sliver maybe.

> *They sit,* BELLA *puts the cake in the centre.* BILL *and* ANT *put their phones on the table.*
>
> *Loud beeping.*

BELLA: Bill!

> *Each man picks up his mobile phone, stares at it, turns away a little.*

ANNIE: What's that?
ANT: It's a message.
BELLA: Who's it from?
BILL: Sorry. I've got to answer this. It's a work thing.
EVERYONE: Great-looking cake.
ANNIE: Gorgeous.

> BELLA *cuts the cake into slices, and gives a slice to* ANNIE.
>
> ANNIE *takes a bite. Notes that* ANT *is too busy to eat. Awkward. And annoying.*

BELLA: Well this is nice. All of us together.
ANNIE: I once had sex in a fountain. In the middle of the day. It was very romantic. Very wet.
BILL: What? Where did that come from?
ANNIE: It wasn't the one up the road. If that's what you're thinking, the one near your place? It wasn't that one.
BILL: Oh, right. Good.
ANT: I don't remember that.
ANNIE: It wasn't with you.

> *Silence.*

ANT: Actually I don't think there is any water in that fountain.
ANNIE: It wasn't you. You've never seen it.
BELLA: There used to be. Water. Vague memory.
ANT: Why don't I google it?

> ANT *waves his phone at them and begins to do just that.*

ANNIE: Anyway, a school group wandered past, on their way to the museum or something. And they didn't notice. It was as if, our passion had made us invisible. Which is odd because. There was a lot of splashing.

ANT: [*googling on phone*] Just as I thought. [*Loudly*] Merci Monsieur Google ...

   No response.

ANNIE: I thought I'd have a lot more fountain sex, but it turned out to be the only time. I would have enjoyed it a lot more if I'd known that then.

ANT: [*reading from his screen*] It is a defunct fountain.

   No response to this.

ANNIE: [*to* ANT] What I'm really asking is: do you think I'm attractive?

BELLA: We used to have a lot of dinner parties.

ANT: [*to* ANNIE] What? Where did that come from?

BILL: [*to* ANNIE] I think you're attractive. I've always thought that.

BELLA: You think I'm attractive?

BILL: [*to* ANNIE] You're an attractive woman. [*To* BELLA] And you also. Still.

   They smile.

ANNIE *and* BELLA: Have some cake.

   He takes a slice, eats.

BILL: I ever tell you about that time I deliberately ran over my neighbour's cat? No? I thought she said the cat was attacking her baby and trying to suffocate it at night but it turned out to be a misunderstanding.

ANT: What about *my* cake?

ANNIE: Why don't you google yourself some? [*To* BILL] So what was it then?

BILL: What was what?

ANNIE: The misunderstanding ?

BILL: Oh that. It was crossed wires.

ANNIE: Yes. I know what you mean.

BILL: Things have changed.

BELLA: Things *have* changed.

More beeping. BELLA *starts to hiccup.*

BILL *picks up the phone. Reads the message.* ANNIE *begins rubbing at her wrists, as if she has strained herself giving* ANT *the shoulder massage.*

BILL *starts to text back. Now both men are texting.*

ANNIE *is rubbing more vigorously at hands and wrists. Rhythmic.*

You know, in my—

ANNIE *softly does the animal mating noise.* BILL *does the reply.*

… I know about evolved thumbs. I know about fairies. I know about innocence. I know about shame.

She hiccups.

ANT *finishes texting. Puts his phone on the table. Holds up his thumbs and begins to do his thumb exercises again.*

BILL *finishes texting. Puts his phone on the table. He also holds up his thumbs and begins to do thumb exercises.*

BELLA *hiccups.*

We were in the garden. He asked if he could see my … panties. And I said … yes.

BELLA *hiccups.*

ANNIE: Have you tried drinking a glass of water backwards?
BELLA: I'll be fine.

BELLA *hiccups.*

ANT: You were a child.
BELLA: Yes. And he was a tiny mythological creature.
ANT: Still.
BELLA: Still.

She thinks.

And part of me might have … wanted to show him. The panties.
BILL: Well that's a bit …
BELLA: I know. Wait. No. I don't know.

Beat.

This is not a moment of physical violence.

ANT: Sometimes bad things do happen.

She hiccups.

ANNIE: Well, I think that's weird ... you use the word panties.

BELLA: What other word am I meant to use?

ANNIE: Undies. Grundies. Knickers. Or daks. Underdaks.

BILL: Under-dungers?

ANNIE: Under-dungers. Or scungies! Did anyone ever say scungies at their school?

OTHERS: No.

ANNIE: It's just ... panties ... it's very ...

ANT: It's not about the panties. She finds it troubling. You're meant to be her friend.

BELLA *hiccups.*

ANNIE: I *am* her friend.

BELLA: My oldest friend.

ANNIE: We met at uni. [*To* BELLA] I do care for you. I do.

BELLA *hiccups.*

BELLA: Not ... troubling. Confusing. I don't know when things became so ...

She hiccups again. They stare at her.

Sorry.

She hiccups again.

ANNIE: I thought we were having cake.

ANT: We are.

BELLA: We have a lot of cake.

BILL: We just don't have a lot of time, that's all. We used to. All the time in the world. That's what we used to have.

BELLA *hiccups. The* STAGE MANAGER *enters and gives her a glass of water.* BELLA *drinks it backwards. Gives the glass to the* STAGE MANAGER *who leaves.*

BELLA: I'm fine. Everyone.

ANNIE: People say I haven't changed but those people haven't seen my stomach. Not up close. Not the way it wrinkles softly around my belly button which has itself changed, at some point it's started sticking out instead of pressing in.

BILL: I don't know my stomach, I don't recognise it.

We are strangers to each other. We don't speak the same language. We don't share the same interests. We don't laugh at the same things. We don't even vote the same way.

ANT: I'm trying to build some upper body strength, not for any other reason except that I can, whereas all attempts to return my stomach to a previous, familiar, flatter existence have met with dismal failure.

BELLA: There are other changes, odd things, quirks, unattractive but still, at this point, slightly endearing. I know that will change again. I learned that lesson.

ANT: We may as well eat cake.

They eat cake ... ANNIE *breaks away and looks at the audience.*

ANNIE: Porn cake. Infidelity cake. Google cake. Love cake. Confusion cake. Hope cake.

BILL *breaks away and looks at the audience.*

BILL: I've been asked to speak on clicking beetles which is cute really, it's quite a retro sort of object which I admit I am into. Not deliberately I have to admit, it doesn't take long for something you bought new to move, without any effort of your own, into the retro stage. Mad Magazine becomes the new Enid Blyton and then Harry Potter becomes the new Mad Magazine and then Twilight becomes the new Harry Potter and it gets faster and faster. I was walking past a pub the other day and there was a sign advertising music from three years ago as 'old skool'. That's with a 'k'.

I had a birthday party as a child and clicking beetles were the essential party-bag item, now it's iPods but back then, everyone gave away clicking beetles, those brightly coloured pressed tin insects with the sharp tab of flexible metal. How I loved them. No matter how many times I sliced my fingers open on the razor-like edges.

I remember this birthday party where my mother had bought all these clicking beetles for everyone to just click and click and it was loud and joyous, right up til the moment that Sally Keenan slipped one into her mouth and sliced open her tongue. I think she was trying to make the clicking noise by biting on the beetle which is not as silly an idea as first sounds. I remember the blood on her white cotton frock. I heard my mother say to my father that night: *Thank God we had already cut the cake.*

Sally and I were childhood lovers, or at least I had given her a small bouquet of daisies out of my mother's garden and, in my cubby house, she let me look at her nipples.

We were seven.

She got tongue stitches after the clicking beetle incident and it took a while for her to be able to talk properly and in that time children teased her, as they do, and in fact I teased her, because she made me feel vulnerable and fragile. I made her cry. She's on Facebook now so we do stay in touch, we are after all 'friends'.

She has a husband, children, nice house and I congratulate her on these achievements.

She has long weekends away but her job's pretty shitty in my opinion and she lives in a fairly mediocre town about three hours from here.

I was tossing up about whether to stalk her but frankly, with Facebook, there's no need.

Of course the spark's probably gone, her and her husband, you can have all the long weekends in the world together, in the end you won't be happy and fulfilled. You might say you are. Good sex and all that. But you won't be.

Beeping.

He looks at his phone.

He reads a list of porn titles.

Sperminator
    Growlers in the Mist
    Drilling Miss Daisy
    Inspect Her Gadget
    Edward PenisHands
    Lawrence of a Labia

Pornocchio

Beat.

Shaving Ryan's Privates.

Nothing excites him.

It's only now, when I think back to my cubby house, with the hum of distant lawn mowers and the smells of summer; the cut grass and the wet-the-bed daisies and the chalk-white dog turds and Sally Keenan's nipples and her green-apple-shampoo hair, that I realise: somewhere in there was the happiest moment of my life.

Everyone wipes crumbs from their face.

BELLA: Well this is nice. All of us together.

Lighting change.

9.0 *DROWNING*

Reset.

Loud beeping.

ANT *and* ANNIE *sitting at a table. Cake between them.*

BILL *and* BELLA *stand close by, watching.*

Beeping stops.

BELLA: What's /
BILL: Text /
BELLA: Who /
ANT: It's a work thing.
BELLA: What's /
BILL: Text /
BELLA: Who /
ANT: It's a work thing.

As they repeat these lines, ANNIE *picks up the knife.*

BELLA: What's /
BILL: Text /
BELLA: Who /
ANT: It's a work thing.

> *She suddenly stabs the knife down into* ANT's *hand ...* ANT *screams.*

Is this about the message? Because if it is I'm sorry. It's a work thing. That's a great-looking cake and I loved you when we first met and it's been years and you turned into a stranger.

ANNIE: [*to* ANT] What's your name?

> *A pause.*

ANT: Jamie? Oliver?

> *She twists the knife and he screams again.*

Put the knife down! Please.

BELLA: Annie. Look what you did to his thumb.

BILL: Put the knife down Annie.

ANNIE: So which one is it? Jamie? Or Oliver?

ANT: It's just ... Ant. It's a nickname. I'm sorry. Things change. Things do change. I know it's disappointing. And all the stories are lies. It's my birthday soon. I'm dreading it. Please, we won't worry about the thumb. It's not evolved in any way. It's a work thing. I'm lonely.

BILL: I'm lonely.

BELLA: I'm lonely.

ANNIE: I'm lonely. They said getting old together would be lovely but it's not, it's just getting old.

> *She starts stabbing viciously at the cake.*

Porn. Cake. Infidelity. Google. Love. Confusion. Hope.

> *Lighting change.*

10.0 *COPING*

Reset.

BILL, ANNIE *and* BELLA *sitting at a table.*

ANT *enters, carrying a luscious-looking cake, puts it down between them. Sits. They look at him.*

ANT: It's ... just cake.

> *Beeping, sound of a text message coming through.*

BILL *picks up his phone, he stares at it, turns away a little.*

[*Disappointed*] Is that a work thing?

BILL: Sorry.

BELLA: Bill.

ANNIE: Ant made us a cake.

ANT: It's okay.

BILL: Sorry, I thought it was just cake.

He continues texting.

ANT: Don't worry about it.

He cuts a slice and hands it to BILL. ANNIE *sniffs at the air.*

ANNIE: Is it Jamie?

BELLA: Is it Nigella? I can't quite pick the flavour.

She sniffs.

Wait, is it Green Apple?

BILL, *still texting, stuffs the cake in his mouth.*

ANT *watches* BILL.

ANT: [*with venom*] No. It's olive.

Lighting change.

11.0 SEARCHING

ANT, *stands to one side, makes an odd noise with his mouth, stretching his neck one side to the other, a sort of half-gag, half-choke noise. He tries to stick his tongue out and winces a little.*

ANT: I've still.

Noise.

My tongue ...

Noise.

The root of my tongue, still.

Noise. Stretches his mouth, his tongue. Better.

Last weekend, I got this text message in the middle of the night.

I wasn't asleep. I was drifting, in a very peaceful way. As if I was dying or on heroin or my body had become an empty plastic bag floating on a wave of sewage.

And I thought, sort of hoped, it could be this woman I met last week.

I mean we didn't do all that much, some kissing but there was, I think, I think there was a real connection.

Despite what happened.

No, Annie doesn't know.

I find people tend to judge too quickly, you know? They get a small snippet of information and then it's like an alarm's gone off, and they ... recoil. Especially older people, it's a habit I try not to fall into. [*Correcting*] I'm going to try not to fall into.

We were kissing and it was, she was, quite rough. At first it was okay, it was, I was.

It was sexy.

And then, it crossed the line, past sexy towards excruciating, and I tried to pull back a bit and she, she, sort of, sort of, sucked really hard and wrenched her head sideways and that's when I felt something in my mouth go pop.

Pop.

It really did make that sound.

She didn't say she wanted to see me again (but) I gave her my number anyway.

So, when I heard my phone go off, I thought ... *hello.*

The kiss, I was sure I could taste blood but I didn't want to slow things down you know, it was exciting at the same time.

But then, blood. You have to be careful.

Anyway, it wasn't her texting me. But maybe this was better.

This text message, it was saying that I, that my phone number, had been selected in a lottery run by the Thai government.

And I had won three hundred thousand dollars Australian.

I mean. It's probably a hoax but you have to say … wouldn't it be amazing if it was true?

I think … I always thought I would have quite a lot of money. Sometime. Around now. Maybe a bit earlier.

I think … I always thought I'd have kids. Quite a few, maybe, say, four? I come from a family of six, so.

My oldest sister is always on at me to, I don't know. She doesn't get on with Annie and when I'm venting, just blowing off steam really, she tells me I deserve to be happy.

I think … I always thought I *would* be happy.

I try to stay healthy, I do long walks by the beach.
And I eat well. A lot of men my age don't, but I do.
No saturated fats, mostly vegetarian.
We're eating a lot of cake at the moment and that's. That's not good.

I told my sister about that text message, I thought she'd be thrilled for me but I could tell right away: she was suspicious.

Well I was too of course, but the thing is … there was … it sounded like it could be plausible; the Thai government wanting to promote Thailand. And look, with that Australian woman they jailed for being drunk and having a good time, they need all the positive publicity they can get right? That's plausible.

It's a lot of money though, isn't it?

But they have riots and things. Bangkok. Redshirts. People try and take over. Yeah? So.

She can be quite negative, actually. My sister. She's not happy herself, you know, she has kids and a job she likes but her husband's a dick.

So the first thing they needed, the Thai government, was for me to text them to say I had received their text and give them my email address.

I did that. I know I know, identity fraud, that was what I was thinking too but I didn't give them any info per se. My hotmail address. That's it.

And I thought that's the last I'll hear of that but then *beep beep beep beep.* Another text! This one saying they were sending an email and I only had a few hours to take advantage of their offer.

I went to the library. I told Annie it was a … work thing.

Luckily there were no pensioners around, they hog the computers like you wouldn't believe and of course they're all researching their family trees! Why? They're old, what use is it to them? It's not like if they found a cousin or something they could just hop on a train or a plane and go see them. Actually maybe they could. There are some very good discounts for senior citizens I've noticed.

I check my hotmail account and there's the email from the Thai lottery people. They want me to fill out a form and send it back. I print it off, look at it closely of course. They want some fairly detailed information. Name, address, date of birth but also copies of your drivers licence and/or passport—I guess that's so they have photo identification. It is a lot of money after all. It would be terrible to give it to the wrong person.

But I have to admit, the English is not very good. I don't want to judge them but I do think the Thai government could afford to have people who speak fluent English. I'm not being racist, I enjoy Thai food and at work sometimes I'll have a Pad Thai for lunch or a Tom Yum Goong. Or sometimes I'll just get porn crackers and eat them at my desk.

Stops, corrects.

Prawn crackers.

That was when my sister rang, while I was in the library. I had to go outside to take the call and of course as soon as I stood up this old lady jumped in my seat, literally barged me out of the way and plopped herself down. Then before I could stop her she was on Google. She was incredibly rude and I hope she breaks a hip with that sort of behaviour.

I mean. I hope she *realises she might* break a hip with that sort of behaviour.

My sister wanted to know about my weekend. I told her about the Thai Government Lottery and the three hundred thousand dollars. She said it had to be a hoax although when I said wouldn't it be great if it was true, she admitted it would. But highly unlikely they'd text me, she said. She also said not to read messages from unknown sources anymore; text messages apparently can trap people, they think they're just reading them, but actually it racks up your phone bill.

I already knew about that.

She didn't ask about Annie or about how I've been feeling. Which is not great, actually.

Not great.

I think what I'm going to do is send the form, but not read any more text messages.

I'm not interested in incurring unwanted debt just now although how am I supposed to know if the message I receive is from the Thai lottery people or someone else?

I wish I hadn't said anything about the rough kissing.

I didn't want to ruin the moment between us. I didn't want to criticise her technique even though the truth is she could benefit from some constructive criticism.

She wouldn't listen and I finally had to spit in my hand and show her the blood.

And she left almost straight away. She actually seemed angry.

But that could just be me jumping to conclusions, which I try not to do.

I called after her: *Wait this is my phone number, call me.*

And I shouted my number. Which was embarrassing because we were in Coles.

In the sauce and mustard aisle.

I'm pretty sure she heard. And memorised it, it's quite an easy number to memorise.

I want her to text me. I want to apologise for spoiling her morning and for not having a more robust tongue.

I want to tell her I'll make it up to her when my money comes in. I'll buy her a car. Wouldn't that be amazing?

I didn't tell my sister about the woman I met at the supermarket. I didn't say she found me attractive. I didn't say my whole life I've been waiting to feel like that. Or that I will never look at a display of condiments in the same way again.

I don't feel strong enough to surf that wave of pity and frustration and jealousy.

She's my nearest relative. And the only person that remembers me from when … I had all that time.

It's not that I think she'll disapprove.

Long pause.

Yes I do.

12.0 CLICKING

Reset.

ANT *sitting alone at the table.*

Beeping, sound of a text message coming through. ANT *ignores it.*

ANNIE *enters, holding a cake. Behind her are* BELLA *and* BILL. *There are sparklers in the cake, it looks far more festive than previous cakes. The three stand to one side, obviously waiting to present the cake to* ANT.

More beeping. Another text message. ANT *pushes it to one side.*

As the three of them open their mouths to sing, ANT *begins to cry.*

ANNIE, BELLA, BILL *close their mouths and stand there, unsure of how to respond.*

The sparklers keep burning.

ANT *keeps crying. Desolate. Heartbreaking. Grief-ridden sobs.*

More beeping and this time ANT *grabs the phone and smashes it against the table until it stops.*

Eventually the sparklers splutter out.

BELLA *steps forward. Puts her hand on his arm.*

BELLA: Ant? We um … we got you a cake.
ANT: Cake?

BILL: Happy birthday mate!

> ANNIE *puts the cake down in front of* ANT.

BELLA: We went for a random number of sparklers. Rather than exact number of candles.

BILL: Didn't want to add to global warming. Ha!

ANNIE: It's not just cake.

> *Beat.*

We love you.

> *She cuts a slice for him.*

BELLA: We love you Ant.

BILL: Yeah.

> BELLA *gives him the laser look.*

We love you.

> *She continues to cut the cake into many slices and put them onto a plate. She hands the first plate of cake to* BELLA *who moves into the audience and gives them out. She hands the second plate of cake to* BILL *who does the same.*
>
> *As they do, lights on the audience begin to lift.* ANT *sees them.*
>
> BELLA *and* BILL *return to the stage.*
>
> *All four stand looking out to the audience.*

BELLA: I should explain. A cubby house. And wet-the-bed daisies.

BILL: This is not. Enid Blyton. This is not that.

ANT: This is just. A creeping realisation. Mustard. And fountains.

ANNIE: And rosebuds on the bedlinen. A tiny heart.

> ANT *reaches into his mouth and pulls something out. There is an odd metallic clicking noise and* ANT *holds up a brightly painted tin beetle, the sort you used to get at parties before too many kids sliced their fingers off with them. He holds it up as one may hold a tiny lantern in the dark.*
>
> *We can see his thumb pressing and repressing the metal tab.*
>
> *The other three take beetles out of their mouths and hold them up.*

They click them alongside ANT. *They stop.*

ANT: Happiness.

Lights begin to fade. Actors lowering their arms in unison.

The clicking slows and comes to a stop. Pause and then, before lights fade out entirely, they suddenly hold up their beetles and start clicking again, in this moment, defiant, hope full. Glee full. Joy full.

The stage is full of clicking beetle sounds.

THE END

THE DAPHNE MASSACRE
Donna Abela

The Daphne Massacre was first produced produced at The Blue Room Theatre, Artshouse Complex, Northbridge on the lands of the Whadjuk Nyoongar peoples of the Noongar Nation, on 30 August 2001, with the following cast and creatives:

ISABELLA / TEACHER	Krysia Wiechecki
COOK / A MUM / A BOY	Ronnie Vickers
NURSE / A MUM / A BOY	Honor Humphrys
DENTIST / FATHER PAT	Stephen Whiley
DAPHNE	Natalie Ryan-Brand

Director, Arn Madgin
Set & costume design, Arn Madgin
Lighting design, Fiona Reid
Lighting operation, Fiona Reid and Glenn J. E. Bell
Front of house, Heather Robinson

This script received dramaturgical support from Playworks The Women Performance Writers' Network.

CHARACTERS

ISABELLA. A bride-to-be.
THE MUMS. Isabella's mother figures.
THE BOYS. Orphans.
NURSE. The Dentist's assistant.
COOK. The Dentist's cook.
DAPHNE. A bride-to-be who has had the pleasure.
THE TEACHER. Miss Laurel, who taught at the orphanage.
DENTIST. A dentist (voice only).
FATHER PAT. Superintendent of the orphanage (voice only).

DOUBLING

Isabella / Teacher
Cook / A Mum / A Boy
Nurse / A Mum / A Boy
Dentist / Father Pat
Daphne

SETTING

The play is set in a waiting room, near a river, in an orphanage and in Isabella's imagination and memory.

PRODUCTION NOTES

The play is an ensemble piece for four women. Scenes merge and respond to each other. As such, blackouts, costume changes and a fixed set are likely to impede the work.

The Mums and the Boys speak as choruses. However, the lines may be shared or staggered between the actors playing these roles.

1.

ISABELLA *is on the floor devouring a diary.* THE MUMS *scoop her up.*

THE MUMS:	Ready Isabella?
	For the best for the future for the best future?
	Yes!
ISABELLA:	She wants to prepare properly prepare for a whole life together with someone a husband properly To do right right things so I can't harm—
THE MUMS:	The boys! How are the boys? Better off without you!
	Little darlings locked themselves in when you left starved themselves refused to eat thanks to you and your uppity influence
	And you can't do what you did to men! Men like them important men some of them priests
	Some jokes you silly bitch just aren't funny
	So forget it

| | it wasn't a proper job
you helped out
that's all
did your dash |
|---|---|
| ISABELLA:
THE MUMS: | You're lucky Baxter didn't take back his ring!
He's paying for this
This visit
yes
and others
fittings and what not
up to ten if need be |
| ISABELLA:
THE MUMS: | Her wedding present but early
I'm getting him boots
and he's getting you dentures!
So don't blow it!
Chop chop!
We've gotta get back
cook tea
bath kids
and brick the house! |
| ISABELLA: | Miss Laurel
that teacher whose place I took |
| THE MUMS: | Quick quick
on the double |
ISABELLA:	Did you know her?
THE MUMS:	Move it!
ISABELLA:	No
THE MUMS:	No?
What?
Excuse me?
ISABELLA:	This
it's not compulsory
Coughing up all my
my teeth
it's elective surgery

	a trend
	maybe not necessary at all
THE MUMS:	Oooooh
	isn't she a bold article?

	Stop it!
ISABELLA:	What?
THE MUMS:	Upsetting the apple cart!
	Like that teacher
	don't be like the teacher
ISABELLA:	Miss Laurel
	I know *why* she died
THE MUMS:	Look

We've had it
had the pleasure
had the benefit of dentures almost all our lives
See?
Plastic
doesn't rot stain or stink
Changed our lives it did
God yes
'cause two dentures
think about it
instead of thirty-two teeth
mathematically speaking
is quite a convenience
Drop 'em in the washing up
the nappy bucket
the twin tub
bit of a swish
then pop them on the sill
while you
free from the drudgery of dental hygiene
mow the road
make hay
mince words
and don't think!

	Once kids start popping out
	it's one less worry
	you'll see
ISABELLA:	So ditching my
	teeth
	before my Big Day
THE MUMS:	is normal
	a very normal
	very necessary
	routine operation
ISABELLA:	for the best
THE MUMS:	for the future
	for the best future
	yes!
ISABELLA:	Thanks for coming with me then
	for taking the trouble
THE MUMS:	Darling!
	What's a bridesmaid-mother-best-friend for?
	But to be there
	completely
	for you
	with magazines and that
	and brochures
	swatches and cakes
	hair dos and don'ts
	kitchen teas
	and now this
ISABELLA:	this this this
THE MUMS:	harmless
	little
	itty bitty
	quite painless really
ISABELLA:	appointment

2.

ISABELLA *becomes the* TEACHER *at the orphanage.* THE MUMS *become two* BOYS *who taunt her while she speaks.*

THE BOYS: You're lying Miss Laurel
about the lesson
making it up

Who'd believe you?
Father Pat doesn't

'Your sums add up to vanity
to a liar's advantage'

Don't bother
you stupid slut

I bet this lesson's bullshit

TEACHER: Father Pat
the boys
they're only
not that bad but
one or two
a prank
a few pranks
and sometimes
others are
they're in on it too and
I ignore them
it's nothing
I can manage
prepare lessons properly
you know that
but since
ever since that assembly when

you laughed at me

the boys
since then
won't listen

If you could just come to class Father Pat

       stop it
       tell them to stop
       then maybe
FATHER PAT: [*off*] Miss Laurel

 THE BOYS *stop, as if caught.*

       These boys are orphans
       they need to be mothered

       Only you have trouble teaching them
       so the trouble must be you

       See you at tea

 THE BOYS *resume their taunt more viciously.*

3.

DAPHNE'*s mouth is covered by a scarf, hair-do or surgical mask. She is waiting patiently to see the Dentist.*

ISABELLA:	My
	my mouth
	already
	it aches
THE MUMS:	Does not
	Get a grip
ISABELLA:	here near my ear where my jaw
	on both sides
	inside
	already
	it aches
	it's digging into
DAPHNE:	But I had no trouble
ISABELLA:	What?
DAPHNE:	No trouble at all
ISABELLA:	You've had the
	had the … ?
DAPHNE:	pleasure
	yes

	just last week
	I've healed beautifully too
ISABELLA:	It's it's it's … ?
DAPHNE:	for the best
THE MUMS:	See!
	Hello
	Who are you?
DAPHNE:	Daphne
	actually
THE MUMS:	We're her bridesmaid-mother-best-friend
	Isabella's
	She likes to fiddle-fart around a bit
	It's showy
	we don't like showy
DAPHNE:	Didn't she prepare properly for her appointment?
	Practise patience?
	Instil composure
	Self-control?
THE MUMS:	Oh
	no
DAPHNE:	Oh
	I did
ISABELLA:	But
	how?
DAPHNE:	Discipline darl
	I refused sleep
	laid down all day on broken sticks
	all night too
	fasting
	My mind concocted horrible things
	yummy deceiving smells like
	roasting chickens
	hot buttered potatoes
	but luckily
	I knew my naughty body would torture my resolve

	so
	I strapped chains around my waist
	and my True Love
	he bound them for me
	tight

                        Weakening
                        eating
                        wasn't possible

                        and now
                        without chains
                        or teeth
                        I sincerely
                        prefer bones to meat

THE MUMS: Oooooh
                        we're impressed!

                        You listening to this?

ISABELLA: this this

DAPHNE: It's our womanly privilege
                        to eat the food of suffering
                        to die daily
                        until all want stops

                        Hunger for nothing
                        It brings such happiness!

ISABELLA: It'll hurt hurt
                        like hurt
                        like
                        it'll hurt like

DAPHNE: Well
                        it
                        was a bit
                        dry
                        my mouth
                        after the procedure
                        but that's all

                        Trust me

>   Imagination
>   the made-up stuff
>   if you haven't prepared properly
>   that's the worst bit
>
> ISABELLA *sinks to the floor imagining the pain.*

4.

THE MUMS *become* THE BOYS *lying to the police.*

THE BOYS: Yes Officer
Miss Laurel met a man
near the river
had packed her bags
we saw her packing

But that night
the man yelled at her
and drove off
the tyres skidded
it woke us up

We could see her
from the window
alone
with her bag open
her clothes out all over the riverbank
We went to bed
and that's when she must've done it

FATHER PAT: [*off*] Cut her clothes up
hung her underwear everywhere
had no shame
none
was trouble from the start
Then went
and drowned herself
in the river
because of him
that man

	not because of the boys
THE BOYS:	Only she had trouble teaching us
	Officer
	so the trouble must've been her
ISABELLA:	inside
	inside
	it's digging into

5.

ISABELLA *is on the floor imagining the pain. A* MUM *becomes the* NURSE.

NURSE:	There's gas on tap
	there there there and there
	Help yourself
ISABELLA:	Did you know Miss Laurel?
NURSE:	Flavoured too!
	Lime
	chocolate
	strawberry-cordial-like
	and if you're adventurous
	guava!
	Now I'm the Nurse here
	for this normal
	very normal
	very necessary
	routine operation
	and you're on the floor
	Off
	off it
	girls today
	dear God
	off it!
ISABELLA:	Sorry
	I'm sorry I'm here having this this this
NURSE:	That Daphne

	that delight over there
	wasn't on the floor last week!
	No
	She was clean
	considerate
	on a chair
	hands together in her innocent lap
	thinking up something comfy!
	Weren't you darl?
DAPHNE:	Yes Nurse
	I was actually
NURSE:	But this little piggy
	besmirching herself
	The Dentist has a right to a nice experience you know!
DAPHNE:	He's an angel
NURSE:	a high priest
	a genius
	selflessly devoted to giving you this essential
	and fashionable
	service
DAPHNE:	I didn't feel a thing
NURSE:	didn't utter a peep
DAPHNE:	except at the beginning bit
	before the gas
	a
	twinge
	thrilled my whole
	being
NURSE:	then she fainted
	made it easier for all of us
DAPHNE:	and when I woke up
	I nearly didn't believe I'd had the
NURSE:	the pleasure!
DAPHNE:	except a small bead of red was on my lips
	but milk
	the next day

	it was like milk
	not red
	and a sweet scent was coming from my mouth
ISABELLA:	How
	exactly
	will he extract my
	all my teeth?
DAPHNE:	His surgery room
	truly
	you'll just love it
	It's the colour of clouds
NURSE:	Happy fluffy ones
DAPHNE:	And his hands
	squeaky clean
	you can still taste the lavender suds
NURSE:	His father abluted with lavender soap too
	Tradition
	and a nice touch
	don't you think?
ISABELLA:	But
	exactly
	extracting my
	arc
	it's a dental arc isn't it?
	Just how will he … ?
NURSE:	You're the home-wrecker-type aren't you?
	who won't rationalise
	see sense?
	Who's bent on wrecking her future home
	with budgetary disaster!
ISABELLA:	No
	I'm I'm sorry I'm
	so lucky
	But will he rip the top row out
	or the bottom first
	or both?

	One tooth at a time
	or in clumps?
DAPHNE:	She didn't read the pamphlet
NURSE:	Why didn't you read the pamphlet!
ISABELLA:	Pamphlet?
DAPHNE:	Look
	Just think of afterwards
	when you're at peace
	with yourself
	with your well-fed family-to-be
	with a severe but delectable sort of burning desire
	to do it all again
	Think of that
NURSE:	Yes Daphne
	Think of that
ISABELLA:	Daphne?
	Am I a Daphne too?
NURSE:	It's a nickname
	no big deal
	just a little joke

Offstage, from the surgery, the DENTIST *bursts out laughing. It carries over into ...*

6.

ISABELLA *becomes the* TEACHER *tied to a tree.* THE MUMS *become* THE BOYS *laughing at her.*

TEACHER:	Father Pat
	you said
	I did what you
	mothered them
	made toffees and
	thought a picnic might
	by the river
	improve things
	but

I joined in
a game
a laugh at first
got caught
tied up
they got their ties and

please
this job
I need this
I have no-one
I moved here especially
but they

Father Pat
they tied me
to a tree
and
my legs
up my legs
stuck
I made toffees
I
Father Pat
you said
but up my legs
covered in ants
bull ants!
hundreds!
but if
if I moved
they

THE BOYS: [*threatening*] Don't!
FATHER PAT: [*off*] Miss Laurel

Boys are hearty
It's their way

I refuse to believe that exuberance is a problem

See you at tea

THE BOYS *and the* DENTIST *laugh more viciously. It carries over into ...*

7.

One of THE BOYS *becomes the* COOK.

COOK: That bastard finished yet?

All laughter abruptly stops. The other BOY *becomes the* NURSE.

NURSE: Enough said
none of your lip
put a sock in it
shut your trap!
COOK: Don't throttle yourself

I need me plate back
to put his lunch on
Are you gonna get it?
NURSE: Nuh
COOK: Cow
Go on
I hate going in there
NURSE: Well Daphne here's champing at the bit
aren't you darl?
DAPHNE: Yes actually Nurse
I
COOK: Spare me

Move you
I'll get it myself
NURSE: You wait till you're wanted!
COOK: No
NURSE: The Dentist deserves his teacake in peace!
ISABELLA: Teacake?
COOK: Yeah

	Special treat today too
	apple and arsenic
DAPHNE:	What!
COOK:	Acid Daphne
	think of it
	eating into such a precious oesophagus
DAPHNE:	Nurse!
	He hasn't finished fitting my
NURSE:	She's kidding Daphne
COOK:	Yeah
	Daphne
	just a little joke
ISABELLA:	So
	he
	hmmm
	eats
	does he
	on the job?
COOK:	All day long
	the pig
NURSE:	Radical Premarital Extraction is no easy procedure!
	He
	he needs to eat
	to keep up his strength
	it's sustenance
ISABELLA:	it's
	it's
COOK:	disgusting!

When he's tunnelling into you love
he'll suck marinated bone marrow off crustless bread
demolish chops by the fistful
lick the garlic sauce off
and breathe into your face
And for afters
if nothing hideous happens
there's a blood orange custard

	and a nice posh port to go with it
NURSE:	I know I cook for the cunt The expert! The the consummate professional who by way of of psychological preparation masticates in sympathy with the type of tooth he's pulling!
COOK:	Pate for anteriors spuds for incisors meat for molars and custard for gums!
ISABELLA:	Masticates?
NURSE:	*Chews!* God!
COOK:	Garbage Guts

The COOK *slips into the dental surgery.*

Pause.

NURSE:	Daphne Did she knock?
DAPHNE:	No Nurse she just actually went in
NURSE:	Oh Oh dear

They listen, expecting trouble. Silence. The COOK *returns eating leftover teacake from a plate.*

COOK:	Who's for teacake?
NURSE:	You'll get me killed
COOK:	Apples eggs and cinnamon walnuts and allspice Want some?
NURSE:	Choke
COOK:	Daphne?

DAPHNE:	I couldn't
COOK:	How 'bout you?
ISABELLA:	Me?
COOK:	Yeah
	Go on
	It won't bite

ISABELLA *eats some teacake and suddenly realises ...*

ISABELLA:	Your face
	Half of your face is
	it's black
NURSE:	Guava!
ISABELLA:	completely black
NURSE:	There's guava!
ISABELLA:	down one whole cheek
NURSE:	Gas!
	Isabella?
ISABELLA:	It's a scar
	isn't it?
COOK:	A beauty too
	Nurse hasn't noticed yet
	Some Nurse
NURSE:	Gas
	Have it
	She's not having gas!
COOK:	Shut your neck you

Pause.

ISABELLA:	What happened?
COOK:	I got burnt
	years back
	during a blue
	a domestic
	Some bastard took a cup of tea
	hot black tea
	and threw it in me face

ISABELLA:	It must've hurt
	like hurt
	like
	Did it?
COOK:	Like fucking hell

8.

The NURSE *and the* COOK *become* THE MUMS.

THE MUMS:	Darling!
	Isabella!
	Look!
	Samples
	She must see these samples
	His choppers
	look
	aren't they fabulous?
	Lovingly hand-crafted
	and the range:
	opaque
	translucent
	opalescent!
	Girls today
	honestly
	you're so lucky
	In my day it was basic white
	or sometimes
	not often
	a pastel set for summer
	Although
	once
	I was daring
	well
	you are when you're young
	for a minute
	I hired a most brazen set
	for my debut

Diamantes this big
inset into each incisor
Cost a bomb!
But on the night
my insets sparkled
turned heads
men's heads
girls en masse were spewing
Belle-of-the-fucking-ball I was

Yes
well

But these days
look at these
designer styles to die for:
rustic
anodised
gold-dipped!
And disposables!
Ask about them
Pack of ten
one a week
then toss!

Hello?
Samples!
More samples
they must have more:
perfumed
odour-eating
self-cleaning
surely!

Isabella?
How you going darl?
See anything you like?

ISABELLA: Well
I don't mind the green

THE MUMS:	The green
	hmmm
	neither do we
ISABELLA:	The federation shade
	to match the guttering on that house we might buy
THE MUMS:	Yes
	good thinking but
	Baxter mightn't kiss a mouldy-looking miss
	so
	she might leave the green I think
ISABELLA:	Or chintz?
	Can he do chintz?
	To go with the lounge on lay-by
	Or gingham
	Or
	I know!
	The clan tartan
	to match dad's kilt when he's giving me away!
THE MUMS:	She's off now
	into the swing of it
	mixing and matching
	Isn't this fun?
	Dentures
	back with a vengeance
	all the rage again
	and all this choice!
	Who would've thought?
	So splurge girl
	go on
	it's Baxter's treat
ISABELLA:	my wedding present but early

Isabella exits.

9.

One of THE MUMS *becomes the* COOK.
ISABELLA *enters. She finds the* COOK *burying money by the riverbank.*

ISABELLA:	What are you doing?
COOK:	You worked at the orphanage didn't you?
	Took that Teacher's place
	after she drowned herself?
ISABELLA:	Did you know her?
COOK:	No
ISABELLA:	Oh
	It wasn't a paid job
	I moved into the orphanage to mind the boys for a while
	just helped out
	They were in shock
	It wasn't a real job
COOK:	Still got dismissed but
	didn't you?
ISABELLA:	How do you know?
COOK:	I read ya file
	You're an upstart
	Says so in red letters
ISABELLA:	I am not
COOK:	Aren't you?
ISABELLA:	No

Pause.

	What are you doing?
COOK:	Visiting me bank
	River bank
	Beats a real bank but
	minds my savings and its business
	no worries
ISABELLA:	What are you saving for?

COOK:　　　　A vineyard
　　　　　　My very own

　　　　　　Had one lined up once
　　　　　　someone going halves

　　　　　　Born for it I was
　　　　　　tending and crushing acres of grapes
　　　　　　blending them to a deep dark perfection

　　　　　　I'm leaving here
　　　　　　can't wait
　　　　　　gonna live different
　　　　　　so I'm preparing properly
　　　　　　to set off in style
　　　　　　first class
　　　　　　window seat thanks
　　　　　　with views
　　　　　　sunsets
　　　　　　this shithole
　　　　　　the sight of it
　　　　　　sinking in the distance
　　　　　　with decent feeds in a dining car
　　　　　　not thawed-out pies
　　　　　　plastic-wrapped muck!
　　　　　　I want confit salmon
　　　　　　crisp asparagus
　　　　　　sautéed lobster tails drizzled with lime
　　　　　　not drenched
　　　　　　white chocolate cheesecake
　　　　　　and a bottomless glass of a very cheeky Chablis

　　　　　　But I shouldn't talk like this
　　　　　　You're fasting

ISABELLA:　　Shit
　　　　　　I ate teacake
　　　　　　I smelled it and
　　　　　　I forgot

COOK:　　　　You did too

　　　　　　Did you like it?

ISABELLA:	I did
	It was like eating
	I don't know
	spiced air
COOK:	I use fresh apples
	fresh as anything
	not bruised ones
	not waxed ones that smell like petrol
	But that scumbag bastard Dentist
	I could use vomit and he wouldn't know
	dead parrots
	gobs of spit
	'cause he doesn't get it
	doesn't respect it
ISABELLA:	What?
COOK:	The intimate nature of taste

Pause.

ISABELLA:	I read her diary
	The Teacher Miss Laurel
	they gave me her room
	the same bed
	I found it under the mattress
	devoured every word of it
	The boys hurt her
	broke something inside her
	weren't stopped
	They lifted me
	loved me and needed me
	and I saw new things in me
	But they
	to her
	they
	Why didn't she just leave?
	Why don't you just leave?

COOK:	I will
	when things conclude
ISABELLA:	What things?
COOK:	Well
	I'm in the habit of poisoning his dinners
	Belladonna in his beef stroganoff
	mercury in his savoury mince
	weedkiller pesticide
	borax mould Drano
	you name it
	if it looks lethal
	I've mixed it in or made it into a sauce
	But that monster's got a cast iron gut
	Bloody remarkable
	He should've popped off years ago
	Honestly
	I've tried everything
ISABELLA:	To kill the Dentist?
COOK:	To stop this custom
	Fresh ideas
	Isabella
	on how to stop him
	if you've got any, love
	just speak up

10.

ISABELLA *becomes the* TEACHER. *The* COOK *and the* NURSE *become* BOYS *cutting up her clothes.* FATHER PAT*'s laughter is heard.*

TEACHER:	Out of my room!
	Stop it!
	You can't
	Stop!
	All my clothes
	God!
	Can't believe

Father Pat
he's pleased with all his
all this this
cutting up
ripping

can't stop it
take it
disgusting
it's
I'm so
disgusting
becoming
I'm

That's it
I'm over this
can't anymore cope with this
this
this

11.

A MUM *becomes the* NURSE.

NURSE: appointment!

    FATHER PAT*'s laughter stops.*

Are you committed to this or what?

Ugly girls
they're no trouble
Whip their teeth out for ya they would
wouldn't they darl?

DAPHNE: Too right
wholeheartedly
yes

NURSE: But the pretty ones
always the pretty
coming here with your silly-bugger thoughts

	you want everything:
	marriage
	kids
	a big house
	your own teeth!
	Keep your teeth then!
	Go on!
	It's no skin off my nose
	But mark my words
	one day you'll wake up and think
	my kids?
	where are my kids?
	And where will her kids be?
DAPHNE:	Sniffing petrol
NURSE:	Yes
	because petrol puts fumes where food should be
	food that couldn't be bought 'cause Mum robbed the coffers
	spent the money on herself
	on crowns
	on caps
	on fillings
	on root canal therapy!
DAPHNE:	It's so selfish
	so
	unsacrificial
ISABELLA:	No
	Those boys
	they were in shock when I got there
	and I stayed with them
	day and night
	sacrificed everything 'till they came good again
	I got them better
	Me
	alone

DAPHNE:
    I did that
    No
    people get over shock eventually

    Lucky timing
    that's what you had

    I wouldn't boast

12.

As ISABELLA *speaks,* THE MUMS *become* THE BOYS *in a troubled sleep.*

ISABELLA:
    Before I worked at the orphanage
    I kept the church clean
    poured morning teas
    starched altar cloths
    took great pride in how white they were
    Thought that was important
    making a difference
    my lot

    But the boys
    I watched over them
    rid their sleep of rot
    saw the future take root in their eyes

    Me
    alone
    I did that

    And they'll be okay
    most of them

    Like Danny
    he'll be fine
    fearless
    working one day
    skylarking on building sites
    twenty storeys up in the air

    And Frances
    he'll be a professor for sure

                'cause even asleep he's solving things
                sums and theories and problems he hasn't got yet

                But then
                then there's Salvador
                the one you worry about
                the one with the shock of something unspeakable on
                his face
                He'll carry tinned meat
                white bread
                no butter
                back to a boarding house
                Be greeted by nothing but the smell of grilled fat
                He'll open his tin
                cut slices so thin I could cry
                He'll chew slowly to make it last
                the shock of something unspeakable still on his face

13.

THE BOYS *wake from their troubled sleep and recount their nightmare.*

THE BOYS: Her feet!
                In my dream
                Miss Laurel's feet are upside down
                and blue
                and talking underwater
                in the river
                but the soles of her feet are upwards
                facing the sky
                talking about us underwater
                and blue

                But then they become boots!
                Men's boots
                coming after me
                bigger then me

                I'm running
                and I run up a wall

up the drainpipe
onto the water tank
and jump in
but there's no splash
it's empty
and I yell
help!
but no sound comes out
the water tank eats my voice up

And the boots
they're on the roof
jumping on the tin
I'm inside
inside
it's digging into
my ears
my brain
I yell
but nothing comes out
Isabella
it's terrible
but the boots keep coming!

Pause.

It was us
Miss Laurel drowned herself
in the river
because of us

We got lollies if we made her cry

We went too far

We're sorry!

Don't tell Father Pat we told you

14.

THE BOYS *become* THE MUMS.

THE MUMS:	So Daphne!
	Nice day for it
	hmmm?
	for a fitting?
	you're here for a fitting then?
	hmmm?
DAPHNE:	Yes
	I've been beside myself all week
THE MUMS:	Well it is a big moment
	Isabella
	Look interested darl
	Which delightful dentures did you pick?
DAPHNE:	Well
	one special set the Nurse showed me
	they were like milky glass
	see-through almost
	with angels etched on every second tooth
THE MUMS:	Angels?
	Oooooooo
DAPHNE:	outlined too
	in real gold
	but I declined them ones
	they were showy
THE MUMS:	we don't like showy
DAPHNE:	And actually
	I thought about not even getting dentures
THE MUMS:	You mean
	going natural?
DAPHNE:	Yes
THE MUMS:	living modestly
	on mashed potato and tea?

DAPHNE:	Beyond bother
	yes
THE MUMS:	Bless her heart!
DAPHNE:	But then I thought
	What about my True Love?
	Would he like bare pink flesh smiling up at him?
	Nude uncovered gums?
	I didn't think so
	So I've gone for simple
	wood
	pine actually
	not oak or nothing
THE MUMS:	It sorts the girls out
	doesn't it?
	all this
	the goats from the sheep
	the sheep from the goats
ISABELLA:	It's commendable
DAPHNE:	No
	it's nothing
	it's just
	a way to display my devotion
	My True Love
	when we first met
	he couldn't take his eyes off me
	like one of them paintings
	his eyes following me
	around the room
	out the door
	down the road
	up the shops
	and everywhere I went after that
	And last week
	after I'd had
THE MUMS:	the pleasure!

DAPHNE: I was groggy
from the happy gas
and forgot to wait for my True Love
he was picking me up
but
I walked home
went to the wrong house
his brother's house
and I laid down on the front lawn
and fell asleep

Luckily
he found me
my True Love
he was so worried
said
What if you'd been raped?
I couldn't marry you then
could I?

I hadn't thought of that

So
there on the lawn
in front of his brother
he got his penknife
and into my skin
he cut his name address and phone number
just above my heart
saying
your love is mine alright?
I won't share you with no-one

Look

15.

ISABELLA *becomes the* TEACHER.

TEACHER: Stop

No
stop
stay in your seats please
I'm sorry to interrupt
but I must speak

FATHER PAT: [*off*] Miss Laurel
Assembly is over

TEACHER: I know
but this is important Father Pat
so if everyone could just wait
stay seated
for one minute more

I must speak

Pause.

16.

A MUM *becomes the* NURSE.

NURSE: Enough said
none of your lip
put a sock in it
shut your trap!

Every pregnancy costs a tooth!
Don't you know that?
don't you care?
that our hormones
sex hormones
run amok when we're pregnant?
leach minerals
soften oral tissue

dilate our gum flaps
and upset our once-snug teeth
which wriggle
twist
up
upwards
arrrghhh
the pain
then before you know it
oops
too late
pop!

Our hormones
sex hormones
evict milk teeth from little girls too early
Their succeeding teeth
half-dressed
half-asleep
are exposed to extra years of decay-producing
influences!
Boys' teeth sleep in longer
enter the oral cavity slower
fully enamelled
and rot
consequently
much much later

And crevicular fluid!
there's statistics on this!
Women have more of it
more sores
inflammations
infatuations
the lot!

Men should live longer than us
They're fit for it

But women
our hormones
sex hormones
ambush epithelium
cripple bone growth

I won't go on

It's
all this
drawing the short straw
as we women have
it's embarrassing
disgusting

and avoidable

So
face facts
Daphne

Your dental crypt will cark it
because your teeth
your female teeth
are weak

So strike them
before they strike you!

Get this procedure over with
and you won't look back

ISABELLA: No

I was strong

I got them through it

Me
alone
I did that

17.

THE MUMS *become* THE BOYS. *They cover* ISABELLA*'s eyes, twirl her around, and sing while they lead her to the centre of the stage.*

THE BOYS:	*star of wonder*
	star of might
	star with royal beauty bright
	westward leading
	still proceeding
	guide us with your perfect light

They uncover Isabella's eyes. She realises she is on stage, that this means trouble.

FATHER PAT:	[*off*] Isabella
	You are
	like that teacher
	don't be like that teacher!
	Leave the stage immediately
	You are interrupting the concert!
ISABELLA:	Yes yes of course
	I
THE BOYS:	Don't
	Father Pat?
	I know we didn't ask you first
	but we wanted to surprise Isabella
	and thank her
	for stepping in
	and staying with us
	and helping us
	But we didn't have a gift
	or money for one
	so we thought that
	when you and the committee
	after our concert
	come up on stage and leave presents for us
	we thought that this year

> instead of all around the tree
> you could put all our presents all around Isabella
> near her feet
> and take her picture!
> And we could make a nice frame for it
> then give it to her
> to say thank you
>
> And we thought that you
> Father Pat
> that you could go first!
>
> Ready?
>
> And we'll sing!

THE BOYS *sing.*

> *We three kings of orient are*
> *bearing gifts we traverse far*
> *field and fountain*
> *moor and mountain*
> *following yonder star*

A terrible pause.

18.

THE BOYS *become the* COOK *and the* NURSE. *They are young again, fighting. The* NURSE *has a teacup.*

COOK:	Acres of grapes
	blending them to a deep dark perfection
NURSE:	He wants me by his side
COOK:	But a vineyard
	running one together
	we were born for it
	we've planned it for years
NURSE:	He needs me
COOK:	But you're young
	plump with summers and promise and
	all that life ahead of you

	Don't let him do this!
NURSE:	You're jealous
COOK:	You're stupid!
	Desperate!
	In love with a monster
NURSE:	An angel
COOK:	But we've got the deposit
NURSE:	I'll need my half now
	for my trousseau
COOK:	Has he proposed yet?
	Popped the question?
	Where's the ring?
NURSE:	It's coming
	He's busy
	Radical Pre-marital Extraction is no easy procedure!
COOK:	He won't love you for it
NURSE:	He will
COOK:	He doesn't love you
NURSE:	He's busy
COOK:	Doesn't even look at you
	or think of you
	ever!

The NURSE *throws a cup of tea in the* COOK*'s face. The* COOK *clutches her face. They sink to the floor.*

19.

The COOK *and the* NURSE *become* BOYS *whimpering at* ISABELLA*'s feet.*

FATHER PAT:	[*off*] You are interrupting the concert!
	Enough said
	none of your lip
	put a sock in it
	shut your trap!
ISABELLA:	Father Pat
	The boys meant no harm

	no disrespect
	but have been through hell because of you
FATHER PAT:	[*off*] Off that stage!
	Off it!
	Girls today
	dear God
	off it!
ISABELLA:	No
	Miss Laurel is dead
	You urged the boys on
	hurt her through them
	rewarded their viciousness
	then lied about it
	I know everything
	The boys told me everything
	I read her diary
	will go to the papers or the police
	unless you
	listen
	yes listen to the boys
	do what they ask
	and thank me for everything I did for them
FATHER PAT:	[*off*] Isabella!
	You're dismissed!

20.

One of THE BOYS *becomes the* NURSE. *She approaches* ISABELLA *with a gas mask.*

NURSE:	You're going through with this normal
	very normal
	very necessary routine operation
	if it kills me!
	You've got a choice
	Lime

	chocolate
	strawberry-cordial-like
	and if you're adventurous
ISABELLA:	Nurse?
NURSE:	Help yourself!
	There there and
ISABELLA:	Why 'Daphne'?
NURSE:	What?
	Look at you!
	You've got it chronic you have
	Vanity
	Stark raving vanity!
	Feed that to your flaming kids
	you're so clever!
ISABELLA:	Tell me
NURSE:	Gas!
	Just
	have it
	have it!
ISABELLA:	Women having their teeth ripped out
	why do you call them 'Daphne'?
NURSE:	It was good enough for me
	didn't hurt me
	made me what I am
	made me
ISABELLA:	A Daphne too?
NURSE:	So?

So the little children
suffer
you must
for the little children
like I did
suffer
I

Oooooo

I'll tell the Dentist

	yes
	to be less careful with you!
	Now be a darl!
ISABELLA:	It's a joke
	isn't it?
NURSE:	Bugger it!
	Come here!
	Come on!
	I'll do it myself
	Arrr
	say arrr Daphne
	big breath Daphne
	come on Daphne
ISABELLA:	It's a joke
	isn't it?
	At our expense
NURSE:	Maybe
	It might be
	So?
ISABELLA:	So some jokes
	you silly bitch
	just aren't funny

21.

THE MUMS *implore* ISABELLA.

THE MUMS:	Why
	Isabella
	why keep what will hurt you?
	You're just flesh and blood
	unfit to resist the confused forces of life
	Just
	this adjustment
	it's minor
	a tad inconvenient
	that's all

You lose
nothing essential
nothing to fret about
but you get
peace of mind
save everyone
in the long run
from all manner of pain
trouble
trust me

I mean
no teeth no decay
no words no hurt
no brain no strain
no wonder

And Baxter
he stood by you
saved hard for you
for this luxury
this head start

so you can't go home untreated
can you?
walk in
an insult
to him
to what he's worked hard for?

Sweetheart?
Sweetheart?
Don't upset the apple cart
Please?

They're only teeth
Rip 'em out before the rot sets in

Avoid strife
we did

　　　　　　　　please
　　　　　　　　We're begging

　　　DAPHNE *rises.*

DAPHNE:　　　Go on
　　　　　　　　Everyone'll be so jealous

　　　　　　　　Before I'd had
　　　　　　　　the pleasure
　　　　　　　　I was a normal girl
　　　　　　　　nothing special
　　　　　　　　but afterwards
　　　　　　　　I had honour
　　　　　　　　instant respect
　　　　　　　　I never asked for it
　　　　　　　　but people just started treating me like
　　　　　　　　like I was
　　　　　　　　awesome

　　　　　　　　I took my teeth home
　　　　　　　　in a jar
　　　　　　　　to bury in the backyard
　　　　　　　　and the dog next door dug them up
　　　　　　　　He had bad ears
　　　　　　　　red and infected
　　　　　　　　with flies eating the tips off
　　　　　　　　but when he chewed on my teeth
　　　　　　　　his ears
　　　　　　　　miraculously
　　　　　　　　got better

　　　　　　　　Word spread

　　　　　　　　People brought their sick pets into the yard
　　　　　　　　to adore my teeth
　　　　　　　　chew them
　　　　　　　　Pigs with diarrhoea
　　　　　　　　ferrets with frost bite
　　　　　　　　cats with colic

they all got healed
And some owners
some of them
they had visions

I had a vision

A visit actually

Mary came
the Blessed Virgin
to pay her respects
I was in the house
she was in the yard
in the sky
but I knew she was around
I could feel a divine presence
like
like a tongue up my back
My back blistered
I nearly combusted
split down the middle
but it didn't hurt
it didn't hurt
because I was lifted up
above my bed
so I could float
like her
but not in the hot sun
I was inside
in the air conditioning
just
floating

For the sake of the neighbours
I pulled down my nighty
soothed my hair
because it's not right is it?
for holy ones

> who others are jealous of
> to look shabby in her hour of triumph
> when everyone's looking
> and taking pictures of me
> because now
> I'm awesome now
>
> It's just not right

A MUM *becomes a* NURSE.

NURSE:	Daphne
DAPHNE:	Yes Nurse?
NURSE:	The Dentist is ready to see you now
DAPHNE:	Splendid

DAPHNE *enters the dental surgery.*

Pause.

A MUM *becomes the* COOK.

COOK:	I've had a gutful of this
NURSE:	Good
	Fuck off
	Get lost
	We've got work to do
COOK:	Work?
NURSE:	Yes
	Look
	I didn't start it!
COOK:	You were there at the start!
NURSE:	And by God yes
	I'm proud
	I'm
	it's an institution now
	good enough for me
	my aunts
	cousins
	didn't hurt us
	made us what we are
	made me

ISABELLA:	The first Daphne?

Pause.

NURSE:	I
	He's an angel
	a high priest
	a genius
	he
ISABELLA:	Were you?
	The first one?
COOK:	Tell her
NURSE:	Leave
COOK:	Go on
NURSE:	Just leave it
COOK:	Women having this procedure are called 'Daphne' because
NURSE:	Don't!
COOK:	because when the Dentist set up his practice and advertised for an assistant
	you
NURSE:	Don't laugh!
COOK:	I never do
	Not at this

Pause.

NURSE:	He
	I can't
COOK:	advertised for an assistant and
NURSE:	and I
	got the job

He was young and
I was young and

He wanted to specialise in something
and thought

He did it for free

Took photos

                         for the posters
                         was a hit

                         The trend
                         a resurgence
                         like wild fire
                         took off
                         and

                         He was so successful
                         busy
                         so busy and
                         marriage
                         he just didn't

                         So I stay
                         he needs me
                         I make sure he eats properly and
ISABELLA: When your teeth were out
NURSE: on the floor

                         like pristine pearls
ISABELLA: What happened then?
NURSE: He
                         looked at me and
                         real close
                         close enough to kiss
                         and said
                         'say Daphne'

                         I
                         uttered
                         it

                         It sounded
                         awful
                         it was

                         And he laughed
                         all day
                         at
                         me

Pause.

ISABELLA: I'm leaving
NURSE: No
Don't
Just

    the little children
suffer
you must
for the little children
like I did
didn't have
I

    otherwise
I
what happened to me
just
doesn't
matter

    so Daphne
be a Daphne
you have to

    for me

23.

ISABELLA *becomes the* TEACHER.

TEACHER: Stop

    No
stop
stay in your seats please
I'm sorry to interrupt
but I must speak
FATHER PAT: [*off*] Miss Laurel
Assembly is over
TEACHER: I know

	but this is important Father Pat
	so if everyone could just wait
	stay seated
	for one minute more

                                  I must speak

Pause.

                                  I assure you
it's in the best interests of the boys

Father Pat?
Father Pat?

FATHER PAT: [*off*] One minute
TEACHER: Thank you

Now
with respect
I disagree with your decision
to present Stephen Sanes
with this year's prize for Maths
You see
I've just found the grade book
it's been missing most of the week
and I'm sure an honest mistake has been made
but by my calculations
Jimmy Donavon from my class
has scored better than Stephen Sanes from yours
by two marks

So Stephen
your result was outstanding
but if you could return to the stage please
and hand the prize over to Jimmy

FATHER PAT: [*off*] Hand me the grade book!
TEACHER: Certainly
My calculations have been thoroughly checked

Male voices murmur and calculate.

FATHER PAT: [*off*] Miss Laurel
Your sums add up to vanity

	to a liar's advantage
TEACHER:	I wouldn't call you a liar
FATHER PAT:	[*off*] No
	But we're calling you one
	Aren't we, chaps?

FATHER PAT laughs.

THE MUMS become two BOYS and imitate his laughter.

Off, the DENTIST laughs.

The humiliated TEACHER sinks to the ground.

24.

The humiliated TEACHER remains on the ground. THE BOYS become the COOK and the NURSE. They look at each other, then towards the surgery. The DENTIST stops laughing.

DENTIST:	[*off*] Now darl
	Say
	'Daphne'

DAPHNE, off, tries to say the word 'Daphne' with no teeth. It is a horrible sound.

The DENTIST, off, bursts out laughing.

NURSE and COOK brace themselves until his laugh splutters to a contented stop.

Pause.

DENTIST:	[*off*] Nurse!
NURSE:	Yes?
DENTIST:	[*off*] It's time for Saint Apollonia's blessing!

ISABELLA gets up from the ground.

ISABELLA:	Who?
NURSE:	Saint Apollonia
	Patron saint of dentists
	I stand there
	hear a prayer

	kiss his hand
	that's all
	No big deal

NURSE *puts on a black saintly cloak.*

ISABELLA:	Don't
NURSE:	What?
	But it's his way
	a custom
	my job
ISABELLA:	Let me
NURSE:	But he needs me
COOK:	He feeds you nothing
ISABELLA:	Then let me
NURSE:	What?
ISABELLA:	Bite the hand that feeds you nothing

Pause.

NURSE:	Yes
	Okay
	Yes

NURSE *takes off the cloak and puts it around* ISABELLA. COOK *and* NURSE *prepare her, kiss her, then stand back proudly. They nod.*

ISABELLA *enters the surgery.*

Pause.

Prayerful murmuring from the DENTIST *is heard offstage. The murmuring stops. He screams.*

Pause.

25.

COOK *and* NURSE *become* THE BOYS.

THE BOYS:	Isabella!
	Come back!
	Bring her back!

> We'll starve ourselves
> won't come out
> or go to lessons
> we don't care
> will lock our door forever!
> Don't dismiss her
> bring her back
> Please
> or we won't ever eat anything ever again
> Isabella!

26.

ISABELLA *emerges from the surgery eating a slice from a full teacake.*

ISABELLA: Mmmm
apple
eggs and cinnamon
walnuts
allspice

> THE BOYS *become the* COOK *and* NURSE *crushing grapes with their feet.*

COOK / NURSE: And grapes!
Acres of grapes!
Blending them to a deep dark perfection
We were born for it
ISABELLA: Smell
COOK / NURSE: Mmmm
ALL: Like spiced air
ISABELLA: Have a taste
Go on
It won't bite

> *They laugh.*

THE END

Left to right: Donna Abela, Ned Manning, Vanessa Bates, Noëlle Janaczewska, Verity Laughton, Hilary Bell and Catherine Zimdahl in 2007. (Photo: Keith Saunders)

About the authors

Catherine Zimdahl is a writer and visual artist. Her plays include *Gifted, The Halo Effect, The Cold Spell, Deviant Art for the Degenerate, HereNowThenThere, Clark in Sarajevo, Family Running for Mr Whippy, Left Breathless a Question, The Fox, A World into A Child, A Child into the World, Moonfleet* and *The Family Name*. She has had productions at the Sydney Theatre Company, Melbourne Theatre Company, the Griffin Theatre Company, Windmill National Children's Theatre and ABC Radio, amongst others. Awards include Griffin Playwriting Award, Victorian Premier's Literary Award, New Dramatists Exchange and AACTA Awards for Best Short Film and Best Screenplay. Catherine was a visiting artist with Theatre Kantanka's project experimental play Dream Shutter. She has exhibited in solo and group shows. Her paintings have been noted as finalists in art awards and her upcoming multidisciplinary creations include The Parasomnia Project, The Conversation Maps and My Charitable Works.

Ned Manning is a writer, actor and teacher. His published plays include *Us or Them, Milo, Close to the Bone, Luck of the Draw, Kenny's Coming Home* (Currency Press) and *Alice Dreaming* (Cambridge University Press). *Alice Dreaming* has had over 20 productions by youth groups and schools. His adaptation of *Women of Troy* (ABC Radio) was selected for competition in the Prix Marulic, Croatia's International Festival for radio drama. Ned has written ten plays for schools under the title, *Shakespeare for Australian Schools* (available at apt.org.au) that were originally developed for Bell Shakespeare's Actors at Work program. *Romeo & Juliet Intensive* was nominated for an AWGIE. His latest play, *Tsunami*, was shortlisted for the Patrick White Award. Ned's work of non-fiction, *Playground Duty* (New South Books) is a celebration of the teaching profession and a 'survival guide' for young teachers. As an actor Ned has appeared in many Australian productions, including the cult hit, *Dead End Drive-In*. His first novel, *Painting the Light*, was published in 2023. He is currently working on a follow up book.
https://www.nedmanning.com

(Dr) **Verity Laughton** is an Adelaide-based poet and playwright. Her work has been produced nationally and internationally. Her most recent production is the box office record-setting adaptation of Pip Williams' novel, *The Dictionary of Lost Words*, which won the 2025 AWGIE for Best Stage Adaptation and the 2024 SA Arts Ruby Award for Best Work Outside a Festival. Other work includes *The Mourning After*, *Carrying Light*, *Long Tan*, *The Red Cross Letters*, *Burning*, *The Nargun and the Stars*, *The Lightkeeper*, *Gondwana*, *Lights on Petticoat Lane* and *A World of Paper*. Awards include AWGIES for Radio Drama and Community, the Inscription Open Award, the Griffin Award and the SA Critics' Circle Best New Play Award. Nominations include the Martin Lysicrates Prize, the STC Patrick White Award, the Bruce Dawe Poetry Prize, the Rodney Seaborne Prize (twice), the Blake Poetry Prize, the New Dramatists' Award, the Victorian Premier's Awards. *The Sweetest Thing* was nominated for the Rodney Seaborn Award and the NSW Premier's Award. Her poem, *Welcome Swallow* was the runner up in the 2024 Newcastle Poetry Prize.
https://www.veritylaughton.com

Noëlle Janaczewska is a playwright, poet and essayist. She is the author of *The Book of Thistles* (UWA Publishing) and the collection *Scratchland* (UWA Publishing Poetry Series). She is the recipient of multiple awards, fellowships and residencies, including a Windham-Campbell Prize from Yale for her body of work as a dramatist. Reviewers have described Noëlle's work as 'gloriously innovative' and 'a masterclass in storytelling'. Recent productions include: *The Past is a Wild Party* (Siren Theatre Co, Sydney 2024); *Mrs C Private Detective* and *Experiment Street* both for ABC RN; *The End of Winter* (Siren Theatre Co, Sydney 2022, touring 2023 – 2025); *Yellow Yellow Sometimes Blue* for Q Theatre at The Joan; audio scripts for the National Museum of Australia's Rome: City and Empire exhibition, and *Good With Maps* (Siren Theatre Co, multiple seasons 2016 – 2021). A graduate of Oxford and London Universities with a Doctorate from UTS, Noëlle is currently working on a book about food: *Culinary Inauthentic*.
https://noelle-janaczewska.com/
https://eatthetable.com/

Hilary Bell's plays have been produced by Griffin, Belvoir, Sydney Theatre Company, Black Swan, Sydney Opera House, Arts Centre Melbourne, Deckchair, La Boite, State Theatre Company of South Australia, NORPA, Darlinghurst Theatre Company, City Recital Hall, National Theatre of Parramatta, Ensemble, Vitalstatistix. Internationally, by Atlantic, Steppenwolf, London's National Theatre and the Edinburgh Fringe. They include *Wolf Lullaby*, *The Bloody Bride*, *Perfect Stranger*, *Memmie Le Blanc*, *The Red Balloon*, *The White Divers of Broome*, *Splinter*, *Victim Sidekick Boyfriend Me*, *The Red Tree*, *Summer of Harold* and adaptations of *The Seagull*, *The Comedy of Errors*, *A Christmas Carol* and *The Hypochondriac*. She also writes musicals, most recently *Picnic at Hanging Rock*. A graduate of the Juilliard Playwrights' Program, NIDA and AFTRS, she was the Tennessee Williams Fellow 2003-04 and the 2012 Patrick White Playwrights Fellow. Awards include a Helpmann, three AWGIES, the Jill Blewett, Inscription and the inaugural Philip Parsons Award. https://hilarybell.org/

Vanessa Bates is an award-winning playwright, including NSW Premier's Award, AWGIEs, CONDAs and Inscription awards. Her plays include *A Ghost In My Suitcase* (the play), *Small Hard Truths*, *Trailer*, *Light Begins To Fade*, *Every Second*, *The Magic Hour*, *PORN. CAKE*, *Checklist For An Armed Robber*, *Chipper*, *Darling Oscar*, *The One* and *The Magic Hour* (2024). Vanessa's work has been produced at Sydney Opera House, Victorian Arts Centre, Heath Ledger Theatre, Malthouse Theatre, Barking Gecko, Sydney Theatre Company, Darlinghurst Theatre, Black Swan Theatre, The Ensemble, Griffin, Deckchair, Theatre@Risk, atyp, Tantrum, Newcastle Civic Playhouse and many others. A graduate of NIDA Playwrights' Studio, with a PhD in scriptwriting, Vanessa is also a playwriting teacher and workshop facilitator for tertiary institutions, highschools, theatres and writers' festivals. Currency Press have published several of Vanessa's plays including *A Ghost In My Suitcase*, *Trailer*, *Checklist For An Armed Robber* and *The Magic Hour*.

Donna Abela's works includes plays which have won the Griffin Playwriting Prize and the AWGIE award for Stage (*Jump for Jordan*), AWGIE awards for radio (*Spirit, Aurora's Lament, Mrs Macquarie's Cello*), the Human Rights Award for Drama (*Highest Mountain Fastest River*), and been nominated for NSW Premiers Literary Awards (*Tales From the Arabian Nights, Jump For Jordan*). For Kim Carpenter's Theatre of Image, she wrote two large scale adaptations: *Monkey - Journey to the West* (2014 Brisbane Festival, 2015 Melbourne Festival, 2015 Sydney Opera House program) and *Tales from the Arabian Nights* (east coast tour 2004, published by Currency Press in 2019). Recent work includes *Golden Joinery*, an essay on trauma-informed creative practice (Sydney Review of Books), and the documentary *Missing Magdalens* (ABC Radio National). Donna completed a doctorate at the University of Wollongong, has been a dramaturge and dramatic writing teacher for decades, and is a founding member and co-Chair of PYT Fairfield (aka Powerhouse Youth Theatre).

www.ingramcontent.com/pod-product-compliance
Lightning Source LLC
Chambersburg PA
CBHW040252170426
43191CB00019B/2383